The Children of God

Messianic Jews and Gentile Christians
Nourished by Common Jewish Roots

He was in the world, and the world was made through Him, and the world did not know Him. He came to His own, and His own did not receive Him. But as many as received Him, to them He gave the right to become children of God, to those who believe in His name: who were born, not of blood, nor of the will of the flesh, nor of the will of man, but of God. (John 1:10-13)

Raymond Robert Fischer

Olim Publications
P.O. Box 2111, Tiberias, Israel
E-mail: olim@kinneret.co.il

Cover: A sculpture by Rick Wienecke, used by permission.
Design: David Coddington-Studio Mapal-Israel

ISBN 965-555-034-6

Printed in Israel

To Donna Jean Goade Fischer

For more than forty years: my adored wife; my best friend; my most trusted and respected spiritual advisor; the loving mother of our three precious daughters; the one great love of my life.

In thankful recognition and with great appreciation for her never failing love for me, her deep and abiding faith in Yeshua and her total commitment to Israel.

When the Lord called us home to the Land of our inheritance, never for a moment did she hesitate to make the very difficult sacrifice of no longer being able to actively participate in the lives of our grandchildren: watching them grow up from close at hand. Never once in these past eight years have I heard her express any regret about having forsaken so many of the other well earned "normal" golden year benefits enjoyed by others.

If she had not encouraged me to make *aliyah*: if she had not always been there for me, standing by my side, selflessly pouring out her enduring love and support, constantly blessing me even in the most difficult moments, this book would not have been written.

Acknowledgments

I wish to express my deep gratitude to Paul Jablonowski, Reuven Schmalz and Donna Fischer who reviewed the manuscript and made excellent editorial suggestions.

My profound and enduring thanks also to those who, in the beginning, assisted my company materially, as we struggled to get established in the new and very difficult business environment of Israel: Elmo Geppelt, Harold Kent, Jim and Hannah Johnson, the International Christian Embassy Jerusalem, and the International Christian Chamber of Commerce-Germany.

Finally, I offer my deepest appreciation and acknowledge my great debt to the president, dean, and faculty, past and present of Faith Seminary for the incredibly edifying experience of having benefited from the wonderful Christian education they provided, and also for their continuing bold commitment to trans denominational conservative doctrine and the inerrancy of Scripture.

May the Lord bless each of you as you have so abundantly blessed me.

Table of Contents

Part One

Who is a Jew?

Part Two

WHO IS A GENTILE?
(WHAT IS THE CHRISTIAN CHURCH?)

Part Three

REMOVING THE THORNS OF DISUNITY
DISCOVERING AND EMBRACING THE JEWISH ROOTS OF
CHRISTIANITY

VIII

Foreword

Repent, therefore and return, that your sins may be wiped away, in order that times of refreshing may come from the presence of the Lord; and that He may send back Jesus, the Messiah, appointed for you, whom the heavens must hold back until the time of the restoration of all things about which God spoke through the mouth of His holy prophets from ancient times. (Acts 3: 19-21)

With these words, the apostle Simon Peter declared prophetically that the new born community of faith in Jerusalem, a community birthed by the outpouring of the Holy Spirit Himself in fulfillment of the promise made by Jesus to the disciples before His ascension: this community would surely stray from its foundations and in time to come would be in dire need of a massive restoration to the purity and simplicity that marked its birth.

I seriously doubt that any who listened to him that day, not even Peter himself, could imagine how very far the Church would wander from her origins. They had no concept of the length of time that would elapse until the Lord whom they loved so dearly would indeed return to this earth for it is recorded that the believers throughout the first century lived with the daily expectation of His return.

We who are now privileged to be alive twenty centuries later can appreciate the depth of truth in Peter's prophecy. Every serious student of church history who is also a dedicated adherent to the Word of God is all too well aware of the accumulation of false doctrines, heresies, and ungodly actions promoted by church leaders through the centuries. Particularly tragic is the history of anti-Semitism within the Church which gave birth to multitudes of shameful decrees and flagrant persecutions against the Jewish people through the years, the very people who gave us the Scriptures and through whom came the Messiah, Savior, Redeemer whom the Church professed to worship and serve.

The twentieth century witnessed the beginnings of the restoration which

XI

Peter prophesied as various movements or revivals re-discovered and renewed in the church biblical truths long forgotten or ignored.

The highlight of restoration occurred on May 14, 1948 when the modern State of Israel was born and established as a nation again in the land which God promised to Abraham, Isaac, Jacob and to their descendants so many thousands of years ago. This event sent shock waves of realization through the body of Bible believers who recognized its profound implications. The re-establishment of the nation of Israel was a hallmark event pointing to the return of the Lord Jesus Christ.

Accompanying this restoration of the land, we have witnessed a massive return of her people from around the world. The *Aliyah* (return) of Jews to the land of Israel is a phenomenon of no small significance in our modern age, but it is much more. Paul the apostle taught the Corinthians a principle: "...the spiritual is not first, but the natural, and then the spiritual." (I Cor. 15:46) .

We understand the natural *aliyha*. Is there a spiritual *aliyah* as well? Without question! After the return of Jewish people to the land was well underway, the spiritual counterpart began to appear. We now call it the "Jewish Roots Movement."

It is not a fad; it is not a new idea to tickle someone's ears. It is as much a prophetic fulfillment as the natural return of the Jews to the land of Israel. The prophet Isaiah wrote: "Remember the former things long past, for I am God there is no other; I am God, and there is no one like Me, declaring the end from the beginning and from ancient times things which have not yet been done, saying 'My purpose will be established and I will accomplish all my good pleasure." (Isaiah 46: 9-10)

The prophet Zechariah says this: "In those days ten men from all the nations will grasp the garment of a Jew saying, 'Let us go with you, for we have heard that God is with you.'" (Zech. 8:23)

In very recent years, the Spirit of God has begun to stir in the hearts of men and women of all nations a hunger to know, to understand, and to embrace the Jewish Roots of the Christian faith. It has become nothing less than a new wave of revival within the Church as hundreds and then thousands return to the Word of God to discover such blessings as the true meaning of the Shabbat (Sabbath) as God intended it from the beginning, the beauty and holiness of the Torah which is the very revelation of God's character and which the Church has portrayed in many cases as a negative and oppressive religious system completely unrelated to today's Christian believer.

Nothing could be further from the truth. What pastor in any pulpit today is ready to declare that it is no longer necessary to "Love the Lord your God with all your heart, soul, and strength" since that is a commandment of the Torah and "the Law has been done away with!"

Through the Jewish Roots movement, theological inconsistencies which violate sound Scriptural exegesis are being held up to scrutiny and found seriously wanting, for any interpretation of the Word of God which ignores or omits the Jewish foundation and nature of the Bible will of necessity bring forth error. Jesus Himself said, "Do not think that I came to abolish the Torah but to fulfill it. For I say to you until heaven and earth pass away, not the smallest letter or stroke shall pass away from the Torah until all is accomplished. Whoever then annuls one of the least of these commandments and so teaches others, shall be called least in the kingdom of heaven; but whoever keeps and teaches them, shall be called great in the kingdom of heaven." (Matt. 5: 17-19)

But like every new move of the Spirit during the chronicled history of the community of faith known as the Church, there are the ever present dangers of imbalance and error creeping into the ranks. Most often such imbalances come about because of a lack of clear understanding of God's purposes, of His Word and of church history.

For this reason, Bob Fischer has made a contribution of immense value and significance to the Jewish Roots Movement with this book, *The Children of God*. We must applaud his extensive research and insightful analysis which have produced a masterpiece work that I believe will serve as a foundational classic for all who seek to be a part of this move of the Spirit in our day, a move which is strategically part of the restoration prophesied by the Apostle Peter in Acts chapter three.

I heartily recommend this book to believers in every nation who are seriously seeking to understand and to participate in God's agenda in this hour to bring forth in the earth a people who truly are in nature, in character and in manifest lifestyle, The Children of God.

Barbara Richmond, Doctor of Religious Education
Colorado Springs, Colorado
July 2000

Author's Preface

You worship what you do not know; we know what we worship, for salvation is of the Jews. But the hour is coming, and now is, when the true worshipers will worship the Father in spirit and truth; for the Father is seeking such to worship Him. God is Spirit, and those who worship Him must worship in spirit and truth. (John 4:22-24)

There is nothing optional in this deep longing for worshipers expressed by the Lord God of Israel: YHWH is His name. He created us, His people and the sheep of His pasture, so that we might worship Him. He hungers for our worship, but we must worship Him in spirit, and in truth, in the manner fulfilled in the New Covenant, through grace, by faith, by direct access to Him, made possible by the incredible sacrifice of His only begotten Son, *Yeshua, ha Mashiach* (Jesus Christ).

If we are to worship Him in spirit and in truth, there are, I believe, three great understandings that must already have been put in our minds and written on our hearts.

First, we must know who He is. Such knowledge is infinitely accessible: His identity is written on every page of the Old and New Covenants. Look into the heavens with its multitude of stars; listen to the roar of rushing waters; behold a suckling child at its mother's breast. He is in all these things. He is in every thing. He is everywhere to be found.

Secondly, we must know, with certainty and clarity, who we are: not some make believe creation of our own imagination, some non-existent person who we might desire, or pretend to be; rather, who we really are: the flesh and blood, filled with His Spirit, one of a kind son or daughter whom God lovingly created.

Finally, we must come to perfectly understand and joyfully accept the

XV

position, and substance of our own unique and Divinely appointed place and calling within the Body of all true believers: those brothers and sisters with whom we share the glorious privilege of worshipping Him in spirit and in truth.

For as the body is one and has many members, but all the members of that one body, being many, are one body, so also is Christ. For by one Spirit we were all baptized into one body--whether Jews or Greeks, whether slaves or free-- and have all been made to drink into one Spirit. For in fact the body is not one member but many. (1 Cor 12:12-14)

This world-wide Body of many different members is, I believe, beset by a satanically orchestrated "Identity Crisis" of near epidemic proportions. Driven by the spirit of confusion, this "Identity Crisis," has blurred the vision of myriad Messianic Jews and Gentile Christians alike and sent them groping in horrific disunity, even blindly in search of their rightful, God ordained places within the Body.

Witness the growing segment of the Christian Church that is crumbling in its own apostasy: poisoned by the spores of paganism injected into its very heart at the time of its second birth in the New Babylon called Rome.

Legions of disillusioned and broken-spirited Christians are leaving their life long home churches and even their main line denominations; unable to find solace or direction from pastors and elders who have themselves fallen into apostasy. In North America, for example, in the thirty two years between 1967 and 1999, total membership in the top seven Protestant denominations declined from 29 million to 22.9 million, a shocking loss of twenty-one percent[1].

These are not just numbers. These are deeply traumatized and bewildered brothers and sisters who are fleeing their church homes in droves. These are among the Children of God. Praise Him: for in His unfailing love and boundless mercy, He has not forgotten these precious ones of His own creation.

The Lord God of Israel has laid out a heavenly highway for this satanically displaced Christian remnant of His people who would worship Him in spirit and truth: a highway leading from the depth of the apostasy of Rome to the glory of the heights of Jerusalem. He is pointing the way to Mount Zion: to the sacred Jewish roots of the Christian Church; to the rich Holy ground from whence Nazarene Jewish believers came forth like "shoots" in the Church's first birth.

In rejecting the apostasy of the second Church in Rome, countless thousands of lost, confused and earnestly seeking Christians have taken to this heavenly highway. Some are proceeding slowly and with caution; others are marching as if they were a conquering army set upon a new third millennium crusade; still others are running, blindly, without direction or clear understanding of where they are going and what they can expect to find at the end of their quest.

Recently, a dear Christian sister in the Lord, who temporarily resides in Jerusalem, and is trying to gain permanent residency by relentlessly struggling with a seemingly intractable Israeli Department of Interior, cried out to me in her profound confusion and frustration:

"I don't know what to do. I know I've been called to Israel, but I don't know where or how to worship. Should I worship only with you Messianic Jews? How much of the Law should I keep? Should I act more Jewish; dress more Jewish; associate myself only with Jews; try to make myself more Jewish in every way? I know that I am not Jewish, but I have this deep longing to identify with you and your people; to be more like you."

It has taken a great deal of *chutzpah* (presumption) for me to write this book: to have dared to conclude that part of my own unique place and calling as a Messianic Jewish member of the Body of Yeshua is to endeavor to make lighter the burden, more pleasant the journey; to better illuminate the way for those legions of Christians who are, figuratively, coming home to Mount Zion; who are seeking to find, then gain spiritual nurture from the natural Jewish roots of their faith.

In the past there have been those who have accused me of being "anti-Gentile," and "against the Christian Church." Nothing could be further from the truth. Although I am entirely Jewish, I was raised and educated in a completely Christian world. I sought and found Jesus Christ in an entirely nondenominational Christian Church.

I married a "born again," Christian. We raised three daughters in the Church who, until recently, have had absolutely no understanding of their father's Jewishness or what if anything this meant.

After I had already finished one career and was well established in a second, I was, to my own enduring amazement, called to and graduated from a wonderful conservative Christian Seminary. There I gained an entirely Christian orientation that I have come to appreciate and treasure more and more each day.

It was only after all of this that God in His mercy began to unfold His plan for me by taking me by the hand and introducing me, by way of a highly blessed Messianic Jewish Congregation, to my own Jewish roots. It was only then, after I had finally come to understand who I was, that He called us home to Israel, and it became natural for me to think of His son as Yeshua, the Jewish Messiah.

By no means am I anti-Christian or an adversary of the Christian Church: I love them more than life itself because they led me to my Messiah. My present calling, as I have been given to understand it, is to illuminate and attempt to correct the apostasy introduced by Constantine and those who followed him; to show that the roots of the true Church are in Jerusalem, not Rome; to point the way and facilitate the journey for my Christian brothers and sisters as they enter upon and proceed along the heavenly highway leading from Rome to Mount Zion.

It is my deep and abiding love for Christians and the Church that has motivated me in this work: it is with this love that I now reach out to all of my brothers and sisters, Gentile and Jewish alike. My most earnest prayer is that none of this will be understood as having any other purpose.

LORD, my strength and my fortress, my refuge in the day of affliction, the Gentiles shall come to You from the ends of the earth and say, "Surely our fathers have inherited lies, Worthlessness and unprofitable things. Will a man make gods for himself, which are not gods? Therefore behold, I will this once cause them to know, I will cause them to know my hand and My might; and they shall know that My name is the LORD. (Jer 16:19-21)

In my earlier work, *The Messianic Seal of the Jerusalem Church (Part Two)*[2] I recalled the mathematical axiom, "the whole is equal to the sum of its parts." My approach then was to first examine and explain, in turn, each of the three separate elements of the three part First Century Messianic Jewish symbol (an interlaced Menorah, Star of David and Fish), then to put these separate interpretations together as a means to better understand the symbol's total meaning.

I have used this same "component integration" approach in this work. First, I have examined and defined the two top level "members," of the Body: Jews and Gentiles. Towards this end, I have explored both denominational Judaism and denominational Christianity from theological, organizational and traditional perspectives. Then, building upon thus revealed differences and similarities, I have sought to illuminate the first steps leading to blessed unity: a unity that has evaded the Body since it was first established, through the power of the Holy Spirit, by James, the brother of Yeshua, nearly 2,000 years ago in the Upper Room on Mount Zion.

In the end, I have become totally convinced that there is only one way for the Body of Yeshua to finally achieve this long elusive goal of unity: let us all, in the spirit, return to the Upper Room on Mount Zion. There, in that sacred place, let us together seek, find and restore the deeply sacred Jewish roots of our faith. Then, from these common roots that reach down from the stump of Jesse into the most holy of all ground, let us, even as distinctly different members of the same Body, together draw our spiritual sustenance.

RRF

---

[1] Charisma, March 2000 page 62
[2] Schmalz, Reuven E. and Fischer, Raymond R., *The Messianic Seal of the Jerusalem Church,* Tiberias, Israel, Olim Publications, 1999

Part One

Who is a Jew?

Introduction

For you are a holy people to the LORD your God; the LORD your God has chosen you to be a people for Himself, a special treasure above all the peoples on the face of the earth. The LORD did not set His love on you nor choose you because you were more in number than any other people, for you were the least of all peoples; but because the LORD loves you, and because He would keep the oath which He swore to your fathers--- For the LORD'S portion is His people; Jacob is the place of His inheritance. He found him in a desert land and in the wasteland, a howling wilderness; he encircled him, He instructed him, he kept him as the apple of His eye. (Deut 7:6-8, Deut 32:9-10)

Who are these people, holy to the LORD, the very apple of His eye? The State of Israel, the Body of Yeshua, and the world beyond have relentlessly posed this question for countless generations, and still, for many, the answer remains unclear.

For the State of Israel, the elusive and often hotly debated definition lies at the very heart of determining who or who cannot become citizens of the Land. Further, this lack of clarity has sparked a continuing controversy among the several denominational branches of Judaism with respect to which has or has not the authority to perform recognized conversions to Judaism. This conversion authority issue has not only torn apart internal denominational understanding and acceptance, but also has seriously impacted relationships between the Jews in Israel and those in the Diaspora, especially those in the United States.

For the Body of Yeshua, the question takes on more spiritual dimensions. For those who embrace replacement theology, the Christian Church has

21

replaced biblical Israel, therefore they, as Christians, have become "spiritual Jews" who have taken the place of Jews in the natural. In their thinking, both the continuing Nation of Israel and its 15 million or so ethnic Jews have become irrelevant.

Still others within the Body of Yeshua offer various "proofs" showing they are physically descended from one or more of the "Lost Ten Tribes" of Israel and therefore share the same covenantal relationships with God as do traditionally recognized ethnic Jews. Still others make even more elaborate claims. For example, the "British-Israel" group offer the "documented" assertion that they are the only legitimate descendants of the "Ten Lost Tribes" and therefore the only "true Jews." Thus, they further claim, "Great Britain has now become the 'true Israel'."

Finally, consider the Latter Day Saints (Mormons) who claim themselves to be the only "true Jews." All other persons, they hold, are "Gentiles," *including* all 15 million ethnic Jews.

For the world beyond Israel and the Body, "Who is a Jew?" has even more profound implications. Even while denominational Judaism struggles to establish its own internal pecking order of legitimacy, even while some Christians disallow everything Jewish, principally the Jews themselves and Biblical Israel, the physical enemies of Israel (namely its Arab neighbors on every side, and the Palestinian Authority within) very successfully continue to solidify world support for their contention that they alone have claim to the Land of Israel. In their view, the acceptance of which is ever growing, even in the eyes of the Church, Israel is being illegitimately "occupied" by "Jewish aggressors" who among other things are "Judiazing Jerusalem."

Thus, "Who is a Jew?" is anything but a casual inquiry. Indeed, it is a profoundly important question, the many and various answers to which have historically, are currently and will in the future greatly impact the Nation and State of Israel, the tiny minority of surviving ethnic Jews in the continuing Diaspora, the Body of Yeshua, and even the entire world beyond.

From a fleshly perspective, who and who is not a Jew remains a core issue, the resolution of which will determine when and if there will ever be peace (the absence of terrorism, the threat of war, and/or war itself) in the Middle East.

From the perspective of the Body of Yeshua, I believe there will be no real peace in the world until Yeshua comes again.

In the heavenly, nothing could be more important. Yeshua is waiting for His bride to make herself ready:

Let us rejoice and be glad and give the glory to Him, for the marriage of the Lamb has come and His bride has made herself ready.[1]

1 Rev. 19:7 NASV

Chapter One

Jewish Demographics

"From Adam the promise concerning Christ is passed on to Seth; from Seth to Noah; from Noah to Shem; from Shem to this Eber, from whom the Hebrew nation received its name as the heir for whom the promise about Christ was intended in preference to all other peoples of the world. This knowledge the Holy Scriptures reveal to us. Those who are without them live in error, uncertainty, and boundless ungodliness; for they have no knowledge about who they are and whence they came." (Martin Luther)[1]

Martin Luther, an historically validated pillar of anti-Semitism, would probably have readily agreed with those contemporary biblical commentators who interpret that a Jew, in the natural, is a descendant of the patriarch Judah, the fourth son born to the patriarch Jacob (later Israel) by his first wife, Leah.

The first use of the name "Jew" in Scripture to describe a member of the tribe founded by Judah, is in 2 Kings 16:6, written circa 550 BCE. In the *Tanach* (Old Covenant), there are 78 subsequent uses of "Jew" (rendered in Hebrew: *Yehudi*) Likewise, the word Judaism means literally "Judah-ism" or the religion of the *Yehudim* (Jews).

"Jew" is by no means an exclusively Old Covenant appellation. "Jew" (rendered in Greek: *Ioudaios* [ee-oo-dah-yos]) is used 205 times in the New Covenant.

Originally, the term *Yehuwdim* referred specifically to members of the tribe of Judah, as distinguished from the other tribes of Israel. However, after the death of King Solomon, the nation of Israel was split into two kingdoms: the kingdom of Judah and the Kingdom of Israel. Subsequently, *Yehuwdi* could properly be used to describe any member of the kingdom of Judah, which included three tribes: Judah, Benjamin and Levi.

When the kingdom of Israel was conquered by the Assyrians in 722-721 BCE and the nation of Israel, consisting of the ten tribes that comprised the kingdom, were taken into captivity, only the three tribes in the kingdom of Judah remained in the Land. These people became universally known as "Jews," a name still used to describe all blood descendants of the twelve sons of Israel, as well as those non-blood descendants who converted to Judaism, and their descendants.[2]

Today, by best estimates, there are approximately 15 million *Yehuwdim* in the world. Some 5 million live in Israel. The other 10 million are scattered throughout the nations as a continuing Diaspora in 120 wide spread national segments. By far the largest of these is in the United States with 5.8 million. The next largest segments are in France: 600,000; Russia 550,000; Ukraine 400,000; Canada 360,000; United Kingdom 300,000; Argentina 250,000; Brazil 130,000; South Africa 106,000; and, Australia 100,000.

Most of the remaining segments have fewer than 10,000 *Yehuwdim*. Of these smaller groups, 63 have fewer than 1,000.

Interestingly, groups of *Yehuwdim* ranging in size from 25,000 to less than 1,000 manage to survive in the very camps of their enemies, in such unseemly places as: Iran (25,000); Morocco (7,500); Yemen (800); Syria (250); Iraq (120); and, in Bahrain and Egypt, each with less than 100.[3]

It isn't surprising that the most populous urban Jewish centers are in the United States. The most populous urban Jewish communities are shown in the following table.[4]

Cities with the Largest Jewish Population in the Diaspora

City	Population	City	Population
New York, USA	1,750,000	London, UK	200,000
Miami, USA	535,000	Moscow, Russia	200,000
Los Angeles, USA	490,000	Buenos Aires, Argentina	180,000
Paris, France	350,000	Toronto, Canada	175,000
Chicago, USA	248,000	Kiev, Ukraine	110,000
San Francisco, USA	210,000	Montreal, Canada	100,000
Boston, USA	208,000	St. Petersburg, Russia	100,000

The Jewish people, the Nation of Israel, and the State of Israel have historically occupied a prominent place in the world's list of priorities and concerns. Even today they remain a seemingly central focus of international attention. For example, in the past several years, more than half of the resolutions passed by the United Nations have been pointedly focused upon and against Israel.[5]

It is important, I believe, to recognize just how imponderably disproportionate the scope of this worldly focus is, given the demographic dimensions of the tiny minority who remain the subject of such unceasing attention.

According to the latest estimates, there are currently some 6,073,104,685 people in the world.[6] Of this vast multitude, only 15,000,000 are ethnically Jewish. Stated differently, there is one Jew for every 405 non-Jews. Or, the Jewish people represent less than one quarter of one percent of the world's population.

[1] Martin Luther, *Luther's Works*, Vol. 2, pp 207-209 (Quoted by James Montgomery Boice in his commentary on Genesis, Volume 1)

[2] "Judaism 101," The American-Israeli Cooperative Enterprise, found at www.us-israel.org.

[3] World Jewish Congress (WJC), Lerner Publications Company, 1998, as quoted by the American-Israeli Cooperative Enterprise

[4] Ibid

[5] Editorial comment given to the author by Paul Jablonowski, Awareness Ministry (Director Robert Somerville

[6] U.S Census Bureau, World Population, 1950-2050, at www.census.gov

Chapter Two

Jewish Ethnicity and the Israeli Law of Return

Section One of the Israeli Law of Return, as amended in 1970, proclaims, "Every Jew has the right to come to this country as an *oleh* (immigrant)."

Section 4B defines a "Jew" for the purpose of immigrating to Israel as "—-a person who was born of a Jewish mother or who has become converted to Judaism and is not a member of another religion."

With the passage of this legislation, the government of Israel opened wide the door to full Israeli citizenship for any ethnic Jew who could document his or her *maternal* Jewishness, or failing this was willing to go through the rigorous process of religious conversion.

Then, in order to ensure that families were not broken apart by the immigration of a Jew who happened to be married to a non-Jew, the Law extends the right of immigration to the non-Jewish spouse, their non-Jewish children, and even to their non-Jewish grandchildren and the non-Jewish spouses of such grandchildren. Topping this off, the Law further allows the non-Jewish spouse, children and grandchildren of a certifiable Jew to immigrate to Israel, even if their Jewish sponsor is no longer alive and whether or not he (or she) has immigrated to Israel.

Such "non-Jews" (not Jewish by maternal descent) who are entitled to immigrate under the provisions of this law are granted citizenship but it is noted on their Identity Documents that they are something other than Jewish (usually the country of the person's origin, or sometimes "Christian.")

As the single most glaring exception to the right of all ethnic Jews to immigrate to Israel, only one kind of Jew is automatically excluded under the provisions of this otherwise open invitation —however "iron-clad" the documentation of his or her Jewish ethnicity, any Jew who has "changed his religion" (although not written in the Law as such, in practice, quite pointedly, by accepting Yeshua as the Jewish Messiah) is deemed no longer Jewish, and therefore not entitled to immigrate.

It would probably be difficult to find even one orthodox rabbi in Israel who would deny the historic Jewishness of Yeshua, although the Jewish Messiah Himself would most likely not have qualified for Israeli citizenship under the present Law of Return. He was, after all, a Jew who was more than a little bit involved with the Body. *For the husband is head of the wife, as also Christ is head of the church; and He is the Savior of the body.* (Eph 5:23)

It isn't surprising that this seeming inconsistency in the Law of Return was quickly challenged in the landmark "Brother Daniel" case. This challenge came even before the Law was amended in 1970 to add the provision excluding Jews from Israeli citizenship who had changed their religion.

Brother Daniel (born Oswald Rufeisen), a Polish Jew, converted to Roman Catholicism and later became a Carmelite Monk. Subsequently, this life long Zionist and resistance leader who was responsible for saving many fellow Jews during the Holocaust, applied for Israeli citizenship under the Law of Return, claiming that his nationality under the Law was Jewish, even though his religion was Catholic.

Even though Brother Daniel, the child of a Jewish mother, was clearly Jewish under the provisions of the Law, the State disapproved his application, and he appealed to the Supreme Court. The court found that while the national term "Jew" did not necessarily imply the practice of religious Judaism, "in common parlance" it could not be applied to a person who practiced another faith. Thus, as a practicing Catholic, Brother Daniel could not be recognized by the State of Israel as a Jew.[1]

It was only after this landmark decision that the Law of Return was amended to exclude Jews from citizenship who had converted to another religion . Even so, the Law has subsequently twice been challenged by Messianic Jewish applicants for citizenship. In both cases, the court's previous precedent held and the applicants, although ethnically Jews under the provisions of the Law, were rejected from Israeli citizenship on the sole basis of their faith in Yeshua.

[1] The Anti-Defamation League, "The Conversion Crisis: Testing the Principles," www.adl.org

Chapter Three

Our Father Shem

And Noah begot three sons: Shem, Ham, and Japheth. (Gen 6:10)

Walk down any busy thoroughfare in any Israeli city and you will quickly behold citizens of Israel, both religious and secular, from seemingly every conceivable tribe and nation. There are ebony-black Ethiopians, some with Christian crosses tattooed on their foreheads. There are blonde, blue eyed Europeans, some with felt or knitted *kippa* covered heads who are otherwise indistinguishable from their Scandinavian and Ayrian brothers. There are a variety of Orientals, identical in appearance with their counterparts in every major Far East nation. And, there are red headed Anglo-Saxons with green eyes and freckled faces, still others with roots in India, some traditionally dressed in long silk dresses or white linen suits.

Certainly, there is a preponderance of olive skinned, black headed, prominent nosed, bespectacled, stereotyped targets of the world's anti-Semitism. But, they, like their aforementioned ethnically diverse brethren, except for ever-present Arabs, a smattering of tourists, and a handful of other non-Jews, the great majority of those you will thus behold, despite their many diversities, are *all* citizens of Israel. Many are certifiably Jewish; the rest, non-Jewish spouses, children or grandchildren of Jews; all of them citizens, living in the Land where many of them were born, and to which the rest were called or came in search of "greener" economic pastures.

Scripture provides an explanation for this otherwise inexplicable ethnic potpourri and the basis for a further detailed genealogical study.[1] Since Noah and his family were the only persons left alive after the Flood, the Table of Nations found in Genesis Chapters 10 and 11 naturally begins with them, and it is from Noah's three sons, Shem, Ham and Japeth, that all the inhabitants of

29

the earth are descended.

Japeth, usually mentioned after his two brothers Shem and Ham, is thus presumed to be the youngest. He and his wife were two of the eight people who entered the ark and were saved from the destructive waters of the Flood . Japheth's descendants spread over the north and west regions of the earth: his sons were Gomer, Magog, Madai, Javan, Tubal, Meshech, and Tiras. The Medians, Greeks, Romans, Russians, and Gauls are referred to as his descendants. The Philistines (an ancient, long vanished people in no way related to the contemporary "Palestinian" Arabs) were also descendants of Japheth.[2]

One of Japeth's grandson's, Ashchenaz, and his descendants settled originally in what is now Armenia; although, in later Jewish traditions he was associated, along with his father Gomer, with the Germanic races. Hence, Germanic Jews are still known as "Ashkenazi." It should be pointed out, however, that Ashkenazi Jews, who take their appellation "Askenazi" from the Gentile descendants of Japeth among whom they dwelled, like all Jews, are not ethnic descendants of Japeth but rather of Shem whose descendants are thought to have migrated to this specific part of central Europe after the Assyrian Captivity.[3]

Ham is generally presumed to be Noah's second son. After the waters went down and Noah's household left the ark, Ham found his father, naked and drunk, asleep in his tent.

Ham told his two brothers, who then covered their father without looking on his nakedness. Noah was furious because one of his sons had seen him naked, and he placed a curse on Ham and his descendants. Thus, Ham's offspring were to serve the descendants of Shem and Japheth.

Ham had four sons: Cush, Mizraim, Put and Canaan. The peoples of Ham's line populated parts of Asia Minor, the Arabian Peninsula, and eventually the entire continent of Africa, once known as the Land of Ham. Bill Cooper writes:

"There is--- overwhelming and indisputable archaeological evidence that the early Hamitic peoples were given over to the most debased and degraded systems of thought and worship. Indeed, to say that they were merely deprived of the knowledge of God would be an understatement, for the immediate descendants of Ham were so quick to divest themselves of that knowledge, and so thorough were they in its complete extirpation among themselves, that we can only conclude that they consented to and were partakers in some grand and willful conspiracy to destroy that knowledge altogether. In fact, it is within only a few generations of their migration from Babel, that we read of the Canaanites, the Sodomites and others as having filled their cups of iniquity. And this conclusion is more than adequately confirmed by all the documentary and archaeological evidence that has come down to us.---

"Regarding Ham himself, secular history is almost completely silent save for the fact that Africa was once known as the Land of Ham. The Egyptians likewise called their own land Ham."[4]

Shem, the oldest of the three, was born when Noah was 500 years old. Shem was married at the time of the Flood but had no children. After the Flood he became the father of Elam, Asshur, Arphaxad, Lud, and Aram (usually identified by scholars as Persia, Assyria, Chaldea, Lydia, and Syria, respectively). Thus Shem was the ancestor of the people of the ancient Near East generally, and the Hebrews specifically. Shem died at the age of 600. He is listed by Luke as an ancestor of Yeshua.[5]

Shem is the progenitor of all the Semitic races. At the time of the scattering of the nations from Babel, the descendants of Japheth migrated to the north and north-west of Shinar, mainly towards Europe. They also migrated to the south-east towards the Indian sub-continent, and thence to the Far East. The descendants of Shem and Ham however, shared between them the southern and central regions of Asia Minor and Arabia, with Ham's descendants subsequently spreading onto the African continent.

[1] For an excellent detailed study, see: Cooper, Bill, "The Early History of Man, Parts 1, 2 and 3," www.biblebelievers.org.

[2] "Japeth" (Article: from Nelson's Illustrated Bible Dictionary) Electronic Database (Copyright (C) 1986, Thomas Nelson Publishers)

[3] Cooper, Bill, "The Early History of Man, part 1," www.biblebelievrs.org

[4] Ibid, Part 2

[5] Ibid, Part 3

Chapter Four

The Natural "Seed of Abraham"

Shem was the father of five sons, one of whom was Arphaxad, the father of Shelah who became the father of Eber.

There is, I believe, great significance in this person Eber and his two sons, Peleg and Joktan. While the etymology of the word, "Hebrew," is disputed, many hold it is derived from Eber,[1] or, as others think, from the verb *la'avor*, "to cross over" (people from across the Euphrates).

If, Eber indeed gave his name to all of his descendants, that is, to all "Hebrews," then it can be argued with some authority that not just the Jewish nation, descended several generations later from Jacob through his son Judah, but rather *all* of Eber's descendants were Hebrews, not just those descendants of Peleg. It was Peleg, four generations later, who begat Terah, the father of Abram (later by divine decree named Abraham). Few, however, take notice that Eber also begat the many more descendants of Joktan, the Arab, who were then and remain today the perpetual and bitter enemies of the Nation of Israel, their natural "first cousins," the Jewish people.

There is a common misconception that "Hebrew" and "Jew" are synonymous. Abraham was not the first Jew, as many have erroneously been led to believe. Scripture makes it clear that Judah, the son of Jacob (Israel) was the first Jew.[2] Nor, it seems reasonable to conclude, was Abraham the first Hebrew. Scripture clarifies this point: *Then one who had escaped came and told Abram the* (not **the first**) *Hebrew*—(Gen 14:13a).

While, inarguably, all Jews are indeed the "Seed of Abraham," so are the myriad progeny of another "great" Arab nation, this consisting of the twelve tribes descended through Abram's first son, Ishmael.

Some would argue that Scripture "cancels out" Ishmael's claim to be included in the "Seed of Abraham." The Old Covenant teaches that the promise of the New Covenant will be fulfilled through the seed of Isaac, not Abraham: Paul, later reasserts this truth.[3] Scripture however is speaking here about the "*Spiritual* Seed of Abraham." The descendants of Ishmael nevertheless must, along with their Jewish cousins, be reckoned as "*Natural* Seed of Abraham," that is, his genetic descendants.

In the end, no matter what one's position may be on this interesting issue, more appropriately, and importantly, the descendants of Israel through his son Judah are "Jews," while their cousins, the many descendants of Ishmael are "Arabs."

---

[1] *Unger's Bible Dictonary, "Eber,"* also see: Gen 10:21,24-25

[2] The name "Jew" was first applied to Judah, the Son of Israel, as well as to their territory, Judea: 2 Kin. 25:25; Jer. 32:12; 38:19; 40:11, 41:3; 52:28

[3] Gen 21:12, Rom 9:6-8

Chapter Five

Contemporary Jewish Ethnicity

While there may also be several not clearly defined sub divisions, there are today, two significantly different main Jewish ethnic groups that have evolved from the original twelve tribes: the Ashkenazi and the Sephardi. Both of these groups, like all Jews, are descended from Shem whose third generation removed descendant, Eber, gave his name to all Hebrews. Eber's sixth generation removed descendant Abram (later Abraham) begat Isaac who in turn begat Jacob (later Israel) who begat twelve sons from whom *all* ethnic Jews are considered to be descended.

Ashkenazi: The by far larger of the two groups, the Ashkenazi, take their name from the Hebrew *Ashkenaz*, meaning "Germany." More broadly, this ethnic division includes any of the Jews who lived in the Rhineland valley and in France before their migration eastward to Poland, Lithuania, and Russia after the Crusades of the 11th-13th centuries.

After the 17th century persecutions in eastern Europe, large numbers of Ashkenazi resettled in western Europe, where they assimilated, as they had done in eastern Europe, with other Jewish communities. In time, all Jews who had adopted the "German rite" synagogue ritual were referred to as *Ashkenazim* (plural) to distinguish them from Sephardic (Spanish rite) Jews.

Ashkenazim differ from *Sephardim* in how they pronounce Hebrew, their cultural traditions, in their synagogue chanting, in their widespread use of Yiddish, and especially in their synagogue liturgy. The Sephardic pronunciations, because they are more similar to ancient Hebrew, are used in the contemporary Hebrew language spoken in Israel and elsewhere.

Today *Ashkenazim* constitute more than 80 percent of all the Jews in the world, vastly outnumbering Sephardic Jews. In the late 20th century,

Ashkenazic Jews numbered more than 11,000,000. In Israel the numbers of Ashkenazim and Sephardim are roughly equal and the chief rabbinate has both an Ashkenazic and a Sephardic chief rabbi with equal standing and authority.

All Reform and Conservative Jewish congregations in the United States belong to the Ashkenazic tradition.[1]

Sephardi: take their name from the Hebrew, *Sefarad*, meaning Spain. *Sephardim* (plural) are those Jews (and their descendants) who lived in Spain and Portugal from the Middle Ages until their persecution and mass expulsion from those countries near the end of the 15th century.

The *Sephardim* first fled to North Africa and other parts of the Ottoman Empire, and many of these eventually settled in France, Holland, England, Italy, and the Balkans. Salonika (Thessaloníki) in Macedonia and the city of Amsterdam became major Sephardic population centers.

The thus transplanted *Sephardim* largely retained their native Judeo-Spanish language (Ladino), literature, and customs. They became well known for their cultural and intellectual achievements within the Mediterranean and northern European communities.

The *Sephardim* differ notably from *Ashkenazim* (German-rite) Jews in pre-serving Babylonian rather than Palestinian Jewish ritual traditions. Most of the world's Sephardic Jews now reside in the State of Israel.

The term "Oriental" Jews is perhaps more properly applied to Jews living in or from North Africa (most notably Jews from Morocco, most of whom now live in Israel) and the Middle East who had no ties with either Spain or Germany and who speak Arabic, Persian, or a variant of ancient Aramaic. However, the designation *Sephardim* frequently signifies *all* North African Jews and others who, under the influence of the "Spanish Jews," have adopted the Sephardic rite.[2]

---

[1] Encyclopedia Britannica, Article: "Askenazi," at www.britannica.com

[2] Encyclopedia Britannica, Article: "Sephardi," at www.britannica.com

Chapter Six

The "Denominations" of Judaism

Like the comparatively enormous Christian Church that sprang from its Nazarene Jewish roots, world-wide organized Judaism is a *balagon* (disorder, jumble, mess) of myriad denominational divisions, markedly diverse theological positions and other foundational disagreements that often transcend international borders. In any event, from any perspective, there is certainly nothing even remotely resembling unity within the multifaceted, international, Jewish denominational establishmentæeven a working level of civility would seem to be an optimistic expectation.

All but a relatively few of the world's religious Jews reside in one of two near equally sized national Jewish communities: one in the United States, the other in Israel. Each of these communities differs markedly from the other at almost every level: theological, cultural, political, traditional and social.

The Jewish people themselves generally recognize three major religious denominations: Orthodox Judaism, Conservative Judaism, and Reform Judaism. There is a proliferation of other smaller denominational divisions and sub-divisions, perhaps the most important of which are Humanistic Judaism, Reconstructionist Judaism and the Karaites.

To this, officially "kosher" list of contemporary Jewish denominations, I would, with more than a little trepidation, venture to include *Messianic Judaism*, although even the most liberal of traditional Jews would pronounce individual Jews who accept Yeshua as their Messiah simply "no longer Jews", much less would they favorably acknowledge the legitimacy of any organized body of such believers, who are typically dismissed out of hand with such pronouncements as: " 'Messianic Judaism[sic]' and other groups accepting the tenets of Christianity are not Jewish movements."[1]

Following is a brief overview of the three largest of aforementioned traditional Jewish movements. Messianic Judaism is discussed separately, in following chapters.

Orthodox Judaism: Orthodox Judaism is not a consolidated movement with one central governing body: it is many different movements, all of which adhere to common principles. All of the Orthodox movements share nearly identical observance practices and beliefs, differing only in the details that are emphasized. They also differ in their attitudes toward both modern culture and towards the State of Israel. All do, however share one unshakable core principle: total dedication to both the written and oral *Torah*, which they consider to be inseparable.

Historically, there was no such thing as "Orthodoxy." The term is used primarily in North America (elsewhere the distinction is primarily between "more observant" and "less observant.") The specific term "Orthodox Judaism" is of rather recent origin and is used more as a generic term to differentiate the movements following more traditional practices from the more liberal Jewish movements.

Theologically, Orthodox Judaism views itself as the continuation of the beliefs and practices of the same Judaism, as accepted by the Jewish nation at Mt. Sinai and codified by successive generations of rabbis in an ongoing process that continues to this day.

Orthodox Judaism holds that both the Written *Torah* and Oral *Torah* are of divine origin, and represent the Word of God. This is similar to the view of the Conservative movement, but the Orthodox movement holds that such information (except for scribal errors) is the inerrant word of God and does not represent any human creativity or influence. For the Orthodox, the term *Torah* refers to the "Written Law" as interpreted by the "Oral Law" interpreted in turn by the *Rishonim* (Medieval commentators). As practical questions arise, Orthodox authorities apply the Halachic process (the system of legal reasoning and interpretation described in the Oral *Torah*) using the *Torah* (both Oral and Written) to determine how best to live in accordance with God's will. In this way, Orthodoxy evolves to meet the demands of the times.

One of the distinctions of Orthodox Jews is an openness, even an enthusiasm to question what it is that God requires of them, and then to answer those questions within the system that God gave them.

In addition, among the major movements, only the Orthodox have preserved the "mystical" foundations of Jewish theology, most obviously in the Hasidic movements though no less so in many *yeshiva* movements, both Ashkenazi and Sephardi.[2]

There are several branches of Orthodox Judaism, each with general but not necessarily universally agreed positions. Included are:

"Traditional": This term can be synonymous with "Orthodox" but is usually more in keeping with the term "Conservadox" reflecting varying degrees of Conservative/liberal thinking.

"Centrist/modern/cosmopolitan": These are the Jews who can be seen wearing colorful crocheted skull caps (*kipa sruga*). Adherents usually approve many aspects of secular culture, especially secular education, supplemented by traditional *Torah* study. Most in this group are Zionists.

Yeshivish: These are, colloquially, the "black hat" or "black" Jews, making reference to their manner of dress in all black, very formal attire. Their focus of life is *Torah* study. Secular culture is either tolerated or criticized for its corrupting influences. In general, this group tends to be "non-Zionist" in the sense that they love the Land of Israel and its holiness (many spend a lifetime in Israel studying *Torah*), but they are unenthusiastic about secular Zionism and Israeli secular culture.[3]

Hasidism: The Hasidic movement started in the 1700's CE in Eastern Europe in response to a void felt by many average observant Jews of the day. The founder of *Hasidism*, Rabbi Israel Ba'al Shem Tov (referred to as the "Besht" an acronym of his name) was a great scholar and mystic, devoted to both the revealed, outer aspect and hidden, inner aspect of *Torah*. He and his followers, without veering from a commitment to *Torah*, created a way of Jewish life that emphasized the ability of all Jews to grow closer to God in everything that they did said and thought. In contrast to the somewhat intellectual style of the mainstream Jewish leaders of his day and their emphasis on the centrality of *Torah* study, the Besht emphasized a constant focus on attachment to God and *Torah* in all activities of life.

"Rabbi Ba'al Shem Tov thought and taught that God could be found in the beauty of His creation and therefore that life should be lived in joy. Life should thus be celebrated in the Creator and the *Torah*, not just in the dead letter of the law. It is this celebration that gave birth to the Hassidic dance. Rabbi Ba'al Shem Tov's main point of departure in respect to Zionism is that the only true prophetic ingathering and the reestablishment of the State of Israel will be at the coming of the Messiah. Thus, to their way of thinking, modern Zionism is illegitimate."[4]

Early on, a schism developed between the Hasidic and non-Hasidic Jewish movements, primarily over real or imagined issues of *halachic* observance. The opposition was based on concern that the *Hasidim* were neglecting the laws regarding appropriate times for prayer, and perhaps concern about the exuberance of Hasidic worship, or a concern that it might be an offshoot of false messiahs Shabbtai Zvi or Jacob Frank. Within a generation or two, the rift was closed. Since then, many Hasidic practices have influenced those of their opponents, while their opponents, in turn, have moderated some of the extremes of early *Hasidism*. Nevertheless, the dispute between particular groups of *Hasidim* and their opponents continues to this day, especially in Israel.

Today, *Hasidim* are differentiated from other Orthodox Jews by their devotion to a dynastic leader (referred to as a "Rebbe"), their wearing of formal, conservative black and white distinctive clothing and a greater than average study of the inner aspects of *Torah*.[5]

Conservative Judaism: The name Conservative conveys the founding principle of this movement æthat it is necessary to conserve Jewish traditions in the U.S., a culture in which, they believe, the Reform and Orthodoxy approaches are not viable.

Conservative Judaism attempts to combine a positive attitude toward modern culture, acceptance of critical secular scholarship regarding Judaism's sacred texts and commitment to Jewish observance. Conservative Judaism holds that Judaism has constantly been evolving to meet the needs of the Jewish people in varying circumstances, and that a central halachic authority can continue the halachic evolution today.

In Conservative Judaism, the central halachic authority of the movement, the Committee on Jewish Law and Standards (CJLS), will often set out more than one acceptable position. In such a case, the rabbi of the congregation is free to choose from the range of acceptable positions (or none of them), and his congregation is expected to abide by his choice. The CJLS speaks for the Conservative movement and offers parameters to guide local rabbis who turn to it for assistance. Local rabbis will make use of traditional sources and, when available, religious positions written for the CJLS.

An exception is made in the case of "standards." A "standard" requires an 80% vote of the membership of the CJLS and a majority vote by the plenum of the Rabbinical Assembly. At present, there are three standards:

● The prohibition on rabbis and cantors to attend intermarriages.

● The performance of marriages of divorce(e)s without religious certificates of divorce.(*gittin*)

● The recognition of patrilineal descent.

Willful violations have led to resignations or expulsions from Rabbinical Assembly membership.

Conservative Judaism believes the *Torah* and *Talmud* are of divine origin, and thus mandates the following of Halacha (Jewish law). At the same time, the Conservative movement recognizes the human element in the *Torah* and *Talmud*, and accepts modern scholarship showing that Jewish writings may reflect the influence of other cultures, and in general can be treated as historical documents.

The Conservative movement holds that God is real and His will is made known to humanity through revelation. The revelation at Sinai was the clearest and most public of such divine revelations, but revelation also took place with other people-called prophets and in a more subtle form, and can still occur even today.

Many people misinterpret Conservative Judaism as being like Reform Judaism except with more Hebrew in its services: there are much more profound differences between the two movements. The Conservative movement's leadership is strongly concerned with whether or not the next generation of Conservative Jews will have the commitment to lead an authentic Jewish lifestyle.[6]

Reform Judaism: The most liberal of the major modern Jewish movements, Reform Judaism is at the opposite end of the Jewish theological spectrum from the Orthodox. Some more traditional Jews, reacting angrily to the Reform's liberal practices such as ordaining homosexuals and women as rabbis, etc., would describe the central philosophy of Reform Judaism as: "If it feels good, do it."

A relatively new movement, Reform began in Germany in the 1800s. The early movement, known as "Classic German Reform," that continued on with little philosophical change until the 1960's, was more extreme in its liberalism than contemporary Reform adherents.

Reform differs from Orthodox, Conservative and the other religious movements in its position that the Oral and Written laws are both products of Man in response to divine inspiration. Reform holds that the Written and Oral *Torah* were rendered in the language of the times, and that language changes in its meaning and interpretation over time. Thus, while the laws specifically reflect their times, they retain only the same perpetual basic truths.

The Reform movement continues to emphasize the same key principles of Judaism as the other major movements, with a particular emphasis on individual study, and the freedom, and even encouragement of individual adherents to increase their personal relationship with God by following those practices which lead them into this further intimacy with their creator.

One important difference between Reform and the other two major Jewish movements is that, under unusual circumstances, analogous to a Roman Catholic special dispensation, Reform may consider the offspring of a mixed marriage, where the father is Jewish but the mother not Jewish, to be considered Jewish. Orthodox and conservatives, on the other hand hold exclusively to matrilineal determination of Jewishness.

Today, there are more than 900 Reform congregations in North America with a total membership of more than 300,000.[7]

Perhaps the most striking difference between Reform and the other major movements is Reform's emphasis on the equality of women. In Reform, women are involved at every level of expression and leadership. Such equality of women is by no means to be found elsewhere within Judaism, especially within the various orthodox groups of Israel. It seems clear that the "back seat" status ascribed to Israeli Orthodox women is a central reason for the very small number of North American Jews who have made *aliyah*. In a recent letter to the editor of *The Jerusalem Post*, one frustrated woman wrote:

"Sir, - As one of the all-too-few 'Anglos' who have returned to live in Israel within the past two years, I do not find it difficult to understand the strikingly low numbers of immigrants from English-speaking countries.

"In the Diaspora, a large proportion of Jews identify with their Jewishness through affiliation to a synagogue and their connection with the Jewish religion. There, Judaism is allowed its full range of expression.

"There too, women's voices and active contribution to Judaism are not only tolerated but welcomed, and women take their rightful place alongside their male counterparts as respected leaders, teachers and full members of the Jewish people.

"This is not the case here. Many women and men are not prepared to leave a place of genuine religious pluralism to have to constrict themselves to such realities as the oppression of women in the name of God and the narrowest interpretations of both God and our sacred traditions.

"Sadly, this narrow way of thinking leads to the violation of the rights of many Jews and sometimes, violence." [8]

While both Reform and Conservative movements have begun to take root in Israel, Israeli Judaism is predominately Orthodox, and far and away most new religious *olim* (immigrants) from the West come from Orthodox traditions. Here, the split is more properly reckoned to be along secular/non-secular lines. One recent estimate is that the breakdown is about: 30% secular, 50% traditional (those who to at least some extent practice the Jewish religion, and 20%

religious (orthodox).[9]

The denominational make up of the American Jewish Body is dramatically different from its Israeli counterpart. In America, most religious Jews adhere to the more liberal movements, with only a very few (less than 10% adhering to the more fundamental (Orthodox) expressions.

One survey, although somewhat dated, is still assumed to generally reflect today's American Jewish denominational alignment. This survey[10] found American Jews to be:

Reform...................41.4%	"Traditional"*......................... 3.2%
Conservative...............40.4%	Reconstructionist................... 1.6%
Orthodox...................... 6.8%	Miscellaneous "Jewish"*...... 1.4%
"Just Jewish"*.............. 5.2%	

*self-description, though not a denomination.

[1] Social.,Culture.Jewish Frequently Asked Questions (FAQ): Article: "Who We Are." http://www.faqs.org

[2] The Jewish Student Online Research Center, Article: "Religious Movements," www.us-israel.org

[3] The Jewish Student Online Research Center, Article: "Branches of Orthodox Judaism," www.us-israel.org

[4] Schmalz, Reuven. E., An editorial comment provided to the author.

[5] The Jewish Student Online Research Center, Article: "Hasidism," www.us-israel.org

[6] Ibid

[7] Judaism: Frequently Asked Questions, Part 2: Article: "Reform Judaism" www.faqs.org.

[8] Naomi Oren, "Why Make Aliya?" Letter to the Editor, The Jerusalem Post, Friday, February 25, 2000, page A8

[9] Hillel Applebaum, "Judaism: Frequently Asked Questions, Part 2" : Article: "What are the major Jewish movements?" www.faqs.org.

[10] "Judaism: Frequently Asked Questions, Part 2" : Article: "How many Jews are there today in the U.S.A.?" www.faqs.org.

Chapter Seven

Nazarene Judaism
"The Stump of Jesse" from which Sprouted
Messianic Judaism and the Christian Church

"But these sectarians did not call themselves Christians—but 'Nazarenes.' However, they are simply complete Jews. They use not only the New Testament but the Old Testament as well, as the Jews do—They have no different ideas, but confess everything exactly as the Law proclaims it and in the Jewish fashion—except for their belief in Christ, if you please! For they acknowledge both the resurrection of the dead and the divine creation of all things, and declare that God is one, and that His son is Jesus Christ." [1] Epiphanius (Church Father, 4th Century)

A Brief History: Immediately after Yeshua's ascension into heaven from the Mount of Olives, his disciples: Peter, James, John, and Andrew; Philip and Thomas; Bartholomew and Matthew; James the son of Alphaeus and Simon the Zealot; and Judas the son of James returned to the Upper Room on nearby Mount Zion, the place where, just before His crucifixion, they had celebrated Passover with Yeshua.[2]

It was in this divinely appointed place, located immediately above the very throne upon which King David reigned and where he was later buried, where these first Jewish believers gathered in response to Yeshua's earlier command "---(do not) depart from Jerusalem, but---wait for the Promise of the Father---." [3] There is evidence that the building was owned by John, the Jewish priest,[4] otherwise known to us as the "beloved Disciple."[5]

They waited there obediently as they grew steadily to some one hundred and twenty.

Then, "--- when the Day of Pentecost had fully come, (and) they were all with one accord in one place[6]---suddenly there came a sound from heaven, as of a rushing mighty wind, and it filled the whole house where they were sitting. Then, there appeared to them divided tongues, as of fire, and one sat upon each of them.---."[7]

Thus it was in Jerusalem, the capital of Israel, as chosen and blessed by God,[8] in an unimposing room on top of Mount Zion (the partly original remains of which can still be visited today): here, an incredibly anointed gathering of newly Spirit filled Jews, became the very first Body of Yeshua and inarguably the progenitor of all believers, Jewish and Christian alike—the Body of Yeshua (the Christian Church) in the world today.

THE UPPER ROOM:
Birthplace of the Jewish rooted Christian Church on Mount Zion, Jerusalem, Israel. The Upper Room is located on the second floor, immediately above the throne of King David that later became his tomb.

How could an assembly such as this, with James the Just, the brother of Yeshua as its pastor,[9] and the twelve apostles as its elders, do anything but prosper? And prosper it did.

While there is no available record of the precise number of Jews who ultimately became members of the Nazarene Sect by sealing their belief in Yeshua with a three part baptismal ceremony[10] in sacred grottos, such as the original one located directly behind the Messianic Synagogue on Mount Zion, some sense of their huge number can be found in the Book of Acts as well as in non-biblical sources.

CHAINED CLOSED GROTTO ON MOUNT ZION)

The only remaining entrance, chained closed by the Church, leads to the sacred grotto immediately behind the "Upper Room." It was here that 30-40 First Century artifacts bearing the "Messianic Seal" were found in the late 1960's. There were several other entrances to the extensive catacombs beneath Mount Zion: all have been permanently sealed in recent years.

For example, Scripture records that the original 120 believers before Pentecost (fifty days following Yeshua's ascension) grew by some 3,000 on that one glorious day alone.[11]

Following this, many were added each day until very soon their number totaled 5,000.[12]

The synoptic gospels provide further insight into the rapid growth of the still entirely Jewish Body. By the time Yeshua preached the Sermon on the Mount, he had an audience of "great multitudes" who had come to hear Him from literally all over the country "—*from Galilee, and from Decapolis, Jerusalem, Judea, and beyond the Jordan.*"[13] There are seven other uses of "great multitudes" to describe the excited seeking crowds that followed Yeshua almost wherever He went.[14] Even the most liberal church commentators offer no argument regarding the very large number of Yeshua's early Jewish followers. One traditional estimate is that, at their peak in 135 CE, the Nazarenes totaled about 400,000, some 100,000 of whom were in Jerusalem. [15]

Perhaps one of the most astounding aspects of the Nazarenes was their wide acceptance by other Jewish Sects who did not share their confession of Yeshua as Messiah. While the Upper Room above the Tomb of David could accommodate the original 120 Jewish believers, other meeting places became an almost immediate requirement as their ranks quickly increased. Accordingly, new spin off Nazarene groups, extending from the Mount Zion assembly, met regularly in the Temple courts, in other synagogues, and in private homes where they broke bread together.[16] At these public worship services, teachings and a witness in the name of Yeshua were offered to all within reach.[17]

One explanation for the Nazarene's ready acceptance by other non-believing Jewish sects is the general love and respect afforded by Jews of the time to James the Just, the brother of Yeshua, whom Yeshua, in a post resurrection appearance, had appointed to be the first leader of His newly created Bride.[18] James was named the "Just" by these other non-believing Jewish Sects because of his piety, righteousness, and sweet spirit.[19] James was the first in the line of 15 successive Jewish leaders of the Nazarenes; all of whom, according to tradition, were blood relatives of Yeshua. There is historical support that James' immediate successor, Simeon was a cousin of Yeshua. While the next 13 who followed were certainly all Jewish, their sometimes reported blood relationship to Yeshua is only speculative.[20]

The acceptance of the Nazarenes by other Jewish Sects[21] was to continue as these believers in Yeshua grew to be as formidable as any of the non-believing sects. However, just as Yeshua had predicted, this wonderful peace among Jews wasn't to last,[22] and it disappeared suddenly. In 135 CE, the revered Rabbi of Second Judean Revolt fame; Rabbi Akiva proclaimed Bar Kochba "King Messiah," and invited the Nazarenes to join other Jewish sects in an armed revolt against Rome. When the Nazarenes declined to transfer their allegiance from Yeshua to Bar Kochba, their persecution by other Jews began immediately and continued with a fury.

The Nazarenes, although greatly diminished in number and widely scattered throughout Israel, mostly restricted to mountain communities, lived on quite actively to the end of the fourth century, and then in a state of decline for another two centuries, at least until the end of the fifth century when the "Church of the Circumcision" finally gave way entirely to the "Church of the Gentiles."[23]

De-Judaizing the Mother Church: While the Nazarenes endured and were progressively worn down by unseemly opposition from other Jews, at the same time they were faced with an even more focused and intense persecution by the very Christian Church to which they had given birth.

Even though obedience carried with it seemingly suicidal implications, the Nazarene's, primarily through their Apostle Paul, were intensely dedicated to sharing the gospel by taking to heart Yeshua's imperative : "*Go therefore and make disciples of all the nations, baptizing them in the name of the Father and of the Son and of the Holy Spirit,---.*"[24]

Paul was sent out in obedience by his Nazarene brethren, on three obviously anointed missionary journey's to the Gentiles: the first (46-48), the second (49-52), the third (53-57) and finally, his not exclusively missionary journey to Rome (59-60). It was primarily during these evangelistic outreaches that the Apostle to the Gentiles sewed the seeds of what was to quickly become the Nazarenes' gargantuan Christian Church offspring, which like newly hatched salmon fry, unhesitatingly turned to consume their vulnerable, dying mother.

There was an entirely predictable, natural and almost immediate schism between the Body of Jewish Nazarenes in Jerusalem and the growing army of Christians who were coming to faith in Yeshua as a consequence of the Jerusalem Synagogue's evangelistic outreach. From the Nazarenes' perspective, these Christians who had found salvation in Yeshua were allowed to come and worship in their synagogues, but they were in no way to be considered ethnically, nationally or traditionally Jewish. While they shared the same salvation as joint heirs in Yeshua, they never-the-less remained "strangers" who if they chose to "dwell among them" would be obliged to fully comply with the *Torah*.

"And when a stranger dwells with you and wants to keep the Passover to the LORD, let all his males be circumcised, and then let him come near and keep it; and he shall be as a native of the land. For no uncircumcised person shall eat it. One law shall be for the native-born and for the stranger who dwells among you." (Exod 12:48-49)

On one hand, the more conservative of the Nazarene elders, epitomized by Peter, insisted that the very salvation of such Yeshua professing Christians was conditioned upon full and literal compliance with *all* requirements of *Torah*, including circumcision. On the other hand, the more liberal elders, led by Paul, championed less rigid *Torah* compliance for non-Jewish believers.

As the controversy grew a conference was finally held in Jerusalem in 49 CE between delegates (including Paul and Barnabas) from the church at Antioch of Syria and delegates from the Nazarene Jerusalem Synagogue. This council, presided over by James the Just, met to settle, among other issues, the core dispute over whether Gentile believers in the Jewish Messiah first had to identify with Judaism by being circumcised .

According to Luke, "Certain men came down from Judea and taught the brethren, 'Unless you are circumcised according to the custom of Moses, you cannot be saved' [25] They insisted that Gentiles could not be received into the faith unless they were circumcised and brought under *Torah*. The Apostle Paul, champion of Gentile freedom, said that all people—both Jews and Gentiles—are saved by grace through faith in Yeshua, apart from the works of *Torah*. To require circumcision, he argued, would destroy the good news of God's grace.

In the end, the Jerusalem Council, took up Paul's position. They determined that Gentiles did not have to be circumcised, and that Gentiles should make four reasonable concessions of their own: "We write to them to abstain from things polluted by idols, from sexual immorality, from things strangled, and from blood"[26] In effect, the Gentile believers were simply being required to avoid offending the moral and religious convictions of the Jewish believers.

While the Counsel of Jerusalem was able to quell the controversy regarding Gentile compliance with *Torah*, they were not able to even address the perhaps much more profound fundamental religious, cultural, social, and traditional differences between the two distinctly separate Jewish and Gentile bodies of believers. In short, the Jewish believers shared a strong foundation in *Torah* which they continued to follow in every respect. While *Torah* provided a rich foundation upon which to grow their new found faith in Yeshua, the Nazarenes also shared a distinctly Jewish heritage that was equally rich in tradition, culture and social practice. They also shared the Hebrew and Aramaic languages, which unlike Greek, the *lingua franca* of the time, were for the most part only national in their use and understanding.

The rapidly growing body of non-Jewish Christian believers, however, had nothing, other than their mutual confession and worship of Yeshua, to tie them to the Nazarenes or for that matter to one another. Nor, did they have any understanding of or tradition in *Torah*, which was the very glue that held their Nazarene progenitors together. Before their respective encounters with Yeshua they had been pagans, steeped in a variety of markedly different heathen religions, practices and traditions. To the Nazarenes, these were the *goyim* "untouchables" of their time:

> *Awake, awake! Put on your strength, O Zion; put on your beautiful garments, O Jerusalem, the holy city! For the uncircumcised and the unclean shall no longer come to you.---For the land is defiled; therefore I visit the punishment of its iniquity upon it, and the land vomits out its inhabitants. (Isa 52:1, Lev 18:25)*

It was therefore within this vacuum created by the absence of any real commonality with the Nazarenes (beyond their mutual adherence to Yeshua) that these new non-Jewish Christian believers quickly began to establish a tradition of their own: a tradition that was characterized in part by a conscious effort of its adherents to distance itself from everything Jewish. It was thus here, in this rapidly gestating embryo of the Christian Church, where could be found the spiritual DNA of anti-Semitism and replacement theology.

These unfortunate characteristics of the separately established Christian tradition are well illustrated, for example, by the seeming dismantling and burial of the three-part Nazarene Jewish symbol (Fish, Star of David, Menorah) known as "The Messianic Seal of the Jerusalem Church," and by the suppression of a great body of Hebrew language gospels and other post-resurrection writings that were presumably written and used by the Nazarenes.

50

The Messianic Seal of the Jerusalem Church: I will not elaborate here on the unity message implicit in this three part symbol, which was the subject of my earlier work, co-authored with Reuven Schmalz. I will, however, comment on the Fish, one of the three separate symbols that make up the "Seal."

The fish can be seen as a scripturally supported symbol representing: (1) individual believers, (2) groups of believers, or all believers collectively, and therefore, inferentially, as (3) Yeshua Himself.

VIAL ON TOP OF
ANOINTING OIL STAND

Two of the eight First Century "Messianic Seal" artifacts held privately in Jerusalem. The ancient Aramaic script on the "anointing oil stand" translates: "For the oil of the Spirit." The vial was likely used to hold anointing oil.

The first known written record of the fish as a Christian symbol was made by Clement of Alexandria in about 150 CE, when he suggested to all his readers that they would be well served to include the sign of a fish in their personal seals. Since Clement was a believer, and he didn't find it necessary to expand on why he had made this suggestion, it is easy to infer that the Christian symbolism associated with the fish was by then commonly understood.[27] Indeed, we know from many sources that the symbolic fish was familiar to believers long before the famous Alexandrine was born; in such Roman monuments as the Capella Greca and the Sacrament Chapels of the catacomb of St. Callistus, the fish was depicted as a symbol in the first decades of the second century.

It is most interesting to note that the eight artifacts containing the Messianic Seal, each with the fish as one of its three component symbols, have also been dated to the very beginning of the second century.

51

THE EIGHT ARTIFACTS

Eight of 30-40 "Messianic Seal" artifacts recovered from the grotto on Mount Zion in the early 1960's and now held privately by Ludwig Schneider in Jerusalem. The other artifacts are reportedly held and suppressed by the Church and the government.

In light of the reality of these eight artifacts, each bearing the three-part Messianic Seal, it seems patently obvious that the fish was first used by the Messianic Synagogue on Mount Zion, not as an individual symbol, but as an integral part of a three-part symbol, whose total meaning was considerably different and, if nothing else, at least more inclusive than that of the fish by itself.

Referring back to the time when the Nazarenes left Israel because of unbearable opposition from other Jews and the Christian Church, and considering as well the ongoing intense campaign by this same Christian church to cleanse itself of all things Jewish, it would also seem patently obvious that the fish was purposefully separated from the other two very Jewish rooted elements (the menorah and the Star of David) before it was, by itself, transported to Rome.

Even so, it is very likely that the fish symbol was used by itself as a sign by which early Christians found and identified one another, especially in times of persecution, such as in Rome, before Constantine's conversion, when the early believers had to remain hidden in the catacombs.

I think it also fair to conjecture that Paul and others sent out by the Nazarenes, in their various travels to minister to the Gentiles, could have deliberately presented them with the much more simple singular symbol of the fish.

Certainly, none of the prospective converts would have had any understanding of the significance of the two other very Jewish elements of the Messianic Seal. Also, the detached fish, consisting of two easily drawn intersecting lines, would have been a far more "user friendly" recognition sign than the much more complex three-part Messianic Seal.[28]

The Body of Nazarene New Testament Scripture: While I am an unswerving adherent to the inerrancy of the body of canonized Scripture and believe that the sixty-six books that have come to us through the offices of the Christian Church were by the inspiration of the Holy Spirit, I am never the less fascinated by the great body of relatively recently discovered New Testament apocrypha, much of which, I believe, was originally written in the Hebrew/Aramaic language by the Nazarenes.[29]

Moreover, I am convinced that these writings, perhaps most of which were never serious candidates for canonization, were instead, like the Messianic Seal, purposefully suppressed by the emerging Christian Church. While some may disagree, I believe that several generalizations can be drawn concerning these early New Testament writings:

They have a distinctly Jewish motif and genre.

They are, with some notable exceptions, mostly in consonance with canonized Scripture.

Where new ideas and teachings, not directly supported by canonized Scripture, are presented, these seem to be filling in areas and answering questions not otherwise available, and are generally not seen to be in conflict with any accepted dogma or doctrine derived from the canonized Scripture.

While many of these writings are appropriately labeled as Gnostic,[30] they are never-the-less interesting, instructive, and should be considered in the light of a valuable addition to our understanding of the evolution of the Body of Yeshua.

I believe that the Gnostic label attached by Christian commentators is an accurate reflection of the distinctively Jewish nature of these writings.

Some of these writings have survived only in the form of very small scroll fragments, and in the corroborated quotations of early Gentile Church fathers. Most of the rest were recovered, as fragments, from the ancient Nag Hammadi Library.

The Nag Hammadi Library, a collection of thirteen ancient codices con-

Title and Estimated Date	Extant Condition	Content or Theme
The Gospel of the Nazarenes Late 1st or early 2nd Cent. CE	Several surviving fragments. Also quoted extensively by church fathers, and noted by Josephus	An earlier almost identical and probably the original version of the Gospel According to Matthew. Thought by some scholars to be one and the same as The Gospel According to the Hebrews
The Gospel According to the Hebrews Late 1st or early 2nd Cent CE	Many surviving fragments: extensively quoted by church fathers. Contains 2200 lines, only 300 fewer than canonical Matthew	Strong Jewish character with emphasis on James. Majority of content found in synoptic gospels but also contains hitherto unrecorded events, such as a post resurrection appearance to James wherein Yeshua appointed him as the first leader of the Nazarenes
The Gospel of Peter Early to mid 2nd Cent. CE	One large surviving fragment of sixty verses at Nag Hammadi Library. Existence is further validated by references by church fathers.	Direct parallels with all four canonical gospels. Several familiar gospel accounts of Yeshua's life retold with interesting but not profound variations.
The Gospel of Thomas Late 1st to early 2nd Cent. CE	A single Coptic language (variation of Greek and Egyptian) near complete copy at Nag Hammadi has been dated to about 400 CE.	A collection of sayings by Yeshua. Central themes are salvation as an individual consequence of faith, the nature of God, the Kingdom of Heaven
Epistula Apostolorum Mid to late 2nd Cent. CE	Near complete copies in Coptic and Ethiopic preserved at Nag Hammadi Library	A long and comprehensive instructional letter sent out by the "college of apostles" to the churches. Recounts the life and miracles of Yeshua, and presents many teachings as recorded elsewhere in both the cannon and apocrypha .
The Apocryphon of James Early to mid 2nd Cent. CE	Preserved at Nag Hammadi Library	Records a sharing by the twelve apostles with one another of various sayings and teachings given to them individually by Yeshua.

taining over fifty texts, was discovered in upper Egypt in 1945. This immensely important discovery includes a large number of primary Scriptures: texts once thought to have been entirely destroyed during the early Christian struggle to define "orthodoxy" including the Gospel of Thomas, the Gospel of Philip, and the Gospel of Truth.

The discovery and translation of the Nag Hammadi library, completed in the 1970's, has provided impetus for a major re-evaluation of early Christian history and the nature of Gnosticism.

The table on page 54 is a brief introduction to some of the perhaps more important New Testament Apocrypha. Collectively, I believe at least many of these more than fifty Hebrew/Aramaic writings were available to the Nazarenes and presumably constituted much of their Body of New Covenant Scripture.[31]

"It should be added that most likely many of these early Nazarene Jewish sacred writings were probably reworked and interpolated by later Christian sectarians. In their present form, it cannot be known how extensive have been these alterations from the original writings. There can be no doubt, however, that their core material is Nazarene.

"The very fact that Jewish literature became diversified and spread over three continents in as many and more centuries attests to the truth that Nazarene Judaism was not just some minor blip in Jewish history. The Jewish movement founded upon the life and death of Yeshua the Jew was well on its way to becoming a major, if not *the central* Jewish denomination, before it was snuffed out by the exhaustive efforts of the Church and ultimately, by traditional Judaism itself."[32]

---

[1] Epiphanius: from "Panarion" 29 Quoted from an article, *What is Nazarene Judaism?* By James Trimm and Chris Lingle, The Society for the Advancement of Nazarene Judaism, (www.Nazarene.net) page 1

[2] Acts 1:13

[3] Acts 1:4

[4] Schonfield, Hugh, "The Pentecost Revolution," page 61

[5] Ibid. This John first appears as a disciple called by Yeshua shortly after His baptism (Mark 1:19-20). He does not appear again until the Last Supper(John 13:23). His ownership of the Upper Room would explain the strange story in the other gospels of an unnamed person, evidently greatly trusted by Yeshua, who had been tasked to arrange for the Passover to be celebrated at his house.

[6] It isn't surprising that Jews had assembled in Jerusalem from all over Israel and from the nations. It was Shavuot, one of the three great annual feasts where Jews were commanded by the Torah to do so.

Some hold that these believers only lived in the Upper Room and that they went to the Temple each day to worship, and it was here in this much more open and larger location where Pentecost actually occurred. This position seems reasonable in light of the simple logistics of the situation and is reinforced by the Scriptural teaching that would seem to explain how it was that so many different people could be involved in the momentous event. Surely all of them would not have fit in the relatively small Upper Room, nor were there any sufficient adjacent courts to accommodate a large crowd at this location:

And there were dwelling in Jerusalem Jews, devout men, from every nation under heaven. And when this sound occurred, the multitude came together, and were confused, because everyone heard them speak in his own language. (Acts 2:5-6)

[7] Acts 2:1-4

[8] 2 Sam 5:10

[9] Stated by Jerome as quoted in the *Gospel According to the Hebrews*, recorded in *New Testament Apocrypha, Volume One,* Edited by Wilhelm Schneemelcher, page 178, and affirmed by the Apostle Paul, 1Cor 15:7

[10] The following summary is taken from my earlier work, *The Messianic Seal of the Jerusalem Church, Part Two*, pages 52-53: Bagatti, paraphrasing St. Cyril and Egeria, (both Church Fathers) : "[Those to be baptized] were introduced into the atrium of the baptistery, where, facing the West they renounced Satan, and then facing the East they made a profession of faith with the recital of the creed. Then, each one, divesting [undressing], was anointed with exorcised oil, and then they entered the baptismal basin, immersing themselves three times [in the manner of a ritual Jewish *mikvah* purification rite] ... for the women it seems it was the custom for deaconesses ... to assist [in order to hide] from the gaze of the curious the body of the female being baptized. In fact they [the male officiates] did not carry out any ceremony, much less the anointing with oil of exorcism, since this obliged the baptizer to touch the whole body." See: Bagatti, B., *The Church from the Gentiles in Palestine*, Jerusalem, Franciscan Printing Press, 1984, p.303.

As a matter for further speculation, the traditional Jewish *mikvah* purification rite involves seven successive self-immersions. It would seem an easy reach to describe this shortened (three immersion) Nazarene Jewish baptism as a touching obedient reply of these first on-fire believers in Yeshua literally fulfilling the Great Commission (Matt 28:19) "... baptizing them in the name of the Father and of the Son and of the Holy Spirit ... ."

Emmanuel Testa, O.F.M., in his book, *The Faith of the Mother Church*, pages 146-154, using Cyril of Jerusalem and other church fathers as his source, offers further details of the Nazarene baptismal rite. He suggests that the entire ceremony, including the full body anointing with oil, the three, separate, full body immersions in water, together with the accompanying confessions, professions and liturgy, in sum represent three different baptisms: the Baptism of Fire, the Baptism of Water, and the Baptism of the Spirit.

The Baptism of Fire was the first of the three "rites." The persons to be baptized were instructed on the doctrine of the Way of light (Essene rooted), then many symbolical lamps were lit to brilliantly illuminate the Grotto. One can easily imagine the officiate proclaiming from the just penned Gospel of John, "I am the Light of the world ... ." Interestingly, one of our artifacts recovered in this very place is a small Roman lamp, decorated with both the "Messianic Seal" and many "shoots." I feel certain that it was used in many of these Baptisms of Fire.

The second rite, I would suggest, centered on the three separate immersions "... in the name of the Father, and the Son and the Holy Spirit."

The third "rite" was Baptism of the Spirit, suggested by Cyril to represent that part of Yeshua's baptism when He was filled with the Holy Spirit, symbolized by the dove that rested upon Him. I would further

suggest that this was the Pentecostal "Baptism of the Holy Spirit," which provided an appropriate spiritually charged finale to this incredibly meaningful and exciting initiation of the new believers into "born-
again" membership of the Body.

[11] Acts 2:41

[12] Acts 2:47, 4:4

[13] Matt 4:25

[14] Matt 8:1, 8:18, 12:15, 13:2, 15:30, 19:2; Luke 5:15, 14:15

[15] At least one contemporary topographical reality adds further confirmation. The Mount of Beatitudes is
very near where we live in Tiberias. A seemingly never ending convoy of tour buses transport legions of
"pilgrims" to this site each day to visit a garish Roman Catholic edifice erected on top of the mountain by
the Italian dictator Mussolini. Just out of sight of this crowded tourist attraction, a few meters down the
slope toward Tiberias, there is a natural amphi-theater that was surely carved out by the very hand of God
before the beginning of time. This incredible place is some 500 meters from end to end and about 500
meters from top to bottom. At its upper apex there are several large boulders upon one of which I am
absolutely convinced, Yeshua sat and delivered His famous sermon. Two brothers in the Lord, both engi-
neers, and I tested the perfect acoustics of the place in 1994. They went to the bottom of the slope and
walked from end to end as I, sitting upon each of the boulders, in turn, spoke to them in a normal speaking
voice as we carried on a continuous two-way conversation. The quality and clarity of our hearing was
truly amazing. There is certainly room in this place for a "great multitude" and I am convinced that several hundred thousand Jews were present there that day when Yeshua proclaimed to them among many other
wonderful things: "Do not think that I came to destroy the Law or the Prophets. I did not come to destroy
but to fulfill." (Matt 5:17). It saddens me greatly that today this sacred place is strewn with litter and
fenced by the Church on top of the mountain (since about 1995). If one is insistent, they can gain access
to the place by making a financial contribution of a few shekels to an official of the Church who will in
turn, reluctantly unlock the gate leading to the place. Few take advantage of this great opportunity for a
unique spiritual experience because most are unaware that the place even exists.

[16] Acts 2:46   Perhaps a first reference to "home communion."

[17] Lockyear, Herbert, Sr., " Church: Its Use in the New Testament," *Nelson's Bible Dictionary*. Thomas
Nelson Publishers, 1986, Electronic Database, Biblesoft, 1996

[18] Quoted by Jerome from the *Gospel According to the Hebrews*, recorded in *New Testament
Apocrypha, Volume One,* Edited by Wilhelm Schneemelcher, page 178, as affirmed by the Apostle Paul,
1Cor 15:7

[19] Painter, John, *Just James*, page 1.

[20] Eusebius, *Ecclesiastical History*, Book 4, Chapter 5.

[21] Schonfield, Hugh, *The Pentecost Revolution*, page116. The Jewish people of Jerusalem were strongly
supportive of the Nazarenes. They were pro-Messianism, and the Nazarenes stood for the Messianic
redemption of Israel. It was the leadership of the other Jewish Sects that were to oppose the Nazarenes,
and only then for political, not religious reasons. The Nazareans' rapid growth and strong following made
them a political force to be reckoned with.

[22] Matt 10:23

[23] Mancini, Ignazio, *Archeological Studies Relative to the Judeo-Christians*, pages 176-177

[24] Matt 28:19

[25] Acts 15:1

[26] Acts 15:20

[27] Hasset, Maurice M., *The Catholic Encyclopedia*, Electronic Version, "Symbolism of the Fish."

[28] Schmalz, R.E., and Fischer, R.R., *The Messianic Seal of the Jerusalem Church*, pp 69-70

[29] All references to New Testament Apocryha are taken from: Schneemelcher, Wilhelm, R. McL. Wilson,
translator, *New Testament Apocrypha, Volumes One and Two*, James Clarke & Co., Westminster/Jhon
Knox Press, Cambridge, 1990

30 Dr. Orr writes, "Gnosticism may be described generally as the fantastic product of the blending of certain Christian ideas— particularly that of redemption through Christ— with speculation and imaginings derived from a medley of sources (Greek, Jewish, Parsic; philosophies; religions, theosophies, mysteries) in a period when the human mind was in a kind of ferment, and when opinions of every sort were jumbled together in an unimaginable welter. It involves, as the name denotes, a claim to 'knowledge, ' knowledge of a kind of which the ordinary believer was incapable, and in the possession of which 'salvation' in the full sense consisted. This knowledge of which the Gnostic boasted, related to the subjects ordinarily treated of in religious philosophy; Gnosticism was a species of religious philosophy" (The Early Church, 71).

(from International Standard Bible Encylopaedia, Electronic Database Copyright (C) 1996 by Biblesoft)

31 For a more detail study of this fascinating material I direct the reader to: Schneemelcher, Wilhelm, R. McL. Wilson, translator, *New Testament Apocrypha, Volumes One and Two*, James Clarke & Co., Westminster/John Knox Press, Cambridge, 1990 For the entire The Nag Hammadi Library, in a form that can be searched for words or phrases, I also direct the reader to the Gnostic Society Library's excellent website at: www.gnosis.org

32 Schmalz, Reuven E., Editorial comment given to the author

Chapter Eight

Messianic Judaism in the United States

"Then they shall know that I am the LORD, when I scatter them among the nations and disperse them throughout the countries."
(Ezek 12:15)

Some years ago, soon after I had joyfully embraced my Jewish roots in Beth Simcha, a vibrant Messianic Congregation in Federal Way, Washington, Donna, and I were attending our very first congregational Passover Seder. The event was presided over by our pastor, Frank Stiller.

Frank, like myself, had come full circle. Born of Jewish parents, raised in an orthodox home, he had been "born again" during his twenties. After he graduated from Gordon Cromwell Seminary, Frank was called to pastor a Charismatic Baptist Congregation, a position he held for a number of years until he, like I, was miraculously called by the Holy Spirit to return to his Jewish roots.

In his opening comments to the assembly, more than 300 seated at round tables in the ornate dining room of a posh local country club, Frank, in an inspired moment requested: "Will all fully blooded Jews who are present here this evening please stand."

As I rose from my seat, I was thrilled and perhaps a bit too prideful by this special recognition of my own recently resurrected and now greatly treasured Jewish heritage. However, what immediately followed made a deep and lasting impression:as I looked about the room, I was appalled to see that only five other people were standing.

Looking at this experience from the benefit of ensuing years, I should not have been surprised by the fact that only two percent of a Messianic

Congregation were Jews. According to one estimate, there are some 1.72 billion "Pentecostals/Charismatics" and "Great Commission Christians" in the world today[1] these alongside, by even the most generous estimate, a minuscule 25,000 (.0000213%) ethnically Jewish Messianic Jews. Stated differently, and using round numbers, there are some 50,000 "born again" Christians for every one "born again" Messianic Jew.

From different demographic perspectives, as stated earlier, the Jewish people (all Jews) represent less than one quarter of one percent of the world's population: there is one Jew for every 405 non-Jews. Further, from yet another perspective, there is only one Messianic ("born again") Jew for every 600 non-believing Jews. By any reckoning, Messianic Jews are a tiny minority within a tiny minority.

History and Development: Messianic Judaism, a biblically based movement of Jewish people who accept the truth that Yeshua is the promised Messiah of Israel, is, in effect, a modern day "shoot" from Nazarene Judaism, as it was practiced in the first messianic synagogue on Mount Zion.

The current rapidly growing movement can be traced to Great Britain, where in 1813 a band of Jewish believers were united together in bonds of heritage, witnessing and charitable works as the "Hebrew Christian Alliance and Prayer Union of Great Britain." The movement remained virtually dormant until the Arab-Israeli Six Day War in 1967, then it began to flourish.

Modern Messianic Judaism is an outgrowth of "Hebrew Christianity" as the movement was mostly known prior to its resurgence after 1967. Early "Hebrew Christians" were mostly "fundamentalists" in their Christian orientation, while at the same time they held very strong pro-Jewish, pro-Israel, Zionistic views.[2]

While there had been earlier organizational stirrings, the Hebrew Christian Alliance of America (HCAA) was formally established in 1915. The new organization placed early emphasis on evangelism, and on the Zionistic cause in what was then called "Palestine."

The Christian Synagogue of Philadelphia: the first distinctly Jewish Christian house of worship in the United States, was opened in February, 1922 by John Zacker, a Russian Jew.

During the 1920's and 1930's the HCAA took part in the rising fight against anti-Semitism, and offered strong opposition to Henry Ford's distribution of the forged *Protocols of the Learned Elders of Zion*.[3]

The "First Hebrew Christian Church" was established in Chicago in 1934 under the umbrella of the Presbyterians. This church, like others that followed, was characterized by typically main stream Christian worship with a "Jewish flavor." The HCAA had established an early policy that they would forever

60

remain a fellowship of Jewish believers, who nevertheless maintained their close ties to the doctrine and worship practices of other "Christian churches."

It was not until the late 1960's when the newly formed Young Hebrew Christian Youth Organization (YHCYO) came into being that the Hebrew Christian movement began to take on an entirely Jewish identity all of its own, quite distinct and separate from main line Christianity.

While older, more traditional members of the HCAA offered strong resistance to the move away from main line denominational Christianity, the younger generation won out in the end, and in June 1975, the Messianic Jewish Alliance of America (MJAA) was officially launched. Its adherents quite deliberately distanced themselves from their earlier Hebrew Christian identification with Gentile Christianity and began to think of themselves as "Messianic Jews," rather than as "Christians."

By generally accepted definition, a Messianic Jew had become a person who was born Jewish or converted to Judaism, who was a "genuine believer" in Yeshua, and who acknowledged his Jewishness.

Paul Lieberman, an American born Messianic Jewish author and leader who has immigrated to Israel, put the transition in "born again" Jewish thinking quite succinctly:

"A tenet of Messianic Judaism asserts that when a Jew accepts a Jewish Messiah, born in a Jewish land, who was foretold by Jewish prophets in the Jewish Scriptures, such a Jew does not become a Gentile. In fact, he becomes a completed Jew---a Jew who believes Yeshua is the Messiah."[4]

In this context, there is no conflict whatsoever between being "Messianic" and being "Jewish," since believing in Yeshua, the Jewish Messiah, is one of the most Jewish things a Jew can do. David Stern, a Messianic theologian and pillar of the movement goes right to the point: "I am religious. Not Orthodox, not Conservative, not Reform, not Reconstructionist but Messianic."[5]

One key aspect of Messianic Judaism's deviance from Hebrew Christianity is the generous introduction of Jewish liturgy and worship practices into most Messianic services. The meeting halls themselves often look similar to other synagogues, with the Israeli flag and the American flag at the front on either side, a Star of David, a menorah, and (in some cases) a *Torah* scroll behind a curtain.

Another distinctively Messianic Jewish practice is the use of original Hebrew terms in place of traditional (Gentile) Christian terms, such as: *Abba* (God the Father), *HaBen* (God the Son), *Yeshua HaMashiach* (Jesus Christ), *Ruach HaKodesh* (Holy Spirit), *B'rit Hadasha* (New Testament), *Mikveh* (baptism), *Jochanan* (John), *Miriam* (Mary), *Sha'ul* (Paul), and *Shilush* (Trinity).[6]

The leading organization of this movement is still the MJAA (the former HCAA), the largest of its kind: there are three other smaller alliances in the Untied States. Collectively, by my personal estimate, the four alliances represent, in the United States, no more than 20,000 Messianic Jews and 80,000 associated "Messianic Gentiles."

In 1975, there were only seven of these distinctively Jewish congregations; a decade ago, there were only fifteen. Today, there are at least ten times that number scattered across the United States.

Over ninety percent of the Messianic congregations in the United States are "charismatic" in their theological orientation (believing in the gifts [charisms] of the Holy Spirit: tongues, healing, etc.), with one-third having been created by the Pentecostal Assemblies of God denomination.

Interestingly, these congregations are not "overtly evangelistic." They see their purpose as being fellowship and worship "in a fashion more conducive to the Jewish heritage" than would be the case in a traditional Christian setting.[7]

Opposition: A two-edged Sword: Jewish believers in Yeshua, whether labeled Hebrew Christians or Messianic Jews, have encountered much opposition over the years, from both other Jews and Christians. Many early Hebrew believers themselves retreated from their own rich Jewish heritage. For example, the Chicago-based American Messianic Fellowship (AMF), established by the Christian Zionist W.E. Blackstone in 1887, called the movement "utterly unscriptural," stating its belief that "while still a Jew by birth, in spiritual condition the believing Jew is now a Christian and totally removed from the religion of Judaism." Also, in 1975, the Fellowship of Christian Testimonies to the Jews (FCTJ) officially opposed Messianic Judaism as a "fourth branch of Judaism, and as distinct from mainline Christianity.[8]

Of course, Jews have opposed the movement as well. In the United States, the opposition, while sometimes very vocal, has not been characterized by life threatening violence as it has been in Israel.

Since the beginning of the last century, most American Jews have not accepted Jewish believers in Yeshua as being genuine in their expressed convictions. Common belief among traditional Jews is that any Jew who becomes a believer in Yeshua must either be deranged or have adopted this view for material gain.

In summary, Messianic Jews are a tiny minority who find themselves caught between two opposing groups. On one side Christians oppose them for their supposed grave sin of "Judaizing" main line Christianity. On the other side, traditional Judaism opposes them because they commit the grave sin of making Jesus, who they see as an entirely Gentile God, an idol.[9]

In the end, I believe that the real genesis of growing opposition to Messianic Judaism is not primarily in response to their different religious conviction and practice, but rather out of a genuine fear: perhaps even an unrecognized fear on both sides who feel increasingly threatened by the movement that is so strongly emerging between them. As shown previously, despite efforts on both sides to hold the resurgent group in check, Messianic Judaism is growing exponentially and by all accounts it will continue to do so.

[1] David B. Barrett and Todd M. Johnson, " International Bulletin of Missionary Research," January 2000

[2] Greene, William, The Ascendence of "Messianic Judaism" in the Context of "Hebrew Christianity," Article, found at www.mcu.edu/papers/mess, page 1

[3] Ibid, page 2

[4] Ibid., page 3

[5] Ibid

[6] Ibid, page 4

[7] Ibid

[8] Ibid, pages 5-6

[9] Ibid, page 6

Chapter Nine

Messianic Judaism in Israel

'For thus says the Lord GOD: "Indeed I Myself will search for My sheep and seek them out. "As a shepherd seeks out his flock on the day he is among his scattered sheep, so will I seek out My sheep and deliver them from all the places where they were scattered on a cloudy and dark day. "And I will bring them out from the peoples and gather them from the countries, and will bring them to their own land; I will feed them on the mountains of Israel, in the valleys and in all the inhabited places of the country. "I will feed them in good pasture, and their fold shall be on the high mountains of Israel. There they shall lie down in a good fold and feed in rich pasture on the mountains of Israel.

(Ezek 34:11-14)

As with the much larger Body of traditional Judaism, there are vast differences between the respective bodies of Messianic Jewish believers (including associated Gentiles) in the United States and Israel.

A recent (early 1999) formal survey of the Israeli Body by a Danish Christian group found that there are some 81 organized Messianic Jewish groups in Israel, including 69 that describe themselves as "congregations" and 12 as "home groups."[1] From the data made available by this excellent independent effort, the following observations have been gleaned:

● There are some 2,009 ethnic Messianic Jews along with 1,207 associated Messianic Gentile believers who are identified as "members" of the 69 congregations.[2]

● Geographically, the congregations are scattered throughout the entire country. The three largest are: Grace and Truth Christian Assembly in Rishon

Letzion (165 Jewish and 35 Gentile), Peniel Fellowship in Tiberias (80 Jews and 100 Gentiles) and Carmel Assembly in Haifa (60 Jews and 100 Gentiles).

The rest are quite small by American standards. Statistically, the "average" Israeli congregation has 47 members (29 Jews and 18 Gentiles).

● Theologically and in worship practice less than half, 33 of the 69 congregations, fit into the typical American model/definition of "Messianic Jewish."[3] Eight of these 33 adhere more closely to synagogal worship style and practice (*Torah* service, Jewish rooted liturgy, etc.). The other 25 who identify themselves as "Messianic Jewish" generally limit their association with Israel and things Jewish to celebrating the Jewish holidays and by using Hebrew as a primary language (or by providing a Hebrew translation).

● The remaining 36 congregations either specifically do not identify themselves as "Messianic" (20) and/or are rooted theologically and in practice in traditional main line Protestant denominations (16).

● Among the pastors/leaders of these 69 congregations, 27 have attended either a seminary or bible college. The other 42 have received no formal training and in most cases are the founders of their groups.

● With respect to worship practice, 37 of the congregations describe themselves as "charismatic." The other 29 either call themselves "non-charismatic" or make no mention of this distinction.

As a personal observation, while there have been several persistent attempts by various local leaders to form an effective national level governing organization for the Israeli Body, and several various *ad hoc* organizational structures have succeeded in dealing with major issues and problems that have impacted the entire Body, there is no one such governing and/or advisory organizational structure to which all, or even most of the congregations subscribe. In short, while there have been honest efforts to establish such a structure, there is nothing like an equivalent of the MJAA in Israel.

The primary reason for this situation is, I believe, that many of the congregations are inclined to remain fiercely independent. For example, in addressing outreach beyond his own congregation, one pastor stated to those taking the recent national survey that he "finds it hard to give priority to events organized on a national level."

While the survey is most useful as a tool to study the organized congregations and home groups, it does, necessarily, leave out a considerable number of independent, both Jewish and Gentile, believers who are not affiliated with any organized group. To my personal knowledge, many individual believers have attempted to worship in one or more local congregations but have, for one reason or another, not continued to do so and have thus become "scattered sheep."

By one count, in the greater Tiberias area alone, there are more than 80 such individuals. While there is no way to accurately determine the actual number of such believers nationally, my educated guess is that they would aggregate to about half the size of the affiliated Body. Hence, at least another 1,500 can be added to the total.

On a much more encouraging and exciting note, Barbara Richmond, a well known and highly respected church leader and teacher, who is also an acknowledged leader of the rapidly growing Church-wide "Return to the Jewish Roots" movement, reported an amazing and tremendously encouraging encounter in Jerusalem which is repeated here with her permission. I have known Barbara personally for nearly eight years, and have absolutely no doubt that what she has reported, as recorded by Jim Bramlett, is totally reliable[4]

"A Startling Encounter with a Rabbi in Jerusalem"
by Jim Bramlett, Lt. Col., USAF (retired)
Assistant to the President
Campus Crusade for Christ International

"Barbara Richmond has kept this amazing incident very private but now feels led to share her miraculous experience in Jerusalem in 1995 involving a group of Rabbis. There is no doubt that Barbara is a totally reliable witness. She is director of Women's Ministries at a solid Central Florida church with which I am familiar. I know her pastor. She is a popular Bible teacher, speaker, seminar leader and author.

"In September of 1995, Barbara led a group on a tour to Israel as she frequently does. On their free day with no scheduled activities, she went with several of her group for shopping into the Old City of Jerusalem. She says, "It was a beautiful afternoon and I was leaning against one of the old stone walls, just kind of praying in the Spirit and enjoying where I was"

"Suddenly over her left shoulder she heard a man's voice call 'Barbara.' She turned to look but didn't see anyone she recognized. The only male on the street was a man she described as 'in full black attire, big beard and curls on the side...', an orthodox Rabbi.

"She thought to herself that he could not have been the one to say her name because they do not even speak to women in public. In fact, she avoided eye contact as she knew this sometimes offended them. She turned back, thinking she had been mistaken.

"A few seconds later, she again heard the voice say, 'Barbara - isn't that your name?' She looked again and discovered that the rabbi was looking right at her. "Don't be afraid,' he said 'Come here.' She moved toward him. He told Barbara his first name and said, 'I live here in Jerusalem and I wanted to tell you that I am a believer that Yeshua is Messiah. As a matter of fact there are 40 of us Rabbis and rabbinical students in the community to whom, as we have been studying the *Torah*, the *Ruach ha'Kodesch* (the Holy Spirit) has shown us that Yeshua is the Messiah.'

"Barbara's heart was so moved by this unusual work of the Holy Spirit that she broke into tears. The Rabbi added: 'At present we are secret believers, not because we are afraid, but because the Lord, the Holy Spirit, has not told us to speak out our testimony yet. The Lord has told us to pray for our brethren, so we are meeting at midnight and we are praying.'

"Barbara asked the obvious question: 'But how did you know me? Why are you telling me this?' The Rabbi chuckled and replied, 'I don't know you, but last night when we were praying, one of the other Rabbis came over to me. He put his hand on my shoulder and said to me, 'Tomorrow afternoon at 2 o'clock, you go to...(the name of the street they were standing on) and you will see there an American woman with black hair. Her name is Barbara. Give her this message from the Lord.'

"The Rabbi then gave Barbara a message from the Lord. They talked for a few minutes and before they parted' the Rabbi asked, 'What do you do?' Barbara explained that she was a Bible teacher. His face lit up and he replied, 'Oh, would you be interested in just some simple notes that I have made since I have come to faith in Yeshua and have been studying His words?'

"She said yes, of course and he later had delivered to Barbara's hotel a collection of handwritten notes of Hebrew and cultural insights into the Gospel passages, unique insights not evident in the English or Greek words themselves. These notes form the basis for the book *Jewish Insights into the New Testament*.

"Upon leaving, the Rabbi told her, 'When our testimony becomes public, I am sure we will see each other again.'

"Barbara has been to Israel several times since but has not seen the Rabbi personally, nor has she revealed his name, honoring his request. However in a phone conversation with him (1997), he related that quite a few more have become believers in Yeshua and asked for prayer from the body of Messiah in other parts of the world.

"Why is this testimony being freely shared now? Will it not endanger the believers?

"The Holy Spirit seemed to indicate that the time was now and upon consultation with the Rabbi, he agreed."

Donna and I recently met with Barbara in Tiberias on two separate occasions, while I have been preparing this manuscript. Barbara further recounted to us that she has been in continuing contact with not only the original "Messianic Rabbi" but with other newly born again orthodox Jewish rooted believers as well. While Barbara is unable to accurately quantify the size of this movement in Israel, she is certain from the reports she has received, that it has grown considerably since her first encounter, and it increasingly continues to do so.

[1] Hansen, K.K. and Skjott, B.F., " Facts & Myths about the Messianic Congregations in Israel." Page 57F

[2] Believers identified as members of "International Congregations" and "Home Groups" are not included in this analysis.

[3] The model is taken from the "Statement of Faith" published by the Messianic Jewish alliance of America. See Appendix

[4] A highly respected Israeli Messianic leader, one of my closest spiritual advisors, pointed out to me that Barbara's testimony "had not been confirmed" and therefore should be viewed in that light. I have, prayerfully, reached the following conclusions:

There are two areas of Scripture that are used by some to support the need for such "confirmation." One group of references point to the need for the "testimony of two or three witnesses---." (Deut. 17:6, 19:5; Matt 18:16; 2 Cor 13:1; 1 Tim 5:19; Heb 10:28). However, a review of the cited Old Covenant Scriptures shows that the "two or three witnesses" are required to justify capital punishment, and the cited New Covenant references deal variously with accusations against an elder, the rejection of Yeshua, and the validity of doctrine. None have anything whatsoever to do with establishing the veracity of direct or indirect revelations from God to individual believers, such as Barbara Richmond's testimony in this instance.

There are certainly many instances in Scripture where God revealed Himself either directly or indirectly to *one* individual without any further "confirmation" except by the confirming events which followed. One very familiar example of this is the encounter of Moses with God in the burning bush. Looking into the New Covenant for further examples, if we are to accept the notion that at least some "confirmation" is required to ensure the veracity of a believer's testimony, then, must we, by this stringent standard, dismiss the entire Revelation of John because it was given only to John?

The other Scripture bearing on this matter is 1Thes 5:21, "Test all things; hold fast what is good."

The several Christian commentators I regularly consult agree that "testing" here has two dimensions:

(1) "discerning of Spirits" (see 1 Cor. 12:10; 14:29; 1 John 4:1). (2) Another is to test the professed revelation whether it is in accord with Scripture, as the Bereans did (See: Isa. 8:20; Acts 17:11; Gal. 1:8-9).

With respect to "discerning of Spirits," I have spoken to Barbara at length on this matter and she further testifies that she has received only *one* rejection regarding her testimony, it being a highly vitriolic commentary given, and widely disseminated by an individual Israeli Messianic believer. She also shared that she has received literally several thousand responses from believers all over the world that were all highly supportive, positive, with some of these even being "confirming."

Barbara has, quite in accordance with Scripture, asked the individual who rejected her testimony to meet with her in Israel to discuss and hopefully resolve the matter. According to Barbara, he flatly refused to take part in such a meeting.

Testing Barbara's testimony against the Body of Scripture is by far an easier matter. Both the Old and New Covenants abound with numerous examples pointing to the Jews eventually coming into the Kingdom. Many, including myself, believe we are in the end times when the return of Yeshua is imminent. The testimony that there is a large and growing body of orthodox rabbis in Jerusalem who are "closet" believers is, I believe, quite consistent with both Scripture and the realities of how the Orthodox must relate within their own body to gain their material support from the government and to otherwise survive in Israel.

Chapter 10

The "Lost Tribes" of Israel
The More Bizarre Claims to Israeli Tribal Origin

The considerable mythology associated with the supposed "Lost Tribes of Israel" has arisen from the several dispersions of the Jewish people. The most significant of these were the fall of Israel to the Assyrians in 722 BCE, and the collapse of Judah before Babylonian and Chaldean attacks in 597-581 BCE.[1]

After the death of King Solomon, the nation of Israel was divided into two kingdoms. In the South, centered around Jerusalem, the tribes of Judah, Benjamin and Levi were known as the Kingdom of Judah. The other ten of the original twelve tribes: Ephriam, Manasseh, Gad, Rueben, Simeon, Zebulon, Napthali, Asher, Issachar and Dan remained settled in the North, and they continued to be called the Kingdom of Israel.

The Kingdom of Israel regressed into their former practice of idol worship which greatly angered YHWH: so great was His anger that he caused Shalmaneser, King of Assyria to defeat them in battle and to take them into captivity around 722 BCE.[2]

Already in 732 BCE. Tiglath-Pileser III had carried Reuben, Gad, and the half-tribe of Manasseh captive to Mesopotamia when Damascus fell. A decade later the capture of Samaria resulted in the remaining Israelite tribes being carried away to Assyria as captives.

The end of national life in Judah began with the first attack on Jerusalem by the Babylonians in 597 BCE. The final attack in 581 BCE marked the end completely. By the end of this period, a total of some 4,600 prominent persons had been deported from Judah. This number probably did not include family members or servants. The total may well have been at least double the number recorded by Jeremiah.[3]

It is important to emphasize that "a close examination of Assyrian records reveals that the deportations approximated only a limited percentage of the population, usually consisting of noble families. Agricultural workers, no doubt the majority, were deliberately left to care for the crops."[4] An important conclusion can perhaps be drawn from these two separate reports that large numbers of members of all the tribes were allowed to remain in both the Northern and the Southern Kingdoms. The inference is that there was always a remnant in the Land: in this case a very large remnant. Hence, the case is considerably weakened for the popular notion that Ten Tribes totally vanished, and may one day reappear. It would seem from the evidence that they never left, at least the majority of each, and, at the very least, a substantial remnant of each has always endured.

There is another very interesting and little known part of this saga of deportation:

"The sequel is provided by the inscriptions of Sargon: 'the Arabs who live far away in the desert, who know neither overseers nor officials, and who had not yet brought their tribute to any king, I deported...and settled them in Samaria.'"[5]

One could conjecture that these rootless Arabs who were called to physically take over the land and otherwise fill the places of the deported tribes of Samaria were in fact the progenitors of the contemporary so called "Palestinian Arabs." These Arabs, through their blatantly terrorist organization, the Palestine Liberation Organization (PLO), are quite successfully maneuvering, for starters, to seize Samaria, Judea, and all of Jerusalem, the very heartland of the State of Israel (what is now referred to by the world as "the West Bank"). At this writing, the PLO already controls 40% of this heartland and expects to soon control the rest, more than half of which has already been promised to them by the current Israeli government as a "good will gesture." The Palestinians envision the so called "West Bank" as the heart of their hoped for independent Palestinian State, which they unabashedly and openly proclaim will ultimately consist of *all* the Land of the current State of Israel, cleansed entirely of *all* its Jewish inhabitants.

In any event, there has been much mythology developed around the theme of the so-called ten tribes of Israel. Numerous conjectures, a few plausible, but most highly bizarre, have persisted about the fate of these peoples. They have been variously identified with an amazingly wide range of "tribes and nations," such as, to name a few of many: the people of India, Great Britain, the Americas (North, Central and South), the Nestorians of Mesopotamia, the Afghans, the high-caste Hindus and the holy Shidai class of Japan.

Even so, belief persists that these ten tribes, thus seemingly lost to history and assimilated by other peoples, will one day miraculously reemerge and be restored to their inheritance: the Land, now the State of Israel.

There is, perhaps, a much more rationale and scriptural explanation as to what actually did happen to the ten tribes after they were freed from captivity. In about 530 BCE, Persian King Cyrus II issued a decree permitting the Babylonian captives to return to Jerusalem.[6] In 468 BCE, more captives returned to Israel with Ezra.[7] Even more possibly returned with Nehemiah.[8]

According to a detailed list prepared by Ezra many from the captivity did return to Israel after the captivity. The following table shows examples of some of these returnees, their tribal origins and the Scripture proof to this effect:

Tribal Origin/Descended From:	Proof Text
Arah from the tribe of Asher	Ezra 2:5 with 1 Chronicles 7:39, 40
Bani from the tribe of Gad	Ezra 2:10 with Nehemiah 7:15
Bethlehem from the tribe of Zebulun	Ezra 2:21 with Joshua 19:15-16
Ramah from the tribe of Nephtali	Ezra 2:26 with Joshua 19:32-39
Nebo from the tribe of Reuben	Ezra 2:29 with 1 Chronicles 5:1-8

There is, of course, no absolute proof that *all* of the former captives returned to Israel. In my view, the sense of both history and Scripture lead to the conclusion that many (but certainly by no means all) did return to Israel, and that any, however few or many who did not, were perhaps, but not necessarily entirely absorbed by other peoples and nations. There is certainly no basis, however, to believe that *all* of these tribes may one day re-enter the scene and demand their rightful place in Israel.

On the other hand, in all fairness and objectivity, there is compelling, if not absolutely certain, evidence that scattered descendants from the captivity did manage to survive down to this day while retaining enough of their Jewish identity to make a convincing case as to their origins. Thus, refreshingly these plausible exceptions will be presented: but first, let us examine some of the more bizarre claims of Israeli tribal identity.

"British Israel"

"British-Israelism" has a long history. The Puritan colonists in America viewed themselves as spiritual descendants of the ancient Israelites. However, it was not until 1840 that John Wilson published "Lectures on our Israelitish Origin" which first proclaimed that the British people were the actual descendants of God's chosen people. "British Israel" is a well organized movement in the United Kingdom with many adherents. Their claim:

"The literal descendants of the lost ten-tribed House of Israel are found today in the British Commonwealth of Nations, the United States of America, and certain areas of north-western Europe, particularly Denmark, Sweden, Norway and Holland. Without a knowledge of this amazing truth, a full understanding of the prophecies of the Bible is impossible. Two-thirds of the Bible is devoted to the formation of the Israel nation, its history, its prophetic role in world happenings over the last 2,000 years, and its ultimate destiny in the coming age of Christ's reign on earth. Identifying the Anglo-Saxon-Celtic nations with the Israel of the Bible is a key that unlocks the mysteries of Bible prophecy."[9]

"Proof" of the "British Israel" claim is offered in several remarkable subclaims, for example:

"Brit-*ish:"* *"Brit" in Hebrew means, literally, "covenant"*

History of the Monarchy: The British monarchy is traced back to David who, the "British Israelites" claim, was appointed King of Israel in the 11th Cent. BCE. Using Samuel 7:8, 10, 16 as a proof text, by implication it is asserted that Israel is replaced by Great Britain with no further explanation.[10]

A "Fulfillment" of God's Promise to Abraham: YHWH promised Abraham: *I will make you a **great** nation; I will bless you and make your name **great**; and you shall be a blessing.*[11] Using only the semantical coincidence of the word "great" in this verse, the "British Israelites" take a giant leap in claiming: "The only nation today that may be identified by name with this verse is ***Great*** Britain."[12]

David's Throne: "British Israel" makes the claim: "*Tradition* (alone) records the coming of the royal princess, Tamar Tephi, to Ireland in an ancient sailing ship in the year 583 BCE. Princess Tephi (a direct descendant of King

David of the Bible) was the daughter of Zedekiah (the last King of Judah in Jerusalem) who was taken captive to Babylon. It is believed that after she made her escape to Ireland with Jeremiah (famous prophet of the Old Testament), she married Eochaid the Heremon, a prince of Israelite descent and closely allied with the tribe of Dan."[13] While Zedekiah is mentioned 63 times in Scripture, and several of these references are to his sons, there is no mention whatsoever of any daughter, much less, one named Tamar Tephi, or of any journey by any of Zedekiah's descendants to Ireland or elsewhere.

The "Stone of Scone:" A further claim is offered by "British Israel" that "The Stone of Scone," which is found in the base of the coronation chair in Westminster Abbey, provides a further link with the Bible, being identified with Jacob, the father of the Israelites. The official Westminster Abbey guide, reportedly, refers to this stone as the stone upon which Jacob laid his head when he had the famous dream of a ladder reaching to Heaven.[14] There is, however, absolutely no mention of when and how this stone supposedly found its way to Westminster Abbey.

King James and the Union Jack: "British Israel" makes much out of the notion that "no version of the Bible has so significantly influenced the lives of people world-wide as the Authorized King James Version of 1611. It has been the standard version used by English speaking Protestants for 350 years, and is still in common use by millions of Bible-believers today. The accession of King James to the throne of England is very significant in English history." The significance would seem to be that the name "James" is said to be the English equivalent for "Jacob" thus establishing a connection between this King James and the founder of the Tribe of Judah. This is an interesting point, given Judah was one of the three tribes in the Southern Kingdom: not one of the supposed ten lost tribes of the North. Further "Proof" is offered in the name "Union Jack" given to the flag of Great Britain, again supposing that the "Jack" is a direct link to Jacob.[15]

The word "Jack" however, comes from the name of the flag on the jack-staff of a navy warship. In slang, all flags became known as "Jacks." The flag called a jack is strictly one displayed from a jackstaff on the end of a bowsprit, but is now loosely used as in "Union Jack." The name Union Jack, means therefore, a flag of the Union of England, Scotland, and Ireland and has nothing whatsoever to do with any supposed "Union of Jacob."[16]

In summary, there is no historical or Scriptural reason for equating the British peoples with the Ten Lost Tribes of Israel. Nick Greer concludes, quoting the *Encyclopedia Britannica* :

"The theory (of British-Israelism)...rests on premises which are deemed by scholars—both theological and anthropological—to be utterly unsound. The most minimal investigation usually proves British-Israelists wrong. It is a dangerous doctrine leading to 'King James only' philosophies, distorted end-time thinking, and racism. It has no place in a Christian assembly."[17]

The "Migration" to North and South America

There is another theory expounded in and supported by various publications[18] that the ten tribes, while they were in Assyria, took counsel together to leave and come into a land where mankind never dwelt which was called *Arsareth*. Today this region is supposedly known as the Americas.

Support for this "migration" theory is taken from the Old Testament Apocrypha writing: 2 Edras 13:40-45 which is translated:

Those are the ten tribes, which were carried away prisoners out of their own land in the time of Osea the king, whom Salmanaser king of Assyria led away captive and he carried them over the **waters** *and so they came to another land.*

The entire theory hangs on the word translated "waters." The meaning here suggested is a trans-oceanic migration (by some unspecified conveyance, several centuries before Columbus) from Assyria to the Americas.

The theory, however, immediately breaks down in the light of a proper translation which finds "waters" more accurately rendered "river," contextually, the Euphrates river over which the Tribes crossed, then eventually recrossed, on their way back to the land of Israel from which they had been taken captive.[19]

The "Black Hebrews"

The name "Black Hebrews" is an invention of the predominately white media used to describe a markedly non-homogeneous movement of Afro-Americans who subscribe, variously to Christian, Muslim and/or Jewish religious practices and traditions.

While some but not all "Black Hebrews" claim to be descendants from one or more of the "Lost Tribes" of Israel, there is no apparent anthropological or scriptural evidence to support their origin as anything but tribal Africa.

It is important to point out that these "Black Hebrews" have no connection to the Black Jews of Ethiopia whose Jewishness is officially recognized by the State of Israel.

There are two significant national manifestations of the "Black Hebrew" movement: the original group began and has prospered in the Untied States, and its offshoot in Israel that began in the late 1960's.

The "Black Hebrews" of America: Many members of this group make no claim to being Jewish—quite to the contrary, some groups practice a fundamentalist form of Christianity, while others are militantly Muslim and even openly anti-Semitic.

The "Black Jews of Harlem," however, are an interesting exception. The group has its origins in the Commandment Keepers Congregation founded in Harlem in 1919 by "Rabbi" W.A. Matthew. The original members of this group had in common a not clearly understood identification with Judaism and Jewish tradition. Some claimed, as do some contemporary members, that the African tribes from which they had descended were in fact one or more of the "Lost Tribes" of Israel.

While the tribal roots of these believers may be unclear, their strict adherence to a form of orthodox Judaism is not. Under Halakhic Law, as interpreted by the non-black Rabbis of both the United States and Israel, the central Judaism of this Black American group could not be officially acknowledged. Even so, the group has become a credible sect of Judaism in its own right with a trained and organized rabbinate and prospering congregations beyond New York in: Ohio, Chicago, Philadelphia, Barbados, and Atlanta.[20]

Estimates of the size and scope of the Black Hebrew groups vary greatly from 40,000 to 500,000 primarily because of the various understandings of which sub-groups should properly be included. According to the Council of Jewish Federations, 2.2% (121,000) of America's 5.5 million Jews identify themselves as black.[21]

The "Black Hebrews" of Israel: A still much smaller group of Afro-Americans began migrating to Israel in the late 1960's. Most settled in the largely isolated city of Dimona in the Negev Desert. The religious identities of this group were and remain greatly varied.

Some in the group who felt called to Israel as religious Jews have since converted to Judaism according to Israel Orthodox Jewish Law and have subsequently been granted Israeli citizenship under the Law of Return.

All others in the group: Christians, Muslims, and secular alike remain problematic, to the Ministry of Interior. Despite the general claim of the group that they are "true" descendants of the "Hebrew race," those who have not converted to Israeli Orthodox Judaism eventually are forced to leave the country.

The Ibo: The Ibo are a major group numbering about 15 million who reside chiefly in Southeast Nigeria. The group seceded from Nigeria in the late 1960's to form the Republic of Biafra. A civil war followed and by 1970 Biafra had been defeated.

Edward Oniolo, an Ibo, arrived in Israel in 1989 claiming that the Ibo tribe's dietary laws, monotheism and practice of male circumcision were evidence that some two million Ibo are descendants of an ancient "Lost tribe of Israel."

In a legal showdown in March 1995, testing the legitimacy of the Ibo's claim, the Supreme Court ruled in favor of the Ministry of Interior which denied Oniolo status as a Jew.

According to the Itim news agency, the Ito are among some 40 million people around the world who have at one time or another made official claims to be descendants of the "Lost Tribes," and therefore entitled to Israeli citizenship under the Law of Return. Included among such claimants have been some four million Ethiopians, many of whom have been recognized by Israel as legitimate claimants, and some 15 million people in Southwest Asia, some of whom, most notably a relative few from India, who have been so recognized by Israel.[22]

[1] Nelson's Bible Dictionary, Biblesoft, Electronic Version, Article: "Dispersion of the Jewish People."

[2] 1 Kings 17:1-7

[3] Nelson's Bible Dictionary, Biblesoft, Electronic Version, Article: "Dispersion of the Jewish People."

[4] NIV Study Bible, Article: "Exile of the Northern Kingdom," page 556

[5] Ibid Note: Sargon was the name of the Assyrian king who reigned during the captivity of the Northern and Southern Kingdoms.

[6] Ezra 1:1-4

[7] Ezra 7:1-8:32

[8] Neh. 2:5, 6, 11; 13:6, 7

[9] Revival Fellowship, Article: "British Israel," found at: www.trf.org.au/bi.htm

[10] Ibid

[11] Gen 12:2

[12] Revival Fellowship, Article: "British Israel," found at: www.trf.org.au/bi.htm

[13] Ibid

[14] Ibid

[15] Ibid

[16] Nick Greer, "British-Israelism and the Revival Centres," Article: found at www.preteristarchive.com

[17] Ibid

[18] Ronald Sanders, in his book, *Lost Tribes and Promised Lands,* suggests that Columbus and the Spanish were well acquainted with Hebrew Scriptures and knew that the people throughout the Americas are Israelites. Martin Gilbert, in his book, *The Illustrated Atlas of Jewish Civilization*, suggests that the Ten Tribes migrated to North, Central and South America and to the islands of Puerto Rico, Cuba and the Dominican Republic. Article: "The Migration," found at: www.12tribes.com

[19] Oxford University Press, *The New Oxford Annotated Apocrypha*, footnote commentary on

2 Edras 13:40, page 333, and NIV Study Bible, Article: "Exile of the Northern Kingdom," page 556

[20] Rabbi Shlomo Ben Levy, "General Description of the Black Jewish or Hebrew Israelite Community," Article: www.members.aol.com/Blackjews

[21] "I've heard of a group called 'Black Hebrews.' Who are they?" Article: www.faq.org

[22] "Washington Report on Middle East Affairs," March, 1995. Article: "Israeli Court Says No to Ibo."

Chapter 11

The "Lost Tribes" of Israel
The More Credible Claims to Israeli Tribal Origin

In those days the house of Judah shall walk with the house of Israel, and they shall come together out of the land of the north to the land that I have given as an inheritance to your fathers. (Jer 3:18)

While most claims to Jewish heritage via the "Lost Tribes" are flights of fancy, some clearly are quite credible. In two cases, the Israel government has seen fit to honor such tribal claims under the Law of Return, and in at least one more case there seems to be justification for yet another such recognition. Perhaps, as more evidence is presented, there may even be further recognition. The two thus far recognized claims are those of the Ethiopian Jews and the *Bnei Menashe* people of India. To my mind, the *Pathans* of Pakistan and Afganistan make a very convincing claim that has not yet been accepted by Israel.

The Ethiopian Jews: Most Ethiopian immigrants came to Israel in two major waves. Operation Moses in the early and mid 1980's brought nearly 8,000 immigrants. Operation Solomon in 1991 brought over 14,000 more. But, in Operation Solomon, due to questions regarding their Judaism, the *Falash Mura*, those Ethiopian Jews who had converted to Christianity, were left behind.

Surprisingly, Israel's rabbinical authorities have determined that the *Falash Mura* are the descendants of Jews, therefore, they do not need to undergo conversion. Even so, for many years the Israeli government denied the claims of the *Falash Mura* to come to Israel under the Law of Return. Finally, in 1997 and 1998, permission was given to almost 5,000 *Falash Mura*, many of whom had deliberately been left behind.

According to a report by Larry Thompson, Director of Advocacy for Refugees International, "there are now an additional estimated 15,000 *Falash Mura*, primarily in the cities of Addis Ababa and Gonder, who desire immigration to Israel."

The plight of the *Falash Mura*, both in Israel and in Ethiopia, has yet to be resolved.[1]

Chatsrot Yasef is an absorption center on the northern coast of Israel that has admitted since 1996 over 2,000 *Falash Mura*, Ethiopian Jews. According to Rabbi Waldman who is associated with this absorption center:

"The *Falash Mura* used to be immersed in Christianity. They want to erase the past and become part of Israel. That process begins with religion classes at a refugee camp in Addis Ababa and ends with immersion in a *mikvah,* which signifies conversion to Judaism and attainment of the ultimate goal: an Israeli identity card marked 'Jewish.'---*Falash Mura* don't go back to the ways of the kessim [Ethiopian Jewish priests] or Reform movements or anything else. They return to the Judaism that is accepted in Israel, Orthodox Juda-ism. The final stage of their conversion is a test before a committee from the chief rabbinate's office, which allows them to register as Jewish citizens.

"According to most strains of Orthodox Halacha, a Jew who converts to Christianity is still considered Jewish. We treat them as returners to the faith, rather than as Christians. We make it easier [for them] because they are from the seed of the Jewish people.[2] (emphasis my own)

"Despite rulings by the Sephardic and Ashkenazic chief rabbis declaring Ethiopian Jews to be descendants of the tribe of Dan, many rabbis doubt the authenticity of Ethiopian Judaism. The rabbinate initially mandated symbolic conversion and re-circumcision for all Ethiopian Jews as a condition of immigration. After a month-long strike by Ethiopian Israelis, the requirements were dropped, but most Orthodox rabbis still refuse to marry Ethiopian Jews who do not ritually immerse themselves. The battle has left Ethiopian Israelis bitter at suspicions of their Judaism and hostile toward conversion."[3]

In the most recent development, Interior Minister Natan Sharansky said:

"'The problem of the *Falash Mura* is a difficult humanitarian problem that must be solved speedily. However, we will not give blanket entry permits for them.' Minister Sharansky was in Ethiopia for a four-day trip in order to examine the issues relating to the *Falash Mura* who wish to immigrate to Israel. His decisions include:

1. To allow requests for immigration to be submitted in Ethiopia itself, in order to shorten examination procedures and make them more efficient.

2. To increase staff at the Interior Ministry dealing with these requests, both in Israel and in Ethiopia.

"The Interior Minister noted that the survey conducted a few years ago by David Efrati (then director of the census administration at the Interior Ministry), gave a figure of 26,000 *Falash Mura* living in Ethiopia who had returned to Judaism. This figure is the basis for examining immigration requests today. Each request will be individually examined based on the Law of Return and the Law of Entry, uniting first degree kin.

"Minister Sharansky stated that Israel faces a critical moment, with pressures regarding the Law of Return. On one hand, there are demands to tighten the Law in light of the number of non-Jews arriving in Israel from Russia, while on the other, there are demands to expand the Law due to the situation in Ethiopia. 'The problem of the *Falash Mura* must be solved humanely, but the issue must not be entangled with the Law of Return. It must be quickly decided who has the right to immigrate based on the Law of Return and who will be permitted to immigrate based on the Law of Entry and uniting of families,' he said."[4]

The *Bnei Menashe* of India: Thirty seven members of the *Bnei Menashe* (Sons of Menashe) tribe of India were allowed to immigrate to Israel in February, 2000. These new immigrants joined with another 450 of their fellow tribesmen who have immigrated from India over the past five years.

The *Bnei Menashe*, who have a rich tradition in the Oral Law, trace themselves back to the Tribe of Menashe. They continue to practice many uniquely Jewish traditions and customs.

About 3,500 *Bnei Menashe* tribesmen decided to return to formal Judaism about 30 years ago and to the best of their ability have been following Jewish law since that time.

Leading Israeli rabbinical authorities became convinced of the authenticity of the *Bnei Menashe* claim to Israeli heritage based on what they concluded was convincing evidence, including: their ancient tradition speaking of the patriarchs Abraham, Isaac and Jacob; their custom of circumcising male children on the 8th day after birth; and their sacrificial ceremony on an altar reminiscent of the Jewish Temple in which the Hebrew Biblical name of God, Mount Sinai, Mount Moriah and Mount Zion are mentioned.[5]

The *Pathans* of Pakistan and Afghanistan: The *Pathans* are about 15 million people living mainly in Pakistan and Afghanistan as well as in Persia and India. They have a tradition of being of the Lost Tribes and have quite remarkable Israeli customs, some of which are:[6]

● The *Pathans* circumcise their male children on the 8th day following their birth.

● The *Pathans* have a sort of small *Tallit* called *Kafan*. This is a four cornered garment to which they tie strings similar to the fringes that other Jews call *Tsitsit*.

● The *Pathans* strictly keep the Jewish Sabbath, during which they practice many of the traditional Jewish customs, including: preparing *hallot* (traditional Jewish bread) and the lighting of the *Shabbat* candle.

● *Pathans* keep the Kosher dietary laws in accordance with the *Torah*.

● Some *Pathans* wear a small box which other Jews call *Tefillin* (phylactery) containing the prescribed verses of the *Torah*.

● Many *Pathans* retain family names of the Lost Tribes such as Asher, Gad, Naphtali, Reuben and Manasseh and Ephraim.

● The legal system which is known as *Pashtunwali,* the law of the *Pashtu,* is very similar to the *Torah*. There are pages and even complete books among the *Pathans* and they honor greatly what is called *Tavrad El Sharif* (the *Torah* of Moses), and they rise at the mention of the name of Moses.

● The physical similarity between the *Pathans* and other Jews is exemplified by the British who ruled Afghanistan for a great length of time and called the *Pathans* Jews.

● When not wearing their traditional clothing, *Pathans* are indistinguishable from other Jews of the area. Among the 21 nations of Afghanistan only the *Pathans* and the Jews have Semitic features, their faces are longer and lighter, and some even have blue eyes. Like the Jews of the area, *Pathans* grow beards and sidelocks which further serve to make them indistinguishable from Jews.

● *Pathans* celebrate *Yom Kippur* in accordance with the *Torah*.

● The symbol of Shield of David (Star of David) is found in almost every *Pathan* house. The wealthy make it out of expensive metals and the poor out of simple wood. It can be seen in towers, in schools and also in tools, bracelets, and jewelry. (I find this especially interesting since, up to the appearance of the Star of David as one of the three component symbols of the First Century CE *Messianic Seal*, this distinctly Jewish symbol was thought to have first been used for religious purposes as late as the 13th Century. Its appearance as a Jewish symbol used by the *Pathans* dating from the Assyrian dispersion in 722 BCE is truly remarkable.

● Besides the oral tradition related by the elders of the tribe, the *Pathans* also keep scrolls of genealogy, reaching back to the original twelve tribes of

Israel. These scrolls are well preserved and some are written in gold on the skins of a doe. No less interesting and significant are the names of the tribes which bear close resemblance to the Tribes of Israel. The Rabbani Tribe is really Reuben, the Shinware Tribe is Simeon, the Lewani Tribe is Levi, The Daftani Tribe is Naphtali, the Jaji Tribe is Gad, and the Ashuri Tribe is Asher, The Yusefsai Tribe is children of Joseph, and the Afridi Tribe is really Ephraim. These are the names of the Ten Lost Tribes of Israel. The *Pathans* themselves point out the differences between the original names of the tribes and their present names are because of the different dialects of the languages so that, for instance, Jaji was actually called Gaji for the tribe of Gad.[7]

The *Pathans* number six to seven million in Afghanistan and seven to eight million in Pakistan. They live in the border area between these two countries and about two million live as nomads. These *Pathans* desire for their independence, which is supported by Afghanistan and is a cause of constant tension in Pakistan which does not desire their independence.

To my knowledge, there has not yet been a formal *Pathan* claim to Israeli citizenship under the Law of Return. Given the very convincing evidence (much of which has been omitted from the brief summary above) that would seem to validate such a *Pathan* claim, it is mind boggling to consider the many implications of a potential addition of up to 15 million newly recognized Jews to an already stressed Israeli Jewish population of some six million. Such an addition would in effect double the recognized world-wide Jewish population.

Considering that such a potential *Pathan* claim to Israeli citizenship may one day soon become a reality, it would seem well advised for the Israeli government to be looking for ways to expand the land of Israel rather than instead seeking both domestic and international support to legitimize giving away Samaria, Judea, Gaza, the Jordan Valley, the Golan and even parts of Jerusalem to the traditional Arab enemies of Israel.

---

[1] Article: "Caravan City, Dateline: 06/14/99," www. About.com

[2] The acceptance as still Jews, of those Ethiopian Jews who have converted to Christianity is an extraordinary *ad hoc* exception to the Law of Return that is not applicable to any other Jewish converts to Christianity. As previously noted, Messianic Jews are sometimes militantly pursued æ some have been exported after losing lengthy court battles.

[3] Sari Bashi, *Forward,* Article: "Ethiopian Jews Face Stricter Standards in Israel æParticularly Falash Mura, Those Who Converted to Christianity Under Pressure in Homeland." www.forward.com

[4] Bradley Antolovich, "Problem Of Ethiopian Falash Mura Is Humanitarian," News Report From Jerusalem 4/18/2000   forzion@netvision.net.il

[5] Bradley Antolovich, "Jewish Tribe Returns Home after 2,600 years," News Report from Jerusalem 2/15/2000   forzion@netvision.net.il

6 "The Mystery of the Ten Lost Tribes," Article: "The *Pathans* of Pakistan and Afghanistan" www.moshi-ach.com

7 Arimasa Kubo, *Israelites Came To Ancient Japan,* Chapter Two: Rabbi Marvin Tokayer, (cited) "*Pathans* as the Descendants of the Lost Tribes of Israel," www.ask.ne.jp/~remnant/isracame.htm

Chapter 12

Who is a Jew?—Summing Up

> *And what one nation on the earth is like Your people Israel, whom God went to redeem for Himself as a people and to make a name for Himself, and to do a great thing for You and awesome things for Your land, before Your people whom You have redeemed for Yourself from Egypt, {from} nations and their gods? For You have established for Yourself Your people Israel as Your own people forever, and You, O LORD, have become their God.* (2 Sam 7:23-24 NAU)

A realistic, scripturally sound, and widely understood (if not universally acceptable) answer to this question: "Who is a Jew?" is an important prerequisite: even the very cornerstone upon which the ever elusive *unity* in the Body of Yeshua can at long last be constructed. Said differently, I believe that satan and his legion of demons relish in a widespread misunderstanding of the proper answer to this foundational question. Certainly, this problem doesn't stand alone in explaining the contemporary chaos within the Body of Yeshua, but it is, clearly, one of several major contributory factors.

There have long been many widely different understandings of who and who is not a Jew. At one end of this spectrum of understanding is the official State of Israel, absolutely non-negotiable, *Halachic* understanding: A Jew can only be a Jew if he or she is the offspring of a Jewish mother (or) has converted to orthodox Judaism through the long and tedious labyrinthine process established by the orthodox Rabbis that ultimately leads to Jewish identification.

At the other end of the spectrum are ethnically Gentile Christians who

never-the-less claim to be Jewish for a variety of reasons, all of which ultimately come back to the same central, wrong understanding: the Church has
replaced Biblical Israel making the State of Israel, Judaism, non-believing ethnic Jews and all things Jewish irrelevant. Accordingly, these born again believers, irrespective of any other consideration, have thus become the "true Jews."

It is often further understood that this identification of "true Jew" carries
with it material as well as spiritual implications: the New Covenant has canceled the Old. Therefore, YHWH's eternal granting of the Land of Israel to the
blood descendants of Abraham through, Isaac, Jacob and the twelve sons of
Jacob is no longer operative

It follows then, in this manner of thinking, that the Church has every right
to claim sovereign dominion over Jerusalem and to share the City of David
with whomever it may please, including the avowed and traditional enemies of
Israel. And, therefore, "Born again" believers have every right to respond to
their frequent call to "come home" to Israel, and, as "true Jews," to reside in
the Land for as long as they may please without benefit of any further license
from the State of Israel.

Between these two extremes there are all manner of other interpretations
and claims. Moving toward the center from the Orthodox Jewish perspective,
there are to be found converts to Judaism through the Conservative and Reform
movements outside of Israel whose claims to Jewish identification and Israeli
citizenship are strongly resisted.

Moving toward the center from the other end of the spectrum there are to
be found a legion of Christians: the "Seed of Abraham (as numerous) as the
stars of the heaven and as the sand which is on the seashore" who while sometimes understanding the futility of any official claim, nevertheless feel so
called to Israel and so completely and passionately identify with everything
Jewish that they somehow *know,* deep within their respective beings, that they
must be Jewish.

Others, to me the most heartbreaking, are those dear brothers and sisters in
Yeshua who *are* certifiably Jewish, but have somehow been "found out" by the
Israeli Department of Interior and thus "entered into the computer" to forever
be denied by man their God-given inheritance.

Still others "*know*" to varying degrees that they have Jewish roots but for
a variety of reasons are unable to provide documentary evidence to this effect.

Then there are the many, even the majority of those who would be Jewish,
who stake their claim exclusively on a "feeling deep within their spirits" that
they must be descended from one or more of the "Lost Ten Tribes."

I would be the last to deny or belittle many of such claims, even some that
at first glance seem outlandish. God works in mysterious ways, and I have

seen instances where He, in His grace, quite miraculously provided proof of Jewish ethnicity. In my own case, the Lord called me to Israel, then led me, supernaturally to documentary evidence proving my Jewishness that had been suppressed by both sides of my family for two generations.

As another example, a dear couple from the United Kingdom who frequently visit the Land, have been our faithful supporters and friends from the very beginning of our new life here. They have encouraged us and several other Messianic families in the Land through prayer, fellowship, and, in our case, materially as faithful customers of our company's products. Throughout their entire Christian walk of many years, although they felt called to support Israel and believers in the Land, both have always assumed they were entirely Gentile. Quite recently, through what can only be characterized as a Divine gift, the lady member, while not so seeking, "discovered" documentary evidence proving her own Jewish ethnicity.

However, let me be clear so as not to further encourage what in so many cases are baseless flights of fancy. While I feel certain that there are many, many legitimately ethnic Jews who would make *aliyah* to Israel but are unable to document their claims, I feel just as certain that the vast majority of such otherwise undocumented claims are dangerous to those making them and can, in the end, only lead to heartbreaking and even faith shattering disappointment.

Getting back to the central question: Who is a Jew? I offer the following further considerations:

Judaism is not a race: Contrary to the understanding of CNN, Bill Clinton and many others that there are "*three* great monotheistic religions." I firmly believe that Judaism is the world's *one* great monotheistic religion: a religion adhered to, originally, by a race of people descended from the twelve sons of Jacob (later named Israel by YHWH) who were from that time forth and who today remain an ethnically identifiable Semitic race, the Jewish people—Jews. Yeshua did not come into the world to start a new religion called Christianity: He came, as repeatedly prophesied in the Old Covenant, as the Jewish "Priest" Messiah, and He is coming back again as the also repeatedly prophesied "King" Messiah.

If Judaism were a race, then no one could join it or leave it without a total revamping of his or her genetic makeup. Anyone who is not ethnically Jewish can convert to Judaism by going through a man made and man administered process. Anyone, Jew and Gentile alike, when given the faith to do so through grace, can accept Yeshua.

The very first believers were a sect of ethnic Jews who called themselves Nazarenes. Believing Jews today might best be described as modern day Nazarenes. According to Paul, believing Gentiles have been from the beginning of the Christian Church, and remain today, *grafted in* among the natural Jewish branches. Here, they are well and equally fed, along with their modern day Nazarene brothers and sisters, by a common Jewish root.

In short, it seems clear to me, that Christianity is not truly a stand alone monotheistic religion: it is rather a continuation, a fulfillment of Judaism. In the same way that Yeshua is the promised Jewish Messiah, Christianity is an extension of the religion that so intricately and completely foretold His coming.

Therefore it is of faith that it might be according to grace, so that the promise might be sure to all the seed, not only to those who are of the law, but also to those who are of the faith of Abraham, who is the father of us all. (Rom 4:16)

Viewing this from the very different perspective of the Israeli Department of Interior: a born Gentile who "properly" converts to Judaism is bestowed the very special distinction of being known as a "righteous convert." Like Ruth, born a Gentile, who married Boaz, a Jew, and together they begat Obed (a genetically half-Jew) in the line of Yeshua, such converts are in every way to be considered Jewish.

Adherence to Jewish religious, traditional, cultural and social practice

While some may disagree, Judaism, even more so Messianic Judaism, has a seemingly magnetic attraction to many, perhaps even most, Christians who rejoice in participating in Jewish religious, traditional, cultural and social practices. By way of illustration, I need only point to the relative participation of Jews and Gentiles in Messianic Jewish congregations, in the United States, where Gentiles constitute well over half of the membership.

To my own way of thinking, this is a wonderful phenomenon. I delight in worshipping with such "Messianic Gentiles,"—their proper recognition of the Jewish roots of our faith is one of the central things that this book is all about. These are brothers and sisters in Yeshua who are truly in unity with the Body and, to use the current vernacular, "on the ground" the result is something truly wonderful. Never have I felt or seen the consistent presence of the Holy Spirit the way I do when I am worshipping joyfully, in spirit and in truth with a mixed congregation of Gentiles and Jews seemingly all of whom are at such perfect peace and unity with their Nazarene Jewish roots on Mount Zion.

Who is a Jew?
My Personal Assessment

It is again with some trepidation that I finally conclude Part One of this book with my own carefully studied conclusion, knowing full well that some, if not many, on both sides will disagree. Even so, having taken the reader thus far, I believe I should share my own conclusions on this vital matter as a basis for your own further consideration.

Quite simply, I take a more "liberal" view than that allowed by the Israeli Law of Return, as most recently amended. I hold that:

● A person is a Jew if it can be clearly established that one or more of his grandparents were themselves certifiably Jewish.

● A person who converts to Judaism through the Israeli Orthodox Jewish or other national Orthodox Jewish rabbinical conversion process, as accepted by the Israeli Orthodox Rabbinate, is Jewish. While others may not agree, I would not include conversions from any other source but Orthodox, either in or external to Israel. I take this position, because I am aware of several "quickie conversions" to Judaism undertaken in the United States as a matter of expediency to gain permanent residence in Israel, rather than as a spiritual commitment to Judaism in any form, including Messianic Judaism.

● There is no other natural or spiritual way that a person can become a Jew except by being born to a Jewish parent(s), being the offspring of a Jewish grandparent, or by proper Orthodox Jewish conversion.

Part Two

Who is a Gentile?
(What is the Christian Church?)

Introduction

For from the rising of the sun, even to its going down, my name shall be great among the Gentiles; in every place incense shall be offered to My name, and a pure offering; for My name shall be great among the nations," says the LORD of hosts.(Mal 1:11)

In Hebrew, the word *goyim* (Gentiles) means "nations." The people of Israel were called by God to be a people who were set apart from other nations. Other nations worshipped various pagan deities, but Israel was called to worship the one true God, who commanded Moses:

'Now therefore, if you will indeed obey My voice and keep My covenant, then you shall be a special treasure to Me above all people; for all the earth is Mine. 'And you shall be to Me a kingdom of priests and a holy nation.' These are the words which you shall speak to the children of Israel. (Exod 19:5-6)

From a Jewish perspective, there are therefore great religious, cultural, social and traditional differences between Jews and Gentiles. According to the Mishna, "---every Gentile child, so soon as born, was to be regarded as unclean, and,--- Gentiles were considered to be heathens who were not to be forced into danger, but not yet to be delivered from it." [1]

During biblical times, the Jew had a low estimate of the Gentile's character. The most vile and unnatural crimes were imputed to Gentiles. Jews considered it unsafe to leave cattle in a Gentile's charge, to allow Gentile women to nurse Jewish infants, or Gentile physicians to attend the Jewish sick. For Jews, the Gentiles, in so far as possible were to be altogether avoided, except in the case of necessity for business.

Gentile feasts and their joyous occasions were polluted by idolatry. A Jew could not leave a room with a Gentile in it because the Gentile might inadvertently defile the wine or food on the table, or the oil and wheat in the cupboard.[2]

Although, in our own personal eight year experience as Messianic Jews living in Israel, while by no means as extreme in practice, we have observed that the essence of this same self imposed Jewish separation from Gentiles has come down into contemporary, mostly ultra-orthodox perceptions, attitudes, and relationships.

In counterpoint, I greatly admire Donna's lovingly persistent and continuing outreach to establish meaningful relationships with our orthodox Jewish neighbors. The genuine, to my thinking, hard won friendships she has developed over the years have been the product of her dedicated and unceasing Hebrew language and culture studies, and her own quite remarkable reflection of being one with Ruth, who married Boaz, "one who is married into the covenant."

Certainly most Gentiles are not afforded anything like this level of acceptance, especially those who are openly "Christians." These Gentiles are held at arm's length by most Jews: even in some cases by their fellow Messianic believers who are ethnically Jewish.

From a Gentile-Christian perspective, a short definition of "Gentiles" offered by the Luther Seminary is simply "People who are not Jewish." At first glance, one might assume that such a definition would find general acceptance. However, there is wide disagreement regarding who and who is not a "Gentile."

The Roman Catholic Church, for example, defines "Gentiles" as: "---the nations distinct from the Jewish people--- before the coming of Christ, the Jews were in fact the chosen people of God---(and) the non-Jewish nations did not worship the true God---(therefore) since the coming of Christ, the word "Gentiles" designates---those who are neither Jews nor Christians."[3]

This definition is certainly in keeping with the Catholic view that they are the one true church and not a part of any wider more encompassing anointed Body of all believers.

While many in the Body do not include them as even a tacitly legitimate branch of the Body, the Church of Jesus Christ of Latter-day Saints (Mormons), regard themselves as the "true Hebrews": to them, "Gentile" denotes any person, including a Jew, who is not a Mormon.[4]

Going back to biblical basics, "Gentiles" is rooted in the "Table of Nations" that developed from the three sons of Noah and their progeny. As offered previously, I believe that Jews in the natural are those who are direct blood related progeny of Jacob, later called Israel by God. And, in keeping with main line fundamental evangelistic Christianity, it follows that the rest of humanity; i.e., the progeny of Japeth, Ham, and the other descendants of Shem (exclusive of those descended from Jacob/Israel) are all ethnic Gentiles.

In the end, however, as in my earlier endeavor to define "Who is a Jew?" perhaps the most appropriate approach to determine "Who is a Gentile?" is to first examine respective Gentile Christian worship structures, systems and practices: to carefully peer through the multicolored stained glass window into the Christian Church.

---

1 Alfred Edersheim, The Life and Time of Jesus the Messiah, Vol. I, page 90
2 Ibid., page 92
3 The Catholic Encyclopedia, Volume VI, definition, "Gentile," www.newadvent.org
4 Encyclopedia Britannica , Article: "Gentiles," www.britannica.com

Chapter One

The Transition from Nazarene Judaism to the Early Christian Church

Beyond their shared faith in Yeshua, the Jewish Messiah, the early Gentile believers found little basis for fellowship, or other religious, traditional or social commonality with their Nazarene Jewish originators. Therefore, they looked to their own various pagan traditions as a foundation upon which to build a new, unique "Christian" religion.

It is not difficult to understand why these new Christian believers were quick to reward the Nazarenes in kind for the rejection they themselves had endured as "untouchables." Hence this early rush to de-Judaize the incipient Christian Church provided fertile ground from which quickly sprang the first bitter fruit of Christian anti-Semitism: a system of hatred and maleficence which sadly still endures in at least several branches of the Church, most notably in those local churches and their denominations that have not yet come to understand and acknowledge the Jewish versus the Roman roots of their faith.

As noted earlier, there was another factor at work that all but guaranteed the Nazarenes' fall from leadership of the Messianic movement they had founded. The Nazarenes' refusal to participate with the rest of organized Judaism in the second Judean Revolt against Rome (135 CE) had both profound political and spiritual implications.

Until that very year, there on Mount Zion, a hierarchy of heredity from the family of Jesus had guarded the Throne of David.

Then, coincident with Hadrian's defeat of Bar Kochba, the city of Jerusalem was converted into the pagan *Aelia Capitolina.* At the same time, as a further affront to the Jewish people, Hadrian renamed the entire Land

"Palestine." This affront continues even today as one of the major false premises upon which the so called "Palestinian" Arabs base their continuing claim to the Land of Israel. Dr. Thomas S. McCall provides further insight into the name "Palestine:"

"There is a propaganda war going on now with regard to the term 'Palestine.' At one time it might have been argued that Palestine was an innocuous designation of the Middle Eastern area, that is generally thought of as the Holy Land. During the last few decades, however, the term Palestine has been adopted by Arabs living in Israel in the area west of the Jordan River. It is specifically employed to avoid the use of the name Israel, and must be considered an anti-Israel term.

"In all Arab maps published in Jordan, Egypt, etc., the area west of the Jordan River is called Palestine, without any reference to Israel. Palestine is the term now used by those who want to deny the legitimate existence of Israel as a genuine nation among the family of nations. The term now adopted by the political entity within Israel that is gradually obtaining more and more pockets of territory through the "peace process," is "the PA (Palestinian Authority). Although it must deal daily with Israeli officials, the PA hates to use the term Israel in any of its communications.

" Palestine, therefore, must now be considered a political propaganda term with massive anti-Israel implications. The world press uses the term to question the legitimacy of modern Israel. Christians also have used the term Palestine for centuries in referring to the Holy Land. In earlier times this might have been excused (although biblically questionable) because of its common usage. In light of the current propaganda war against Israel, however, Christians must now re-evaluate the term Palestine and consider whether it is biblically, theologically or prophetically accurate.

"The term Palestine is rarely[1] used in the Old Testament, and when it is, it refers specifically to the southwestern coastal area of Israel occupied by the Philistines. It is a translation of the Hebrew word *Pelesheth.* The term is never used to refer to the whole land occupied by Israel. Before Israel occupied the land, it would be generally accurate to say that the southwestern coastal area was called Philistia (the Way of the Philistines, or Palestine), while the central highlands were called Canaan. Both the Canaanites and the Philistines had disappeared as distinct peoples at least by the time of the Babylonian Captivity of Judea (586 BCE), and they no longer exist.

"In the New Testament, the term Palestine is never used. The term Israel is primarily used to refer to the people of Israel, rather than the Land. However, in at least two passages (Matt 2:20-21; 10:23) Israel is used to refer to the Land.

"It is clear, then, that the Bible never uses the term Palestine to refer to the Holy Land as a whole, and that Bible maps that refer to Palestine in the Old or New Testament are, at best, inaccurate, and, at worst, are a conscious denial of the biblical name of Israel."[2]

Under the new Roman regime that began in 135 CE, Jews were forbidden by Hadrian to reside in Jerusalem, now, officially *Aelia Capitolina,* although a greatly weakened group of Nazarenes were allowed to remain on Mount Zion. Judas, the fifteenth Jewish successor of James the Just, as leader of the Jewish Nazarenes, was deposed and replaced by Marcus, the first of many Gentile "Bishops" who would subsequently reign over the mostly metamorphosed "de-Judaized" Body now turned embryonic Christian Church.[3]

I find it especially interesting to consider the two spiritual incarnations of one "giant" of our faith: both incarnations were very different, yet both remarkably similar in outcome. In his first incarnation *Sha'ul* (Saul) the zealous Pharisee was militantly bent on destroying, in any way he could, incipient Nazarene Judaism and Nazarene Jews. In his second incarnation, as Paul the Apostle, in a totally unplanned by-product of his extraordinarily successful evangelistic outreach to the Gentiles, he indirectly managed to achieve, some would say almost single-handedly, what he had earlier, as the zealous Pharisee, set out to do in the first place: the precipitous demise of Nazarene Judaism.

The Nazarenes, as directed by the Messiah Himself through His "great commission," responded to the call by sending Paul out to the nations: then just as surely in accordance with the oft unfathomable plan of God, it was this very same Christian Church of which Paul was the central architect, that was, within less than 200 years, largely responsible for driving the Nazarenes into virtual non-existence. In the words of Eamon Duffey, noted Roman Catholic historian:

"Within ten years of the Messiah's death---Christianity escaped from Palestine,[4] along the seaways and roads of the Pax Romana, northwards to Antioch, on to Ephesus, Corinth, Thessalonica, and westwards to Cyprus, Crete and Rome. The man chiefly responsible was Paul of Tarsus, a sophisticated Greek-speaking rabbi who, unlike Jesus' twelve Apostles, was himself a Roman citizen. Against opposition from fellow Christians (Nazarene Jewish believers) including Jesus' first disciples, Paul insisted that the life and death of Jesus not only fulfilled the Jewish Law and the Prophets, but made sense of the world, and offered reconciliation and peace with God for the whole human race. In Jesus, Paul believed that God was offering humanity as a whole the life, guidance and transforming power which had once been the possession of Israel. His reshaping of the Christian message provided the vehicle by which an obscure heresy from one of the less appetizing corners of the Roman Empire could enter the bloodstream of late antiquity. In due course, the whole world was changed."[5]

Thus, near the beginning of the second century CE, there was everything to encourage and nothing to prevent a rapid spread of the story about Jesus, among the legions of potential Gentile followers scattered throughout the Roman empire in such places as: Syria, Jordan, Turkey, Balkans, Greece, Cyprus, Italy, Egypt, and Ethiopia.

And so it was, near the middle of the second century, coincident with Hadrian's reign as emperor (117-138) that we can appropriately point to these followers of Yeshua as part of a religion that was now predominantly Gentile Christian as opposed to it being a movement within the umbrella of Judaism.[6]

Two capstone situations occurred at this point that underscore the transformation of the new religion from the Nazarene Jewish Sect to the Christian Church:

● Hadrian's imperial policy indicated a distinction was being drawn between Jews and Christians: his policy regarding the protection of Christians from prosecution; his decision to ban Jews from Jerusalem in the aftermath of the 132-135 revolt; and the rebuilding of Jerusalem as Aelia Capitolina.

● Justin Martyr: a pagan convert to Christianity sought to engage in discussion between pagans and Jews regarding the truth of Christianity from a philosophical perspective. Hence, in his Dialogue with Trypho he spoke of "we" and "you" – the former being the Christians and the latter the Jews. Even allowing for the clear polemical nature of the text it is apparent that Justin did not consider himself to have become part of a group that regarded itself as Jewish. Clearly, the transformation was now well underway and the era of the Christian Church had begun.[7]

Then, some two centuries later, Eusebius, the Gentile Bishop of Caesaria and renown church historian, on instructions from his friend and fellow Mithrain (sun worshipper), the Roman Emperor Constantine, personally engineered a de-Judaized Christianity acceptable to Rome. It was his task among other things to present a selection of sacred writings for potential canonization. Eusebius, a thorough historian, presumably had access to many if not all of the now lost Jewish Nazarene books for his reference in this endeavor. Only one of these lost, now significantly altered Nazarene writings: The Gospel According to Matthew, originally The Gospel According to the Hebrews, was included in Eusebius' selection. It was in this setting that Constantine thus proclaimed "Christianity" to be the official state religion in 313 CE.

At first, mighty Rome fed even Christians to the lions, and, according to tradition, they were forced into the catacombs. Yet, like a wildfire out of control, non-Jewish Christianity increasingly dominated the feeble and fading pagan classes. Constantine was at an impasse. The Empire was at the brink of civil war and chaos, with the rebels set to win. With a genius mind, at the crossroads in history, Constantine made the right choice and his Empire flourished.[8]

THE INTERIOR OF THE OLD BASILICA OF ST. PETER. Begun by Constantine in 333, four years before his "conversion" to "Christianity." This Church endured for twelve centuries until 1506 when its rebuilding to create the modern St. Peter's began. Constantine built this "Mother of all Christian Churches" immediately above a functioning Mithraeum on Vatican Hill, a physical confirmation of his deliberate blending of paganism into the very fabric and heart of Gentile Christianity. (from a fresco in St. Martino ai Monte, Rome)

BUST OF THE EMPEROR CONSTANTINE I.
Originally part of a huge statue erected in Rome in 313 CE. Constantine ruled the Roman empire with an iron hand from 324 until his death in 337. He claims to have had a vision of Christ's cross seen in the sky above Rome on 27 October 312. However, this devout worshiper of Mithra was not baptized until 3 April 337, and then, as many scholars believe, his "conversion" was a matter of political expediency. The architect and founding father of Gentile Christianity, Constantine was instrumental in developing a new religion that was a bizarre mixture of Nazarene Messianic Judaism and blatant paganism. (located at the Palazzo dei Conservatori in Rome)

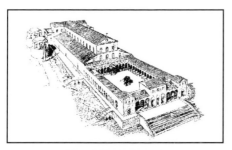

THE EXTERIOR OF THE OLD BASILICA OF ST. PETER. This classic and most imposing edifice, reflecting the genius of its architects, became the model for most subsequently constructed large Roman Catholic Churches. (From a drawing circa 320-335 CE)

1 The fact is, "Palestine" is never used in any of the modern translations. A word search of seven different versions found only one use of "Palestine" in the KJV(Joel 3:4) which was a mistranslation of "Philistia" that was corrected in the NKJV.

2   McCall, Dr. Thomas S., quoted by Zola Levitt in "The Levitt Letter," December 1997

3 Eusebius, Ecclesiastical History, page 466

4 This is a typical misuse of the name "Palestine." Hadrian did not apply the name "Palestine" to the Land of Israel until 135 CE, nearly a century after the time referred to here by Duffy.

5 Eamon Duffy, Saints & Sinners, A History of the Popes, pages 2-3

6 McLaren, James, "From Jewish Movement to Gentile Church," page 1, www.jcrelations.com

7 Ibid

8 Schmalz, Reuven .E., The Messianic Seal of the Jerusalem Church, Part One, pages 37-38

Chapter Two

The Roman Catholic Church
Progenitor of Gentile Christianity

I saw the woman, drunk with the blood of the saints and with the blood of the martyrs of Jesus. And when I saw her, I marveled with great amazement. But the angel said to me, "Why did you marvel? I will tell you the mystery of the woman and of the beast that carries her, which has the seven heads and the ten horns. "The beast that you saw was, and is not, and will ascend out of the bottomless pit and go to perdition. And those who dwell on the earth will marvel, whose names are not written in the Book of Life from the foundation of the world, when they see the beast that was, and is not, and yet is. "Here is the mind which has wisdom: The seven heads are seven mountains on which the woman sits---And the woman whom you saw is that great city which reigns over the kings of the earth. (Rev 17:6-9, 18)

As I have been researching and writing this text, I have sought the Lord for His guidance on what should be brought forth on these pages and how, specifically, these things should be presented as a message from His heart to the Body of Yeshua. I am well aware of the awesome responsibility involved in such an undertaking, and I have entered into this work with considerable "fear and trembling."

While I have long understood the essence of the Roman Catholic Church in its juxtaposition with the Body of Yeshua, I have only recently come to better understand its awesome: or perhaps better stated *fearsome* significance, as it is the very foundation from which all subsequent ecclesiastical Christianity arose.

103

Thus, as I was prayerfully seeking a better understanding of how to proceed with this chapter, the Lord greatly blessed me, and certainly all else who were present at Carmel Assembly in Haifa this past *Shabbat* (25 March 2000), through a divine encounter with Derek Prince[1] and the anointed message he delivered to the congregation.

Given the coincidence of the Pope's presence in Israel that week, and his celebrating mass at the Church of the Annunciation in Nazareth, even as we were meeting in Haifa, Brother Prince was led to preach on the Revelation of John as its relates to Israel, the Jewish people, and the Roman Catholic Church.

Derek Prince is an unimposing, very gentle man. The weight of his message brought tears to his eyes several times during his presentation: he had to pause momentarily before he could continue. What follows is a summary of what he offered relative to the Pope and his church:

"There are sets of opposites that run all through the Book of Revelations. Take for example the bride and the harlot. There is an absolute contrast between the two. The bride is spotless, pure and white. The harlot is quite the opposite. Each represents a city. The bride quite clearly represents the New Jerusalem of Revelations 21:2. Only one city in the world can possibly fit the detailed description given in Revelations 17:18. The harlot can be only one cityæ Rome. There is an absolute contrast between these two cities, and a great and continuing conflict between them.

"I don't want to in any way be controversial---but the Roman Catholic Church has been the number one anti-Semitic force in history. It is also described as a leopard---and you know what the bible says about a leopard, it cannot change its spots.[2] I'm not out to attack anybody but I am just trying to be realistic when I consider what is going on in Israel at this particular moment. (the Pope's overt support of the "Palestinians" during his ongoing visit.)

"The beast or the harlot---Rome or Jerusalem---how very significant on this particular day! Jesus said, "for wherever the carcass is, there the vultures will be gathered together"[3]--- and I see the vultures gathering around Jerusalem---the United States, the European Union, the entire Islamic world, and I would say, all of Christendom: all of them have got a claw to stick into Jerusalem: I am trying to be discrete but still make my meaning clear."

Given its secular historical realities on one side, and its self proclaimed ecclesiastical centrality on the other, I believe it is absolutely necessary for us all to clearly understand the genuine nature of this progenitor of all Western ecclesiastical Christianity. Echoing Derek Prince, I have no polemic desire or intention, but rather I seek only to reach out in love to all within and without the Body: my one heart's desire is to share the truth and love of Yeshua. However sincere my intention, I must confess as the crystal clear truth has been progressively revealed to me: the totally honest, historical, scriptural truth about the Roman Catholic Church,it has been increasingly difficult for me to retain my objectivity. What follows is my best effort to do so.

Two church fathers offer the following about this "mother" of all Christian churches:

Origen says: "Let no man deceive himself. Outside this house; i.e., outside the (Roman) Church none is saved" St. Cyprian speaks to the same effect: "He cannot have God for his father, who has not the (Roman)Church for his mother"[4]

Concerning it's nature and authority (through its own interpretation of Scripture) the Roman Catholic Church proclaims about itself:[5]

● It is to be a kingdom ruled in His (Christ's) absence by men *(Matt.18:18; John 21:17).*

● It is therefore a visible theocracy; and it will be substituted for the Jewish theocracy that has rejected Him *(Matt.21:43).*

● Its extent will be universal (Matt.28:19), and its duration to the end of time *(Matt.13: 49)*

● All powers that oppose it shall be crushed *(Matt.21:44).*

● Moreover, it will be a supernatural kingdom of truth, in the world, though not of it *(John 18:36).*

● It will be one and undivided, and this unity shall be a witness to all men that its founder came from God *(John 17:21).*

Concerning its position within the Body, the Roman Catholic Church itself proclaims:

"In---the Scriptural doctrine regarding the Church, it has been seen how clearly it is laid down that only by entering the Church can we participate in the redemption wrought for us by Christ. Incorporation with the Church can alone unite us to the family of the second Adam, and alone can engraft us into the true Vine. Moreover, it is to the Church that Christ has committed those means of grace through which the gifts He earned for men are communicated to them. The Church alone dispenses the sacraments. It alone makes known the light of revealed truth. Outside the Church these gifts cannot be obtained.

"From all this there is but one conclusion: Union with the Church is not merely one out of various means by which salvation may be obtained: it is the only means."[6]

A Brief Overview of the Papacy

Martin Luther, the "great reformer," was in many ways an enigma. At the dawn of the Reformation, he was more than just conciliatory toward the Jews: his outreach was loving and sincere. Later, however, when the Jews did not respond to the thus offered invitation to accept their Messiah, Luther, in his frustration, became perhaps the most vitriolic of the anti-Semites of his time.

Similarly, as the Reformation began, Luther stressed his continuing loyalty to the Papacy: he intended the Reformation to be short lived. Ultimately, Luther had every intention of returning to the sheep pen of Rome.

It was only later, after other reformers such as Zwingli and Calvin had joined in what quickly grew to an outright rebellion, that Luther began to speak out against the Papacy:

"I would honor the Pope, I would love his person, if he would leave my conscience alone, and not compel me to sin against God. But the Pope wants to be adored himself, and that cannot be done without offending God. Since we must choose between one or the other, let us choose God. The truth is we are commissioned by God to resist the Pope, for it is written, 'We ought to obey God rather than men.' (Acts 5:29)---If the Pope would concede that God alone by His grace through Christ justifies sinners, we would carry him in our arms, we would kiss his feet. But since we cannot obtain this concession, we will give in to nobody, not to all the angels in heaven, not to Peter, not to Paul, not to a hundred emperors, not to a thousand Popes, not to the whole world. If in this matter we were to humble ourselves, they would take from us the God who created us, and Jesus Christ who has redeemed us by His blood. Let this be our resolution, that we will suffer the loss of all things, the loss of our good name, of life itself, but the Gospel and our faith in Jesus Christ—we will not stand for it that anybody take them from us." (Martin Luther)[7]

The Roman Catholic Church makes no attempt to marginalize its various absolute doctrinal positions. Concerning the Pope, the Church itself proclaims:

"The title Pope---denotes the Bishop of Rome, who, in virtue of his position as successor of St. Peter, is the chief pastor of the whole Church, the Vicar (serving in the place) of Christ upon earth.[8] The Pope is declared to possess ordinary, immediate, and episcopal jurisdiction over all the faithful. We teach, moreover, and declare that, by the disposition of God, the Roman Church possesses supreme ordinary authority over all Churches, and that the jurisdiction of the Roman Pontiff, which is true episcopal jurisdiction is immediate in its character. It is further added that this authority extends to all alike, both pastors and faithful, whether singly or collectively---Christ has conferred upon St. Peter---the perpetuity of this office in the person of the Roman pontiff, the

Pope's jurisdiction over the faithful, and his supreme authority to define in all questions of faith and morals."[9]

The Church also proclaims: "Apostolic succession is found in the Catholic Church (and) that none of the separate Churches have any valid claim to it (and) that the Anglican Church, in particular, has broken away from Apostolic unity." [10]

Further to its claim, the Roman Church lists 265 successive Popes by name, showing their respective terms of office. These successive "Vicars of Christ" are listed in an "unbroken chain" beginning with "St. Peter (32-67CE)," and ending with the current Pope, John Paul II (1978-)." Of the 265 Popes, 77 have been canonized as "saints" by the Church.[11]

STATUE OF "ST. PETER"

Claimed by the Vatican to be an ancient statue of St. Peter enthroned. Otherwise claimed by detractors to actually be a pagan statue of Jupiter that was removed from the Pantheon in Rome (a pagan temple), moved into St. Peter's Basilica and renamed "Peter." The foot of this stature has nearly been worn away by the kisses of countless pilgrims. (From Michael Scheifler's "Bible Light" web site. Used with permission)

If, as Derek Prince also suggested in his message, "the spine is the connective channel of the entire body through which all of its various parts are connected and held together;" then, I would further suggest that the Papacy is the "spine" of the Roman Catholic Church.

Central to its claim of universal authority over all Christendom is the assumption that all of its Popes in an unbroken succession since Peter, who, having been appointed by divine inspiration, through their respective lives and ministries in the very place of Christ on earth have been living testimonies and true examples of the scriptural requirements of "an overseer" (bishop, elder, etc.):

A bishop then must be blameless, the husband of one wife, temperate, sober-minded, of good behavior, hospitable, able to teach; not given to wine, not violent, not greedy for money, but gentle, not quarrelsome, not covetous; one who rules his own house well, having his children in submission with all reverence (for if a man does not know how to rule his own house, how will he take care of the church of God?); not a novice, lest being puffed up with pride he fall into the same condemnation as the devil. Moreover he must have a good testimony among those who are outside, lest he fall into reproach and the snare of the devil. Likewise deacons must be reverent, not double-tongued, not given to much wine, not greedy for money, holding the mystery of the faith with a pure conscience. (1Tim 3:2-9)

There is no argument among students of the Papacy, even most Roman Catholic Church historians, that literally dozens of Popes have failed to meet the requirements for a bishop described in 1Timothy 3. It isn't just a matter of some Popes becoming fornicators, bribers, or murderers after becoming Pope, but rather some Popes attained the Papacy by means of committing such sins. Others, while they may not have attained the office by means of those sins, were known to be fornicators, rapists, murderers, etc. when they were appointed Pope. If the Catholic Church allows men to attain the Papacy by means of bribery or murder, and it appoints men as Pope who are known to be fornicators or thieves, how can anybody conclude that the Catholic Church has an unbroken succession of legitimate bishops by any reasonable morale standard, much less the Scriptural requisites of 1 Timothy 3?

While the Roman Catholic Church has, infrequently, removed people from church offices for immorality, it has been inconsistent in doing so. That inconsistency has been worse in its highest office, the Papacy, than anywhere else.

Some Catholics argue that the immorality of Popes is a thing of the past. However, that objection fails for two reasons. Even if only Popes of the past were immoral, and modern Popes had not been, the Catholic Church's claim to authority today rests upon the legitimacy of those past Popes. One missing link would prevent the Catholic Church from being able to claim an unbroken succession from the apostles.

One also might ask: Have recent Popes met the requirements of 1 Timothy 3? Consider, for example, Pope Pius XII, who, was, as is well documented, fully aware of the ongoing extermination of six million Jews by the Nazis, yet, chose to turn his back in silence rather than to offer even the slightest protest concerning the horror of the Holocaust.[12]

In discussing the Papacy of Pius XII, it would be negligent not to mention *La Popessa* - "the female Pope" as she was widely known. Sister Pascalina, a German nun, was, officially, the "housekeeper" of Pius XII. According to

UPI, she was one of the most rarely photographed women in the world. She ruled the Vatican with an iron fist. Nobody saw the Pope without her approval.[13]

Consider also John Paul II, the current "Vicar of Christ," who within the past few days of this writing stood in the sacred Hall of Remembrance (Yad Vashem) in Jerusalem, literally surrounded by the horrible evidence of murdered Jewry, still offering only lip service to the tragedy rather than making an outright apology for the Church's historically well documented complacency and even complicity.

By such heinous sins against the Jews; by teaching so much false doctrine, and by making corrupt alliances with world governments, it seems clear that recent Popes, along with their long line of predecessors, have also fallen far short of the standards for high ecclesiastical office set forth by the Apostle Paul.

While some Catholics, will surely object to the charge that recent Popes have failed to meet these scriptural requirements for ecclesiastical office, not even the most blindly loyal supporter of the Papacy can object to that charge being made against dozens of Roman bishops and Popes of previous centuries. [14]

The following examples (far from a complete list of Papal corruption of the worst sort) are offered by Eamon Duffy, a Roman Catholic historian and author in his book Saints and Sinners: *A History of the Popes* (New Haven and London: Yale University Press, 1997). Duffy writes:

"In the misery of exile, surrounded by imperial clergy and far from home, Liberius [bishop of Rome] weakened. He agreed to the excommunication of Athanasius [a bishop who defended the deity of Christ], and signed a formula which, while it did not actually repudiate the Nicene Creed, weakened it with the meaningless claim that the Logos [Jesus Christ] was 'like the father in being' and in all things. In 358 he was finally allowed to return to Rome. He found the city deeply divided. On Liberius' exile in 355, the Emperor had installed a new Pope, Liberius' former archdeacon Felix. Consecrated by Arian bishops in the imperial palace in Milan, Felix was an obvious fellow traveler, but imperial patronage was a powerful persuader, and many of the Roman clergy had rallied to him. Constantius was now unwilling simply to repudiate Felix, and commanded that Liberius and he should function as joint bishops....

(Note: It is interesting to see how the Church dealt with this fiasco historically: There is no mention of a Pope Felix near the time when he was actually a joint Pope with Liberius. Instead, he is shown as Pope Felix (269-274), some 86 years before he, according to Duffy, actually held the disputed office. As for Pope Liberius, he was passed over for sainthood, the first Pope not to be so honored among the first 36 successors of Saint Peter.)

Duffy continues: "Liberius' successor Damasus (366-84), who had served as deacon under both Liberius and Felix, would inherit some of the consequences of his predecessor's exile. His election in 366 was contested, and he was confronted by a rival Pope, Ursinus, whom he only got rid of with the help of the city police and a murderous rabble.... (Note: The Church lists a canonized Saint Damasus, but there is no mention of the disposed Pope Urinus.)

"Deprived of the support of empire, the Papacy became the possession of the great Roman families, a ticket to local dominance for which men were prepared to rape, murder and steal. A third of the Popes elected between 872 and 1012 died in suspicious circumstances - John VIII (872-82) bludgeoned to death by his own entourage, Stephen VI (896-7) strangled, Leo V (903) murdered by his successor Sergius III (904-11), John X (914-28) suffocated, Stephen VIII (939-42) horribly mutilated, a fate shared by the Greek anti-Pope John XVI (997-8) who, unfortunately for him, did not die from the removal of his eyes, nose, lips, tongue and hands.

(Note: In the official listing of Popes, there is Pope John XV (985-96) and a John XVII (1003), but no John XVI is acknowledged. A Pope Gregory V (996-99) is listed.

"Most of these men were maneuvered into power by a succession of powerful families - the Theophylacts, the Crescentii, and the Tusculani. John X (914-28), one of the few Popes of this period to make a stand against aristocratic domination, was deposed and then murdered in the Castel Sant' Angelo by the Theophylacts, who had appointed him in the first place. The key figure in both John X's appointment and his deposition was the notorious Theophylact matron, Marozia.

"She also appointed Leo VI (928) and Stephen VII (928-31), and she had been the mistress of Pope Sergius III, by whom she bore an illegitimate son whom she eventually appointed as Pope John XI (931-6)....

"Its [the declining Papacy's] symbol is the macabre 'cadaver synod' staged by Stephen VI in January 897, when he put on trial the mummified corpse of his hated predecessor but one, Pope Formosus. The corpse, dressed in pontifical vestments and propped up on a throne, was found guilty of perjury and other crimes, was mutilated by having the fingers used in blessings hacked off, and was then tossed into the Tiber. Stephen himself was subsequently deposed by the disgusted Roman crowd, and strangled in prison....

"Of the twenty-five Popes between 955 and 1057, thirteen were appointed by the local aristocracy, while the other twelve were appointed (and no fewer than five dismissed) by the German emperors. The ancient axiom that no one may judge the Pope was still in the law-books, but in practice had long since been set aside. The Popes themselves were deeply embroiled in the internecine dynastic warfare of the Roman nobility, and election to the chair of Peter, as we have seen, was frequently a commodity for sale or barter.

"Roderigo Borgia's election as Alexander VI in 1492 was accompanied by--naked bribery....Yet, for all his ability, Roderigo was a worldly and ruthless man, and at the time of his election was already the father of eight children, by at least three women...." [15]

The "Vicar Christ on Earth" (He who sits in the place of the Messiah)

If the "spine" of the Roman Catholic Church is the Papacy, then its "heart" is its doctrine that Peter and all the Popes who would follow him was/would be Divinely appointed by God as the "Vicar of Christ on earth": the absolute, supreme and infallible head of the church on earth in the very place of Yeshua.

The life or death importance of this understanding, that its correctness establishes the validity and very existence of the Roman Catholic Church, is clearly stated by the Church itself:

"We have shown (previously) that Christ conferred upon St. Peter the office of chief pastor, and that the permanence of that office is essential to the very being of the Church. It must now be established that it belongs of right to the Roman See---(a) that St. Peter was Bishop of Rome, and (b) that those who succeed him in that See succeed him also in the supreme headship."[16]

The Church begins support for its position on this pinnacle matter:

"It is no longer denied by any writer of weight that St. Peter visited Rome and suffered martyrdom there---. Some, however, of those who admit that he taught and suffered in Rome, deny that he was ever bishop of the city---. It is not, however, difficult to show that the fact of his bishopric is so well attested as to be historically certain."[17]

The Vatican's claim not withstanding, I offer three compelling areas of proof that the Vatican's position regarding Peter, his successors vis-à-vis the Papacy is blatantly false:

● Scripture never mentions or even hints that Peter ever traveled to or ministered in Rome. Rather, Scripture clearly shows that Peter was alive, well and ministering in Jerusalem, some 1,800 miles from Rome, during the entire period the Roman Church claims he was occupying the "Holy See" in Rome as the first Pope.

● There is convincing evidence that Peter died in Jerusalem and was buried there, not in Rome as claimed by the Roman Church. This claim is established by the discovery of what is thought to be Peter's tomb and bones in a 1st Century Nazarene Cemetery on the Mount of Olives, as verified by two eminent Roman Catholic archeologists who made the discovery, thoroughly documented its validity, and, according to the claim of one witness, reported the same personally to Pope Pius XII. This same Pope who had refused to intervene in the ongoing Holocaust or to even comment upon it, could, reportedly, do nothing but agree to the validity of this momentous archeological discovery and its profound implications for the Church. Even so, he reportedly gave instructions that the facts of the discovery were not to be made public, until, perhaps, some later time.

● The entire structure and validity of the Roman Catholic Church is based upon a faulty hermenutical exegesis of two solitary verses of Scripture: Matthew 16:18-19.

The testimony of Scripture: The Roman Church lists "St. Peter" as the first Pope, who reigned in Rome during the period 32-67 CE.[18]

There are many specific references to Peter's ministry detailed in the Book of Acts and elsewhere. At least several of these events recorded in Scripture can be dated with reliable accuracy. The Book of Acts, according to the Roman Church, was written in 64 CE.[19] Hence, all events concerning the life and ministry of Peter recorded in Acts obviously must have occurred at some time prior to 64 CE.

According to specific Scripture references, Peter was in Israel, not Rome during his supposed reign as Pope (32-67):

Event	Reference	Probable Date
Paul visits Peter in Jerusalem	Gal. 1:18	37 CE
Peter witnesses to various persons, along the Mediterranean coast in such places as Lydda and Joppa	Acts 9:32 - 11:18	41 - 43 CE
Peter imprisoned in Jerusalem by Herod.	Acts 12:9	44 CE
Peter in Jerusalem teaching about difference between the Law and Grace	Acts 15:7-11	46 - 52 CE
Peter present on Mount Zion for the Council of Jerusalem	Acts 15:6-11	49 CE
Paul again visits Peter in Jerusalem	Gal. 2:1-9	51 CE
Paul opposes Peter in Antioch	Gal. 2:11	51-52 CE
Paul, just before his death in Rome makes the statement: "---only Luke is with me." Surely, if "Pope Peter" had been in Rome, like Luke, he would have been at Paul's side.	2 Tim. 4:11	66 CE

It should also be clearly noted, albeit foundational to the very existence of the Roman Church: the tradition that Peter visited Rome is only tradition and nothing more, resting as it does partly upon a miscalculation of some of the early Fathers, "who assume that he went to Rome in 42 CE, immediately after his deliverance from prison." This "is irreconcilable with the silence of Scripture, and even with the mere fact of Paul's Epistle to the Romans, written in 58, since the latter says not a word of Peter's previous labors in that city, and he himself never built on other men's foundations"[20]

Although Peter did from time to time reach out to Gentiles, he was first called as an apostle to the Jews.[21] Paul, not Peter, was an apostle to the Gentiles. If there were to be a God called Papacy, it boggles the mind to think that Peter rather than Paul would sit as its "Vicar of Christ." F. Paul Peterson comments:

"If Peter was Pope in Rome, it would have been Peter, not Paul who would have written to the churches. Peter wrote altogether only eight chapters, but Paul wrote 100 chapters. Yes, it would have been Peter's place to have written to the churches in various countries. But not a letter, not a sentence, not a word, not a sermon, not even one admonition came from Peter from Rome."[22]

The Testimony of Archeology: In 1946, the famous Roman Catholic Archeologist P.B. Baggati, in collaboration with equally well known and reliable Church archeologist, J.T. Milik, both Franciscan priests, published their book, written in Italian, entitled *Gli Scavi del Dominus Flevit.* An English language version was printed in 1958 by the original publishers, the Franciscan Printing Press in Jerusalem. I personally visited the Franciscan Printing Press in early June, 2000 in an effort to purchase a copy of the English version of this book, as published in 1958. I was not surprised to learn that the 1958 publication was no longer available, but that a later version in English published in 1964 had apparently "replaced" the earlier English version. I purchased a copy of the 1964 version and found, quite interestingly, that it deals only with "Bronze Age" artifacts found at the Dominus Flevit site: there was absolutely no mention of the momentously much more important First Century artifacts found there, much less that among these artifacts was an ossuary (stone coffin/bone box) which suggested that Peter was buried at this site and not in Rome.

In the Italian language version of their book, Baggatti and Milik do (according to F. Paul Peterson) tell a story of their incredible discovery, excavation and careful study of a First Century Nazarene Christian Cemetery on the Mount of Olives at this place called Dominus Flevit, (the place where Yeshua wept). The discovery of this "burial cave" was initiated by Baggatti in response to another catacomb previously found and investigated at nearby Bethany by the renowned French archaeologist Charles Clermont-Ganneau.

Jean Gilman, a staff reporter, published an account of this find in *The Jerusalem Christian Review,* Volume 9, Issue 2, which is summarized as follows:

Both archaeologists (Baggatti and Clermont-Ganneau) found evidence clearly dating the two catacombs to the first century CE, with the finding of coins minted by Governor Varius Gratus in 15-16 CE. Evidence in both catacombs indicated their use for burial until the middle part of the first century CE, several years before the Nazarenes began writing what was to evolve into the New Testament.

The first catacomb found on the Mount of Olives near the ancient town of Bethany was obviously a family tomb. The investigating archeologist, Clermont-Ganneau, found names which corresponded with names in the New Testament. There were also many signs of the cross etched on several of the ossuaries.

As Claremont-Ganneau further investigated the tomb, he found inscriptions, including the names of "Eleazar,"(another version of "Lazarus"), and his sisters "Martha" and "Mary" on three different coffins. Here was a family tomb, with characters right out of the Gospel of John, suddenly made alive again by the apparent reappearance of their bones.

While these discoveries of Claremont-Ganneau were of great importance and interest, of far greater importance was the other catacomb found by Franciscan priest, P. Bagatti several years later at nearby Dominus Flevit. (So greatly important was Bagatti's discovery that had it not been successfully suppressed, it would surely have shaken the very foundations of the Roman Catholic Church!)

During his investigation of the Dominus Flevit site, Bagatti found evidence which established that the tomb was in use in the early part of the first century CE. Inside, like at the Bethany site, the sign of the cross was found on numerous first-century coffins.

Bagatti found dozens of inscribed ossuaries, which included such names as: Jairus, Jonathan, Joseph, Judah, Matthias, Menahem, Salome, Simon, and Zechariah. In addition, he found one ossuary with crosses and the quite different name "Shappira: a unique name not found anywhere in first century Nazarene Scriptures except where it is used in the familiar story recorded in Acts 5:1.

As he continued his excavations, Bagatti also found a coffin bearing the unusual inscription ***Shimon bar Yonah*** (Simon [Peter] son of Jonah). Other than its existence among the burial tombs of some of the very first Christians, there understandably was nor reasonably could be found any other conclusive evidence to identify this stone coffin as that of the disciple and close companion of Jesus, Simon Peter, who is claimed by the Roman Catholic Church to be the first "Vicar of Christ" on earth.

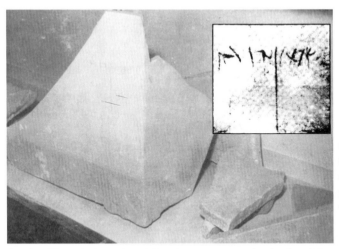

BONE BOX FOUND AT DOMINUS FLEVIT FIRST CENTURY CE NAZARENE CEMETERY ON THE MOUNT OF OLIVES.

Inscription in Aramaic is: Shimon Bar Yonah (Simon Peter son of Jonah)[23]

Like many other important early Christian discoveries in Israel, major finds like this have been unearthed and the results published by the Church (or others) in obscure archeological writings many decades ago. Then, either through deliberate suppression; very limited, or even a total absence of media attention; or even through just simple disinterest, these discoveries, even greatly important ones like the burial cave at Dominus Flevit, were practically forgotten. I believe that it is a matter of God's providence and timing that these ancient tombs once again assume center stage.[24]

Had not F. Paul Peterson, American author and student/critic of the Roman Catholic Church, heard about Bagatti's amazing find, and then been curious enough to travel to Jerusalem to personally investigate the matter, the truth probably would have remained swept under the rug: in much the same way that the Church had, I believe, a few years later, suppressed many of the first century Nazarene artifacts bearing the Messianic Seal of the Jerusalem Church (the subject of our earlier book bearing that title.) But, Peterson did come to Jerusalem and what he found out from those persons, mostly Franciscan priests who had first hand knowledge of the matter, he recorded in his book, *Peter's Tomb Recently Discovered In Jerusalem,* published in 1960.

Having reviewed the evidence provided by Baggatti himself, and by Peterson, along with the fact that the Church has apparently once again suppressed the truth, I believe it is highly probable that what Baggati found in this First Century Nazarene cemetery at Dominus Flevit were indeed the earthly remains of the Apostle Peter.

Peterson's main points:

1. During the course of his investigation in Jerusalem, he (Peterson) spoke to "many" Franciscan priests, including the senior official who was in charge of the printing plant where both Church books on the subject were published. All agreed that Bagatti had discovered the actual burial place and earthly remains of the Apostle Peter.

2. Professional photographs of the tomb, commissioned by Peterson and printed in his book document the physical facts of the story.

3. Marvin Pope, the Yale professor who was at that time director of the American School of Oriental Research in Jerusalem, reportedly told Peterson: "---it would be very improbable that a name with three words, and one so complete, could refer to more than one person, St. Peter. But what makes the possibility of error more remote is that the remains were found in a Christian burial ground, and more yet, of the First Century, the very time in which Peter lived. All of this makes it virtually impossible that the inscription *'Shimon Bar Jona'* could refer to any other than St. Peter."

4. Peterson reportedly spoke with Priest Milik, co-author of the Italian version of the Church published book. In the presence of a Christian Arab, Mr. S.J. Mattar, who was then the warden of the Garden Tomb in Jerusalem, Milik reportedly admitted: "---he knew that the bones of St. Peter are not in Rome, and he agreed---there is a hundred times more evidence that Peter was buried in Jerusalem than in Rome."

5. Peterson relates the following testimony revealed to him by an unnamed Franciscan priest in Bethlehem:

● There is clear evidence that the bones of St. Peter were discovered by Bagatti and that the Franciscan community in Jerusalem, including Bagatti and others, agrees with this assessment.

● He had personal knowledge that Bagatti had taken the evidence directly to Pope Pius XII in Rome, who, in the face of the evidence, agreed with Bagatti's assessment that St. Peter had died and was buried in Jerusalem, and that the Pope had instructed Bagatti to keep the matter quiet for the time being.

Certainly, the validity of all the above testimonial evidence rests entirely upon Peterson's veracity: but, not so the physical evidence of the tomb and its artifacts which remain in Jerusalem, held by the Franciscans in a "semi-private" museum where they can still be seen today by appointment only.[25] By their own physical reality, these stones and bones now cry out for recognition from a silence of 2,000 years.

The "damage control" actions of the Church relative to this matter give all the more credence to its truth:

Peterson Attacked: Instead of simply ignoring Peterson, the Church has attempted to discredit him. Franciscan priest I. Mancini, in his book, *Archeological Discoveries Relative to the Judeo-Christians,* published by the Franciscans in 1984, sub-titles the chapter dealing with Dominus Flevit, "A Romantic Element Enters."[26] An excerpt follows:

"Before ending these short summaries, we cannot pass over an amusing episode to which the discoveries in question happen to give rise. Amongst the inscriptions found on the ossuries of 'Dominus Flevit,' there was one in Hebrew which read *Simon bar Jonah.* Scholars* agree that this name is to be ascribed to some namesake of St. Peter and nothing more. Bagatti thinks there is question of a Christian who took this name either for some family reason or out of devotion to St. Peter. The latter reason would not have been out of common seeing that, in the third century**, many Christians took this name so as 'to be more beloved by the Saviour.'---In his booklet he (Peterson) states that some Franciscans---had confirmed the fact that Fr. Bagatti was convinced that he had found St. Peter's tomb. According to Peterson's 'romance,' this was made known to Pope Pius XII who, while giving it no credence***, ordered the whole business suppressed."

* No such "scholars" are here or elsewhere named.

** Bagatti, Milik and others have dated this find to the first century, not the third.

*** Why would the Pope order the matter suppressed if he gave it no credence. Peterson reported that the Pope did give the matter credence and thus ordered it suppressed.

A Counter-Tomb "Miraculously Discovered" in Rome: After centuries of silence on the subject of Peter's burial and remains, it is most interesting that in 1959, just one year after the Bagatti discovery at Dominus Flevit appeared in English, the Vatican published a further discovery of Peter's tomb: this time in its "rightful" place, under St. Peter's Basilica in Rome.

"In a work issued in 1959, Father Kirschbaum, a member of the archeological commission excavating under the basilica during the 1940's, [27] has given a summary of the findings. These are in brief that it is reasonably certain that the place where St. Peter was buried has been discovered. According to historical records, supplemented by these new discoveries, this is the 'history' of the tomb. The Christians buried the Apostle's body in a simple grave on the southern slope of Vatican Hill and covered it with a few brick slabs. Soon other graves were made near that of St. Peter, and these have been recently discovered. Their existence and inscriptions on the wall make clear that from the very first St. Peter's tomb was a place of pilgrimage so that there was uninterrupted Christian veneration and observation of this spot.

"Pope Paul VI announced to one of the excavators that 'those bones are like gold to us.' On June 26, 1968, he surprised the world by announcing officially that the bones of St. Peter had finally been rediscovered and identified: 'The relics of St. Peter have been identified in a manner which we believe convincing…very patient and accurate investigations were made with the result which we believe positive.' On the following day the Pope, in a solemn ceremony, restored the sacred bones to their ancient resting-place." [28]

On threat of excommunication:: Peterson ends his book with a deep expression of concern for those Roman Catholics who may feel called to read and share it:

"I am sorry that this book has caused so much alarm to some. We have recently learned that my books, *The Rise and Fall of the Roman Catholic Church,* and this one, *Peter's Tomb Recently Discovered in Jerusalem,* are banned in the Philippines and the reading thereof, punishable by 'excommunication.' There must be other places where the same also applies. I have earnestly striven to present the truth in as clear and effective a manner as I would want others to do for me if I, or my loved ones, were lost."[29]

Faulty Hermeneutics: A Misinterpretation of Scripture with Foundational Implications

Jesus answered and said to him, "Blessed are you, Simon Bar-Jonah, for flesh and blood has not revealed this to you, but My Father who is in heaven. "And I also say to you that you are Peter, and on this rock I will build My church, and the gates of Hades shall not prevail against it. (Matt 16:17-18)

Central to the study and application of hermeneutics, defined as the science and methodology of Biblical interpretation, are a collection of well considered inviolable principles; two of which are here germane:[30]

119

The Principle of Harmony: God has spoken without contradicting Himself. We must avoid random dipping into the Scriptures. We must avoid establishing doctrine by proof texting using one reference. The harmony of Scripture is essential. In establishing doctrine, we must look for consistent, repeated themes rather than isolated references. Above all, we must never isolate a text from its context.

The Principle of Context: Scripture should be interpreted in the light of its immediate context and the context of all Scripture. The primary context is the entire bible; the secondary context is the covenant (Old or New); the tertiary context is the Book: the next context is the chapter, and finally the surrounding verses. Within these contexts, one must look for and carefully examine verbal cross references, conceptual cross references and parallel cross references.

The Roman Catholic Church has blatantly violated both of the above principals. In the first instance they have literally constructed their entire Church, with all of its basic teachings and traditions, around Matthew 16:17-18, two isolated verses. In the second instance, there is absolutely no other scriptural contextual support for either their distorted exegesis of these two verses or the mountains of defective doctrines and dogma that have arisen from them.

Through His grace, the gift of Israeli citizenship, and along with it, the continuing opportunity to retrace the steps of Yeshua, affords Messianic believers who permanently reside in the Land, opportunities for some very special, on the scene insights regarding the interpretation of Scripture.

CAESARIA PHILLIPI
(MODERN BANIAS)

Caesaria Phillipi (modern Banias): a truly beautiful and remarkable place where Yeshua gave *Shimon Bar Yona* his new name, *Kefa* (pebble- "Peter").

In this instance, we often visit Caesaria Phillipi (modern Banias), a truly beautiful and remarkable place. It is a wonderful experience to stand there; at the edge of a trout-filled, crystal clear pool; there

120

at the foot of a massive flat faced rock formation, out of which flows the beginnings of the Jordan River. Somehow, transported in the spirit through time back to that moment some 2,000 years ago; standing in the very place where Yeshua stood with Peter, one can almost hear the words He spoke as they are recorded in these two verses.

Other special features of the place seem strikingly germane. There is a huge natural water-cut cave at the base of the massive flat-faced cliff. Next to the cave are niches laboriously hand-carved many centuries past by pagans who once there worshipped their revered stone idols.

The sandy bottom of a large pool is strewn with countless small round pebbles, well polished by centuries of rushing waters, having perhaps taken up their timeless residence there even long before Yeshua addressed Peter in their presence.

Before discussing three possible interpretations of these two verses, let me first point out something Yeshua said, relative to the place where He and Peter stood.

Yeshua said, in part: "---And I also say to you that you are Peter, and on this rock I will build My church---" The Greek word used here for "Peter" is Petros, translated as "a small rock or pebble." The Greek word used here for "rock" is Petra, translated as "a large rock projection, or cliff."

Yeshua was, it would seem, comparing Peter to one of the small round pebbles on the sandy bottom of the pool at their feet. It isn't difficult to imagine Yeshua picking one of these pebbles off the bottom: taking it out of the water and fondly touching its smoothness as He spoke to better make His point.

Peter, like the smooth round pebble in Yeshua's hand, had also been worn smooth and well polished while walking faithfully with his Lord. The many and varied challenges, trails and tribulations he had so endured by Yeshua's side were well symbolized by the several demonic idols then peering down upon this holy scene from their stone niches. Peter had at last come to the place where he could, in profound faith, confess to Yeshua: *Ata Mashiach, Ben Elohim Chiam*---"You are the Messiah, the Son of the living God."[31]

The three possible interpretations of these two vitally important verses hangs on what Yeshua meant to convey when he proclaimed his founding of the church upon this *Petra* (large rock projection, cliff).

1. Some hold that the word *Petra* here refers to Peter's confession, and that Yeshua meant to convey, upon this rock, this truth you have confessed that I am the Messiah and upon confessions of this from all believers who will walk this earth until I come again, I will build my church. Confessions like this shall be the test of piety, and in such confessions shall my church stand amid the flames of persecution, the fury of the gates of hell. This is the view held by Dr.

Arnold G. Fruchtenbaum, widely known and respected Messianic Jewish theologian, author and teacher.[32]

2. Others have suggested that Yeshua, in using *Petra* here, was referring to Himself. Yeshua is called a rock elsewhere in Scripture. (Isa 28:161; Pet 2:7-8)

While standing in this very special place, I have imagined myself watching in awe as Yeshua, in a sweeping gesture, first points to the imposing cliff and then immediately back to Himself as He proclaims, "Upon this rock, this truth that I am the Messiah—upon myself as the Messiah, I will build my church."

3. Another interpretation (the one preferred by Albert Barnes, America's leading commentator) is, that the word "rock" refers to Peter himself. Barnes says:

"This is the obvious meaning of the passage; and had it not been that the Church of Rome has abused it, and applied it to what was never intended, no other interpretation would have been sought for. "Thou art a rock. Thou hast shown thyself firm, and suitable for the work of laying the foundation of the church. Upon thee will I build it. Thou shalt be highly honored; thou shalt be first in making known the gospel to both Jews and Gentiles." This was accomplished. See Acts 2:14-36, where he first preached to the Jews, and Acts 10, where he preached the gospel to Cornelius and his neighbors, who were Gentiles. Peter had thus the honor of laying the foundation of the church among the Jews and Gentiles; and this is the plain meaning of this passage. But Christ did not mean, as the Roman Catholics say he did, to exalt Peter to supreme authority above all the other apostles, or to say that he was the only one upon whom he would rear his church. See Acts 15, where the advice of James, and not that of Peter, was followed. See also Gal. 2:11, where Paul withstood Peter to his face, because he was to be blamed—a thing which could not have happened if Christ (as the Roman Catholics say) meant that Peter was absolute and infallible. More than all, it is not said here, or anywhere else in the Bible, that Peter would have infallible successors who would be the vicegerents of Christ and the head of the church. The whole meaning of the passage is this: 'I will make you the honored instrument of making known my gospel first to Jews and Gentiles, and I will make you a firm and distinguished preacher in building my church.'" [33]

In the end, any of the three possible interpretations are, in my view, plausible, and my personal preference here is not germane. Rather, what is of the greatest importance is the clear understanding that the Roman Catholic interpretation fails to meet even the most meager hermeneutic standard, and must be rejected forthwith.

1 Derek Prince is a greatly beloved and anointed writer, preacher and teacher whose ministry has been centered on his great love for Israel, the Jewish people and their destiny. Nearing age 85, Derek, who is still greatly mourning the death of his second wife, Ruth, is never-the-less relentlessly continuing his wonderful and highly productive international outreach.

2 Jer. 13:23

3 Matt 24:28

4 The Catholic Encyclopedia, Article: "The Church."

5 Ibid

6 The Catholic Encyclopedia, Article: "The Church: The Necessary Means Of Salvation," www. newadvent.org

7 Martin Luther, (Translated by Theodore Graebner) "Commentary on the Epistle to the Galations" (1535) pages 6-7 www.theologywebsite.com

8 From the Catholic Encyclopedia, Article: "The Vicar of Christ":

> "A title of the Pope implying his supreme and universal primacy, both of honor and of jurisdiction, over the Church of Christ. It is founded on the words of the Divine Shepherd to St. Peter: "Feed my lambs... Feed my sheep" (John 21:16-17), by which He constituted the Prince of the Apostles guardian of His entire flock in His own place, thus making him His Vicar and fulfilling the promise made in Matthew 16:18-19. In the course of the ages other vicarial designations have been used for the Pope, as Vicar of St. Peter and even Vicar of the Apostolic See (Pope Gelasius, I, Ep. vi), but the title Vicar of Christ is more expressive of his supreme headship of the Church on earth, which he bears in virtue of the commission of Christ and with vicarial power derived from Him.—-"

9 Ibid. Article: "The Pope."

10 Ibid.

11 Ibid. Article: "List of Popes"

12 "Pope Pius XII, head of the Catholic Church during World War II, was given daily briefings of Nazi atrocities by the British envoy to the Holy See, according to documents recently found in a Rome flea market." Reported in the *Jerusalem Post*, May 25, 2000

13 "The Pope's Palace", Article found at www.Reformation.org

14 Engwer, Jason, "The Corrupt Papacy," Article found at Christian Liberty www.members.aol.com/jasonite

15 Eamon Duffy, *Saints and Sinners: A History of the Popes* (New Haven and London: Yale University Press, 1997). Pages 14 -146 (selected quotes, with permission of the publisher).

16 The Catholic Encyclopedia, Article: "The Pope":

17 Ibid

18 Ibid, Article: "The List of Popes"

19 Ibid Article: "Acts of the Apostles"

20 Rom 15:20; 2 Cor 10:15-16 See Article: "Peter, Simon" International Standard Bible Encyclopedia, Electronic Database Copyright (C) 1996 by Biblesoft)

21 1 Pet 1:1

22 F. Paul Peterson, *Peter's Tomb Recently Discovered In Jerusalem*, page 36

23 Bone Box picture from: F. Paul Peterson, *Peter's Tomb Recently Discovered In Jerusalem*, page 9. Inscription photo from: Gilman, Jean, Article: "Jerusalem Burial Cave Reveals:

Names, Testimonies of First Christians," 1998 *Jerusalem Christian Review,* Volume 9, Issue 2,

24 Gilman, Jean, Article: "Jerusalem Burial Cave Reveals: Names, Testimonies of First Christians," 1998 *Jerusalem Christian Review,* Volume 9, Issue 2, found at www.leadereru.com

25 Franciscan Archeological Museum Jerusalem, "Our guiding purpose is to characterize our collections in such a way as to be correctly perceived as Jerusalem's archaeological museum of Christian origins, at the service of scholars and pilgrims who, in ever greater numbers, visit the Holy Land." Fr. Michele Piccirillo - Director. Open 0900-1130 by Appointment. Phone (972) - 2 - 282936. Groups over 20 persons not accepted. (http://www.christusrex.org/www1/ofm/sbf/SBFmsm.html)

26 Mancini, I., Archeological Discoveries Relative to the Judeo-Christians, pages 60-61

27 It certainly seems an interesting coincidence that this is the same time frame of the Israeli based church sponsored archeological investigations that would ultimately lead to the discovery of Peter's Tomb in Jerusalem

28 Article: "Peter's Tomb," The Catholic Information Network, www.cin.org

29 Peterson, page 94

30 Jim Roane, Phd., Professor of Hermeneutics, Faith Seminary, Lecture notes taken by the author on September 16, 1991

31 Matt. 16:16

32 Dr. Arnold. G. Fruchtenbaum, *The Confession of Peter,* pages 1-10

33 Barnes, Albert, *Notes on the New Testament,* Matthew and Mark, Commentary on Matthew 16:17-18, page 170

Chapter Three

The Pagan Roots and Practices of the Christian Church

Put yourselves in array against Babylon all around, all you who bend the bow; shoot at her, spare no arrows, for she has sinned against the LORD. Shout against her all around; she has given her hand, her foundations have fallen, her walls are thrown down; for it is the vengeance of the LORD. Take vengeance on her. As she has done, so do to her. (Jer 50:14-15)

At one time or another I feel certain that most if not all believers have gotten at least some inkling of how paganism has polluted Christianity. If nothing else, surely all have heard there is something spiritually tainted about how and when most of Christendom celebrates the birth and resurrection of Yeshua. Some even have an understanding that many holiday traditions, including Christmas trees, Yule logs, Easter eggs, etc., extend directly from pagan Babylon, Egypt, Greece, Rome, or indigenous cultures of Western Europe and were deliberately incorporated into "Christian" worship to facilitate conversion of the heathen.

Few, however, have any real understanding of just how completely paganism in its worst forms, from the time it was established by Constantine, like a persistent mold, has eaten its way into the very foundation and fabric of the entire Church. So heinous and extensive is this pollution that its proper revelation would fill at least one separate volume dedicated to that purpose. For the present, however, I will only point out some of the more striking examples.

Mithraism - Worship of Mithra, the Sun God

Mithra is an ancient Iranian god of light who was believed to maintain the cosmic order. Mithra is said to have been born from a rock (or a cave). He fought with the sun and managed to capture the "divine bull" and slayed it before he ascended to heaven. From the blood of the bull came forth all the plants and animals beneficial to humanity.

Mithra is sometimes portrayed as having ten thousand ears and eyes, and

BOTH SIDES OF 3rd CENT ROMAN COIN

Third Century Roman Coin depicting pagan sun god, Mithra. Reverse side shows Mithra driving a chariot drawn by four horses. (From Michael Scheifler's "Bible Light" web site. Used with permission)

he rides in a chariot pulled by white horses.

In the 4th century BCE, Mithra's popularity rose and again he held a high position in the Persian pantheon. Eventually his cult spread beyond Iran and Asia Minor and gradually became a mystery cult.

The ascetic religion of Mithraism (to which only men were allowed) became increasingly popular among the Roman soldiers around 100 CE and at that time Mithra was known in Rome as *Deus sol invictus'* ("the unconquered sun").

Mithra was worshipped in Mithraea, artificially constructed caves that represented his birth-cave. The ceiling looked like the starry sky and at the sides, benches where placed for the ritual meals. In the center of the Mithraea was a niche which held a relief (a raised figure) of the god, dressed in Phrygian clothing (short tunic and cloak, long trousers and a hat with a curled tip), who kills a bull. The Mithraea were spread all over the Roman empire and some 50 of these caves still exist in Rome today.[1]

Interestingly, the early Roman Church fathers transported Constantinian Christianity to Israel. A Mithraeum was found in the ruins of the early Christian Church in Caesaria dating to the 3rd and 4th centuries.[3] This church was first pastored by Bishop Eusibius, noted church historian and loyal follower of his emperor, Constantine.

The Roman Catholic Church took many of its features from pagan mystery religions: vestments, pomp, ritual, wafer, and *mitra* (a divided tiara worn by Catholic Bishops). When Western fundamentalist Christians try to argue that the Church took nothing from the mystery religions, they are not only arguing against skeptics and atheists, they are arguing also against the millions of Protestant Christians whose protest was precisely that the Roman Church had adopted pagan, largely Mithraic, practices.

The Vatican Hill in Rome considered sacred to Peter was previously sacred to the followers of Mithra. The cave of the Vatican was a Mithraeum until December 25, 376 CE, the birthday of the sun god. It was then that a city prefect suppressed Mithraism and seized the grotto in the name of Christ. Mithraic artifacts found in the Vatican Grotto were taken over by the Church.

The head of the Mithraic faith was the *Pater Patrum*, the "Father of Fathers," who sat in the Vatican cave. The Mithraic Holy father wore a red cap and garment and a ring, and carried a shepherd's staff. The head of the Christian faith, the bishop of Rome, adopted the same title and dressed himself in the same manner, becoming the "Papa" or "Father"—the Pope, who subsequently literally sat in the same location in Rome as the *Pater Patrum*. The throne of St. Peter at Rome is older than the Church. From the carved motifs decorating it, it was clearly Mithraic.

SAN CLEMENTE CHURCH IN ROME

Built in the 12th Cent. CE on top of the foundation of a 4th Cent CE Catholic Church. This early Church itself was built directly on top of an enormous cave which held a 2nd Cent. CE Mithraeum, used by early "Christians" to worship their sun god, Mithra. The co-location of this Church and Mithraeum is clear testimony to the blending of paganism and Christianity into a new religion.[2]

The 2nd Cent. Mithraeum in a cave directly under the Catholic Church of San Clemente in Rome

127

THE 3rd TO 4thCENTURY MITHRAEUM USED BY EARLY "CHRIS-
TIANS" AT CAESAREA. (Photo by Joseph Patrich, University of Haifa,
Israel)

A CLOSE-UP VIEW OF THE
ALTAR OF THE 2ND CENT. CE
MITHRAEUM LOCATED IN A
CAVE DIRECTLY UNDER THE
CATHOLIC CHURCH OF SAN
CLEMENTE IN ROME.

THE SUN WHEEL DOME OF ST. PETER'S BASILICA

The light from the sun streams into the center hub of the dome making a genuine sun-lit sunburst image at the center of the wheel. (From Michael
Scheifler's "Bible Light" web site. Used with permission)

SUN WHEEL

Ancient pagan "sun wheel." Mithra
worshippers made chariots dedicated
to their sun god to use in his travel
across the heavens. (From Michael
Scheifler's "Bible Light" web site.
Used with permission)

Ceiling decoration of a Vatican Art Gallery. The sun burst coat of arms of Borgia Pope Alexander VI, 1492-1503. Included are: 3-tiered papal tiara and keys to the kingdom. (From Michael Scheifler's "Bible Light" web site. Used with permission)

Mithraic pagan priests wore robes displaying the sword of Mithras. Identical robes are worn by Roman Catholic priests to this day. Why is the Pope's crown called a tiara, a Persian headdress? Why do Catholic bishops wear a divided tiara called a mitre? Obviously these practices were directly transported from those of their predecessors, the priests of Mithra, who wore a *mitra* (Greek) to signify their office and the duality of the world.

Mithraists commemorated the ascension of Mithra by eating a *mizd*, a

POPE JOHN PAUL II WEARING MITRE, VENERATING STATUE OF CROWNED MARY. The two-horned mitre was worn by Dagon, the fish-god of the Philistines and Babylonians. The Pagan god, Dagon, was the poor defenseless and dumb idol that the Holy Spirit continually knocked down and broke when it sat in the presence of the Ark of the Covenant. (1 Samuel 5). This revelation places the creation of this headdress at least 500 years before Christ.4

MARY WITH INFANT JESUS AND SUNBURST

Statue of Mary with infant Jesus in the Church of the Virgin of the pillar, Zaragoza, Spain. Mary is depicted as the crowned "Queen of Heaven" positioned directly in front of an obvious sun burst. (From Michael Scheifler's "Bible Light" web site. Used with permission)

sun-shaped bun embossed with the sword (cross) of the god. This "hot cross bun," the focus of the Mithratic mass later transported to Roman Christianity, eventually degenerated to the communion wafer, still used today, in the same design, in all Catholic churches.

By the fourth century, Constantine had effectively merged Mithraism with his own understanding of "Christianity" and placed his new, thus formed religion under the control of the Empire, specifically under the guidance of his own closely controlled "bishops."[6]

THE VATICAN'S STATUE OF ST. PETER, FRAMED IN A SUN-BURST, IS REGULARLY DRESSED WEARING THIS JEWELED PAPAL TIARA. The most respected of the ecclesiastical symbols, the tiara, or *trigreno*, is also a symbol of the pope's authority over the Church. No one knows for certain when the tiara originated, and it has undergone many changes since it first appeared at the Papal Court. The tiara comprises three separate crowns, or diadems. The bottom crown appeared in the ninth century as ornamentation at the base of the mitre. When pontiffs assumed the temporal role of sovereign princes, they further adorned the base decorations with the jeweled crown of the princes of the time. The second crown was added by Pope Boniface VIII in 1298 CE to represent his spiritual dominion. By 1315 CE, the *triregno* appears in the documentation of the Papal Treasury.[5]

POPE JOHN XXIII WEARING THE *TRIREGNO* CROWN AT THE TIME OF HIS CORONATION IN 1958.

Pope John Paul I and then John Paul II, in 1978, both refused a formal coronation ceremony with the triple-tiered crown, as it was considered to be out of step with the less pompous tone set by their predecessor Pope Paul VI and Vatican II's recent emphasis on the pastoral role of the Papacy, rather than its temporal authority. However, nothing really prevents the next Pope from returning to the tradition of the coronation and wearing of the triregno crown. (From Michael Scheifler's "Bible

The Halo: Symbol of the Pagan Solar Gods

The sun's corona is traditionally depicted by a halo, a brilliant sunburst, sometimes a crown of thorns, and indeed the halo can be taken as an indication of a sun god in pre-Christian art. Sun gods such as Mithra, Adonis, Horus, and Buddha were shown with haloes long before it was adopted as a Christian convention by the early Gentile Church.

130

For example, Iris, Goddess of the rainbow in Greek mythology, although she was a sister of the winged monsters the Harpies, she (Iris) was represented as a beautiful maiden, with wings and robes of bright colors and a halo of light on her head, tailing across the sky with a rainbow in her wake.

Often Mary, Yeshua and the Roman Catholic Saints are depicted surrounded by a sunburst of rays. The rays of light radiating from the heads of the ancient Pagan gods show that these gods were often given the attributes of the sun. The halo, that originally indicated a solar god, was transferred to the sacred personages of Christianity and are widely depicted in Christian art. The halo thus became the symbol of a god and then a holy person because it is a characteristic of the holy sun.

CORONA OF SUN DURING FULL ECLIPSE

The black body of the moon stands out in relief between the Sun and the Earth during a full solar eclipse. The glowing, corona is the inspiration for the pagan Halo symbol used in worship of the Sun God, to say nothing of its frivolous common wide use to depict angels, etc. throughout the Church.

The halo is to be found nowhere in Scripture. Nowhere do we read that Christ's head was surrounded with a disk, or circle of light. However, what you will never find in the Word of God is found in the artistic representations of the great gods and goddesses of Babylon. The disk or halo, and particularly the circle, "---were the well-known symbols of the Sun-divinity, and figured largely in the symbolism of the East. With the circle or the disk the head of the Sun-divinity was encompassed. The same was the case in Pagan Rome. Apollo, as the child of the Sun, was often thus represented. The goddesses that claimed to be kindred with the Sun were equally entitled to be adorned with the nimbus or luminous circle,....in the very same way as the head of The Roman Madonna is at this day surrounded."[7]

I find it genuinely horrific that the halo remains in such wide use today throughout the Church. What Christian can say that they have never seen members of the church, perhaps, even their own children,

THE VIRGIN MARY WITH HALO

Halos almost universally adorn paintings and other artistic renditions of the Holy family, angels, and saints. This painting of the Virgin Mary is a typical use of the halo, a direct carry-over from pagan sun worship.

adorned with haloes in various dramatic "productions?" Even here, right in our own back yard, the Christian Embassy's internationally adored annual Feast of Tabernacles extravaganza in Jerusalem always features literally scores of characters wearing haloes.

131

Haloes are widely sold by Christian merchants and purchased excitedly by myriad believers who wear them with the expectation that they are somehow giving glory to God. Indeed, they are giving glory to several gods, but most assuredly not to the Lord God of Israel, His son, Yeshua or the Holy Spirit.

This widespread pagan adaptation of haloes by the modern church is an excellent example of how innocently, out of sheer ignorance, we have allowed the pagan roots of the Christian Church to continue on into our contemporary worship practice, and indeed into the very heart of our lives.

The Monstrance, "Wafer God" and Pagan Sun Worship

While I have already introduced the pagan aspects of the Roman Catholic Eucharist (Lord's Supper), the very centrality of the Monstrance or Ostensorium, a blatantly pagan symbol/icon, in the Catholic mass demands further comment.

The Monstrance is a head-size, round metallic sunburst mounted on a stand that normally resides at the center of the altar. The Monstrance is used to display a round wafer of bread, called the "host," which is used in the "communion meal" of the Mass.

The Church itself admits the Monstrance to be a sunburst, hence derived from the Mithratic Mass: "During the baroque period it (the Monstrance) took on a rayed form of a sun-monstrance with a circular window surrounded by a silver or gold frame with rays."[8] This form is further confirmed by the Catholic

POPE JOHN PAUL II HOLDS MONSTRANCE

Pope John Paul II holding a Monstrance or Ostensorium, an obvious pagan sunburst. It is used to display a round wafer of bread, called the host, which is used in the Mass, (Lord's Supper, Communion or Eucharistic meal.) The Catholics believe this wafer of bread turns into the actual body of Christ when consecrated during the Mass. Thus, they bow down before it when they pass by, as if it were actually Yeshua incarnate. (From Michael Scheifler's "Bible Light" web site. Used with permission)

Encyclopedia which states that the most appropriate form for the Ostenorium "is that of the sun emitting its rays to all sides."[9]

Equally as striking as its sunburst form are the raised letters "SFS" directly below the place for the wafer. Each of these letters is a universally understood symbol for the number "6"

132

in the pagan mysteries. Hence, SFS translates to read "666" which is held high by the priest for the congregation to venerate at various times during the Mass.

Virtually, any time the Monstrance is displayed in this way by the priest to the congregation, they are taught to kneel in submission. A Catholic is instructed by the Church not to walk past this sun symbol without acknowledging it by kneeling and/or making the sign of the cross with their hands.[11]

PICTURE OF MONSTRANCE BASE WITH SFS

Monstrance on display in the Vatican Museum. Each of the letters "SFS" in the sunburst is a universal symbol for the number 6, so to the pagan it reads "666." The number, "666" ascribed to satan in the Book of Revelations, is also associated in pagan tradition with what is called "magic square of the sun." (From Michael Scheifler's "Bible Light" web site. Used with permission)[10]

While it might seem so polemically offensive as to make it unbelievable to suggest that the Roman Catholic Church teaches in effect a "Worship of the Eucharist," the Church itself seems to make this point in the new Vatican Catechism of the Catholic Church which states:

"Worship of the Eucharist. In the liturgy of the mass we express our faith in the real presence of Christ under the species of bread and wine by, among other ways, genuflecting or bowing deeply as a sign of adoration of the Lord. The Catholic church has always offered and still offers to the sacrament of the Eucharist the cult of adoration, not only during the Mass, but also

WORSHIP OF THE EUCHARIST

outside it, reserving the consecrated host with the utmost care, exposing them to the solemn veneration of the faithful, and carrying them in procession."[12]

133

Easter-A Paganistic Mockery of the Holiest Event
in the History of the World

I have read several studies regarding the pagan roots of Easter, but none nearly as complete and meaningful as that provided by Dr. C.J. Koster in his book *Come Out of Her My People*, which, with permission, I quote in its entirety:

"The word "Easter" in Acts 12:4 of the King James Version is a mistranslation of the Greek *pascha*. All other translations have subsequently rendered it correctly as 'Passover.' The well-known *Barnes' Notes* comments on this mistranslation, in this single occurrence of the word 'Easter' in the King James Version, as follows, 'There was never a more absurd or unhappy translation than this.' Not only is the name 'Easter' incorrect, but also the time of the feast. No one would ever think of keeping his own birthday every year on the same day of the week. If I were born on a Sunday, I would not think of keeping my birthday on a Sunday each year. I will keep it according to the day of the yearly calendar and not according to the day of the week. This is exactly what happened when Easter Sunday was instituted by Constantine's Church.

"The Passover dispute between the Western Church and the more Scripture-adhering believers of the Near East was finally settled by Constantine's Council of Nicea in the year 325, where it was decided that Easter was to be kept on Sun-day, and on the same Sun-day throughout the world and that 'none should hereafter follow the blindness of the Jews.' Prior to that, Polycarp, the disciple of the Apostle John, had learned from the Apostle himself that the 14th *Abib (Nisan)* was the Scriptural day of the year, which had been legislated in the Old Testament to determine the onset of Passover, which the Saviour kept the night He was betrayed. Polycarp, Polycrates, Apollinariuis and others contended for the correct calculation of the Passover Memorial Supper (and the events following it), to be reckoned as beginning from the 14th *Abib (Nisan)*.

"Now, with Constantine taking the lead, the Council of Nicea decided to reject the Scriptural way of determining the correct date according to the yearly date, in favor of Easter Sun-day, according to the day of the week. Constantine exhorted all bishops to embrace 'the practice which is observed at once in the city of Rome, and in Africa; throughout Italy, and in Egypt.' Another fragment records that Constantine urged all Christians to follow the custom of 'the ancient church of Rome and Alexandria.'

"The case for the yearly Easter Sun-day was held in common with the case for the weekly Sun-day. Origen wrote, 'The resurrection of the master is celebrated not only once a year but constantly every seven days.' Eusibius also stated, 'While the Jews, faithful to Moses, sacrificed the Passover lamb once a year...we men of the New Covenant celebrate our Passover every Sunday.' Pope Innocent I wrote, 'We celebrate Sunday because of the Venerable resurrection...not only at Easter but...every Sunday.'

"But where did this Easter Sun-day originate? Any encyclopedia or dictionary, such as the Oxford English Dictionary, will supply the answer: Easter had a pre-Christian origin, namely a festival in honor of *Eostre*, the Teutonic dawn-goddess, also know as *Eos*, the Greek dawn-goddess, and as *Usha* or *Ushas*, the Hindu dawn-goddess. This *Eostre* was also known to be the spring goddess and the goddess of fertility. Thus, another form of Sun-worship, another variant in the form of a dawn-deity, *Eostre*, also called *Eastre*, *Eostra* or *Ostara* was adopted by, or merged with Christianity. This same dawn-goddess was also well known in the Greek Classics (Homer, Hesiod) as *Eos* (the Roman *Aurora*) and was an amorous deity and the idea of fertility with its fertility-symbols of eggs and rabbits was to be expected. Any reference work will testify to the fact of the origin of Easter eggs and the Easter rabbit or bunny, because "Easter" was not only goddess of dawn but also goddess of spring with all of its fertility-symbols and fertility-rites.

"This word *Eos, Eostre, Ostara*, is related to Sanskrit and Vedic *usra* or *ushas*, the Sendic *ushastara* and the Lithuanian *Ausra*, the old Teutonic *austron*, and the male spring or dawn deity of the Norwegians, *Austri*, of which we read in the *Edda*. Most likely this *Eostre*, dawn deity/fertility deity, is the same as *Astarte*, which is recorded in the Hebrew of the Old Testament as *Ashtaroth* and *Ashtoreth* (the latter being changed because of deliberate Hebrew misvocalization). The name of *Astarte* was *Ishtar* in *Nineve*. She was also known as the 'queen of heaven.'

"Let us further examine the festival of this dawn, or spring-deity. Just like *Eostre*, the dawn-deity of the Germanic tribes, we find *Eos*, the dawn-deity of the Greeks, who although married to *Tithonus*, was consistently faithless to him, which accounts for the blush of dawn. She was known to be the sister of *Helios*, the Sun-deity, and represented in sculpture with radiant sun-rays around her head.

"Similarly, and probably the same origin of this *Eos* and *Eostre*, we find in Hindu mythology the goddess of dawn to be *Ushas*, daughter of Heaven. Other spring festivals were celebrated, with the rites of *Adonis* or of *Tammuz* (well known as the youthful Sun-deity) which were held in the summer in some places, but held in the spring in others, such as in Sicily and Syria, our dead and risen Messiah being assimilated to the pagan celebration of the dead and risen *Adonis* (*Tammuz*). This 'weeping for *Tammuz*' is exactly what Yahuweh included amongst His verdict of 'wicked abominations,' as we read in Eze. 8:9 and 14.

"Rev. Alexander Hislop comments on this fusion of the Scriptural Passover Memorial (and the events following it in the New Testament) with the pagan spring celebrations: 'To conciliate the pagans to normal Christianity, Rome, pursuing its usual policy, took measures to get Christian and pagan festivals amalgamated, and, by a complicated but skillful adjustment of the calendar, it was found no difficult matter, in general, to get paganism into Christianity (which was) now far sunk in idolatry.... .'

"Sir James Frazer similarly comments, 'When we reflect how often the Church has skillfully contrived to plant seeds of the new faith on the old stock of paganism, we may surmise that the Easter celebration of the dead and risen Messiah was grafted upon a similar celebration of the dead and risen Adonis...Taken altogether, the coincidences of the Christian with the heathen festivals are too close and too numerous to be accidental. They mark the compromise which the Church in the hour of its triumph was compelled to make with its vanquished yet still dangerous rivals.'

"*Adonis* was known also as the *Phrygian Attes, Attis, Atys. Attis* was beloved by *Cybele*, the 'Mother of Gods,' the great Asiatic goddess of fertility, who had her chief home in Phrygia. Some held that *Attis* was her son. The worship of *Attis* and *Cybele* was adopted in 204 BCE by the Romans where the great spring festival in their honor became well known. This festival lasted from the 22nd to the 25th of March, the last day, when the mourning was turned to joy for the resurrection of the dead *Attis*. *Attis* was also identified with the Sun. The 25th March was regarded as the vernal (spring) equinox, and we can easily see how the pagan worshippers of many different pagan religions were reconciled with the Messianic Belief, by means of assimilating a similar commemoration, but which had a different date, according to the day of the year, and not according to the day of the week, the Sun-day, Easter Sun-day, year after year. This was the decision taken by the Council of Nicea.

"Furthermore, not only was the time of the Scriptural feast supplanted by the pagan day's date, but also the rites of the pagan Easter took over, namely the fertility pagan symbols of Easter eggs and Easter rabbits (bunnies), and also the Easter buns, the hot-cross buns.

"The 'buns,' known by the identical name *boun*, were used in the worship of the queen of heaven already 1,500 years before the Christian era. They were also known amongst the Teutonic tribes as *osterstoupha* and moon shaped *ostermane*. The Mighty One warns His people against this 'abomination' as he called it in Jer. 7:10, and as is described in Jer. 7:18. Even the round shape of them with the cross on the cross with a circle around it. This was especially known to be the symbol of the Babylonian Sun-deity. The circled cross was later found struck by Caesar's heir, Augustus 20 BCE, and by Hadrian and other Roman emperors.

"How and when were these things ever permitted to enter in? In an attempt to justify this, the Church uses the term 'Christiainization.' The adoption of these pagan Easter eggs, Easter rabbits and Easter buns, are explained by the Catholic Encyclopedia, 'a great many pagan customs celebrating the return of spring, gravitated to Easter...The rabbit is a pagan symbol and has always been an emblem of fertility.' This is in direct contrast to the Word of Yahuweh in Jer.10:2, 'Do not learn the way of the Gentiles' and in Deut. 12:30, 'Do not inquire after their mighty ones, saying, 'How did these nations serve their mighty ones? I also will do likewise.' Israel was commanded to keep the worship pure and undefiled by destroying everything pertaining to pagan worship, even to destroy the names of pagan deities (Deut 12:3), and not even to 'mention the names of other mighty ones, nor let it be heard from your mouth' (Ex.23:13).

"The whole subject of Easter, its Sunday-emphasizing date, and its pagan emblems and rites, such as Easter sunrise services, is crowned by the general admission that the word 'Easter' is derived from the name of a goddess, the dawn-goddess, the spring-deity, the goddess of fertility.

"Let us rather commemorate our Savior's Memorial Passover and the subsequent events according to the Scriptural calendar, starting on the evening of 14 *Abib*. Let us repent of, and eliminate the pagan Easter festival."[13]

The Virgin Mary, Worshipped as the "Queen of Heaven"

The children gather wood, the fathers kindle the fire, and the women knead dough, to make cakes for the queen of heaven; and they pour out drink offerings to other gods, that they may provoke Me to anger. (Jer. 7:18)

The Roman Church makes no effort to conceal their outright veneration of Mary as the "Queen of Heaven." According to the Catholic Encyclopedia, "As early as 540 CE we find a mosaic in which she sits enthroned as Queen of Heaven in the center of the apex of the cathedral of Parenzo in Austria, which was constructed at that date by Bishop Euphrasius."[14]

Pope Pius XII proclaimed the Queenship of Mary in a Papal Encyclical, dated October 11, 1954:

"To the Venerable Brethren, the Patriarchs, Primates, Archbishops, Bishops and other Local Ordinaries in Peace and Communion with the Holy See.

"Venerable Brethren, Health and Apostolic Blessing.

"From the earliest ages of the Catholic Church a Christian people, whether in time of triumph or more especially in time of crisis, has addressed prayers of petition and hymns of praise and veneration to the Queen of Heaven. And never has that hope wavered which they placed in the Mother of the Divine King, Jesus Christ; nor has that faith ever failed by which we are taught that Mary, the Virgin Mother of God, reigns with a mother's solicitude over the entire world, just as she is crowned in heavenly blessedness with the glory of a Queen."[15]

Time magazine well summarized the position of the Church with regard to Mary's heavenly queenship:

"Among all the women who have ever lived, the mother of Jesus Christ is the most celebrated, the most venerated...Among Roman Catholics, the Madonna is recognized not only as the Mother of God, but also, according to modern Popes, as the Queen of Universe, Queen of Heaven, Seat of Wisdom, and even Spouse of the Holy Spirit."[16]

Alexander Hislop provides an excellent study of Mary as the "Queen of Heaven" in his book, *The Two Babylons*, a summary of which follows:

"God's wrath concerning worship of the 'Queen of Heaven' as recorded several times in Jeremiah, is certainly not a casual warning or expression. The 'Queen of Heaven' then being worshipped by the people of Israel and now venerated by the Roman Catholic Church is a pagan counterfeit of the Virgin Mary who dates back to the time of Nimrod, some 400 years after the great flood.

"After Nimrod's death, his wife Semiramis, was determined to retain her power and wealth. She concocted the story that Nimrod's death was for the salvation of mankind.[17] Nimrod was touted as the woman's promised seed, Zero-Asta, who was destined to bruise the serpent's head, and in doing so was to have his own heel bruised.

"It isn't difficult to see the Paganistic parallel of this story as a counterfeit of the true prophecy concerning Yeshua. To enable the Babylonian people to better worship this child, a woodcut portrait was created, depicting him in his mother's arms. The mother obviously drew her glory from her deified son. However, the mother, in the long-run, practically eclipsed the son in worship. The original picture obviously was meant to merely be a pedestal for the upholding of the divine son...But, while this... was the design, it is a plain principle in all idolatries that that which most appeals to the senses must make the most powerful impression. The mother obviously created the most powerful visual impression, both because she was an adult and because she was so magnificently arrayed.

"Once people began to worship the mother more than the child, Babylonian priests felt forced to issue an edict deifying the mother also. After the passage of still more time, 'her son's birth was boldly declared to be miraculous, and therefore she was called ...the Virgin Mother.' The highest titles were then bestowed upon her. She was called the Queen of Heaven.

"Thus, we can see that this ancient Queen of Heaven was a Pagan counterfeit of the Virgin Mary. She was a Divine Mother that had given birth to a Divine Child! Of special note is the connection in Rome where Mary was also called the Dove.

"In Ancient Babylon, both the worship of the Virgin Mother and her symbol, the Dove, identified her with the Spirit of all grace...the Holy

Ghost. Thus, the Pagan Trinity is God the Father, the Son, and the Virgin Mother. Indeed, the Roman Catholic Church has made this same claim— The Madonna of Rome is just the Madonna of Babylon. The Queen of Heaven in the one system is the same as the Queen of Heaven in the other."[18]

The Clerical Appellation "Father"

The Church uses several variations of the title "Holy Father" for the Pope and simply "Father" for its various other myriad clerics. Yeshua couldn't have made it any clearer when He proclaimed:

Do not call anyone on earth your father; for One is your Father, He who is in heaven. And do not be called teachers; for One is your Teacher, the Christ. (Matt 23:9-10)

The Church never-the-less uses the title "Pope," which in its Latin form is a variation of "Father." The *Catholic Encyclopedia* unabashedly informs us of both the replacement/de-Judaizing and pagan roots of this title:

"The most noteworthy of the titles are Papa, Summus Pontifex, Pontifex Maximus, Servus servorum Dei.---The terms Pontifex Maximus, Summus Pontifex, were doubtless originally employed with reference to the Jewish high-priest, whose place the Christian bishops were regarded as holding each in his own diocese. As regards the title Pontifex Maximus, especially in its application to the Pope, there was further a reminiscence of the dignity attached to that title in pagan Rome." [19]

In another article, the *Catholic Encyclopedia* goes on to provide the Church's rationale for ascribing the title "father" to its various other clerics, without any mention, much less attempt to explain Yeshua's clear imperative forbidding such usage.

"The word Father is used in the New Testament to mean a teacher of spiritual things, by whose means the soul of man is born again into the likeness of Christ: "For if you have ten thousand instructors in Christ, yet not many fathers. For in Christ Jesus, by the gospel, I have begotten you. Wherefore I beseech you, be ye followers of me, as I also am of Christ" (I Cor., iv, 15, 16; cf. Gal., iv, 19). The first teachers of Christianity seem to be collectively spoken of as 'the Fathers' (II Peter, iii, 4). Thus St. Irenaeus defines that a teacher is a father, and a disciple is a son, and so says Clement of Alexandria . A bishop is emphatically a 'father in Christ', both because it was he, in early times, who

140

baptized all his flock, and because he is the chief teacher of his church. But he is also regarded by the early Fathers, such as Hegesippus, Irenaeus, and Tertullian as the recipient of the tradition of his predecessors in the see, and consequently as the witness and representative of the faith of his Church before Catholicity and the world. Hence the expression 'the Fathers' comes naturally to be applied to the holy bishops of a preceding age, whether of the last generation or further back, since they are the parents at whose knee the Church of today was taught her belief. It is also applicable in an eminent way to bishops sitting in council, 'the Fathers of Nicea', 'the Fathers of Trent'. Thus Fathers have learnt from Fathers, and in the last resort from the Apostles, who are sometimes called Fathers in this sense: 'They are your Fathers', says St. Leo, of the Princes of the Apostles, speaking to the Romans; St. Hilary of Aries calls them sancti patres; Clement of Alexandria says that his teachers, from Greece, Ionia, Coele-Syria, Egypt, the Orient, Assyria, Palestine, respectively, had handed on to him the tradition of blessed teaching from Peter and James, and John, and Paul, receiving it 'as son from father.'"[20]

The Obelisks of Rome

An "Obelisk," according to the *Encyclopedia Britannica*, is:

"---a tapered monolithic pillar, originally erected in pairs at the entrances of ancient Egyptian temples. The Egyptian obelisk was carved from a single piece of stone, usually red granite from the quarries at Aswan. It was designed to be wider at its square or rectangular base than at its pyramidal top, which was often covered with an alloy of gold and silver called electrum. All four sides of the obelisk's shaft are embellished with hieroglyphs that characteristically include religious dedications, usually to the Sun god, and commemorations of the lives of rulers.--- Other peoples, including the

AN AERIAL VIEW OF THE PIAZZA OR PLAZA AT THE VATICAN.

The sun wheel design is immediately noticeable. Look closely inthe center of the wheel. What you see there is an obelisk. A genuine Egyptian obelisk shipped to Rome by the Roman emperor Caligula. The obelisk is a phallic symbol used in sun worship. (From Michael Scheifler's "Bible Light" web site. Used with permission)

141

Phoenicians and the Canaanites, produced obelisks after Egyptian models, although not generally carved from a single block of stone. "Late in the 19th century the government of Egypt divided a pair of obelisks, giving one to the United States and the other to Great Britain. One

now stands in Central Park, New York City, and the other on the Thames embankment in London---A well-known example of a modern obelisk is the Washington Monument, which was completed in Washington, D.C., in 1884. During the time of the Roman emperors, many obelisks were transported from Egypt to what is now Italy. At least a dozen went to the city of Rome itself---."[21]

A CLOSE-UP OF THE OBELISK IN FRONT OF ST. PETER'S. It is difficult to understand why a pagan Egyptian obelisk, related to sun worship, would be sitting in the middle of a pagan sun wheel, in front of a supposedly Christian church? (From Michael Scheifler's "Bible Light" web site. Used with permission)

The fact is that there are 13 of these "sun-pillars" from ancient Egypt in Rome. According to Dr. C.J. Koster, " --- the most famous of these is at the entrance of St. Peter's Square. It is not a mere copy of an Egyptian obelisk, it is one of the very same obelisks that stood in Egypt in Heliopolis in ancient times! When the mystery religion came to pagan Rome, Egyptian obelisks---were hauled at great expense, and erected by the Roman emperors. Caligula, in 37-41 BCE, had this very same obelisk brought from Heliopolis, Egypt, to his *circus* on the Vatican Hill, where now stands St. Peter's. This solid red granite obelisk in front of St. Peter's is 83 feet high (132 feet with its foundation) and weighs 320 tons. Pope Sixtus V ordered it to be moved a little in 1586, in order to center it in front of St. Peter's. The sun-pillar from Heliopolis, which *Elohim* has ordered to be destroyed, was not destroyed. Rather, it was erected right at the entrance to St. Peter's—a memorial to the merger of Sun-worship with the Messianic Belief.[22]

Pine Cones: Yet another Pagan Symbol Widely Used by the Roman Church

Pine cones were widely revered and used by pagans because they were the "fruit" of the Evergreen and thus, to them, a symbol of eternal life. Pine cones have also been transported from paganism as a widely used ancient and contemporary symbol of the Roman Catholic Church.

142

Pagans have always coveted eternal life, and have sought it by worshipping and revering many objects they find in Nature.

> *They set up for themselves sacred pillars and wooden images on every high hill and under every green tree. There they burned incense on all the high places, like the nations whom the LORD had carried away before them; and they did wicked things to provoke the LORD to anger, for they served idols, of which the LORD had said to them, "You shall not do this thing.* (II Ki 17:10-12)

Some examples of the widespread use of the pine cone as a pagan symbol are:

● The mystery cult of Dionysus during the late period of the Roman Empire worshipped a grotesque idol comprised of a distorted hand with a serpent on one uplifted finger and a pine cone on the thumb.

● In Mexico, pagans worshipped a God who is depicted holding a pine cone and a fir tree, symbols of rebirth and the sun.

● The first virgin mother in pagan history was Semiramis, more than 1,000 years before Yeshua, traceable back to Tammuz of Babylon. Tammuz is depicted as an Assyrian winged god holding a pine cone.

● Bacchus, the ancient Roman pagan god of drunkenness is depicted holding a staff with a pine cone as its head.

● Dionysus, the Greek pagan god of fertility is depicted holding a staff with a pine cone as its head.

The pine cone is also widely used, even today, in Roman Catholic architecture and sacred decorations. For example:

● Since the ultimate goal of religion is securing eternal life, the Pope's special staff is adorned with a pine cone, the ultimate pagan symbol for eternal life.

● Typically, many candles used specifically in Catholic masses are adorned with pine cones, as are other ornaments used in services conducted by the Church.

● Finally, the Church describes a giant pine cone as a highlight of the Vatican's landscape:

"From the cupola of St. Peter's may be seen the whole collection of buildings included under the name of Vatican Palace, a long stretch of edifices with many courts, ending in a row of smaller connected buildings before which stands a great *loggia* (an open arcade/gallery), known as the Nicchione. To the right and left of the loggia and at right angles to it are two narrow buildings, which are connected transversely by the Braccio Nuovo at a distance of 328 feet from the *loggia*. These four buildings enclose the Giardino della Pigna, so called because in the *loggia* stands a *gigantic pine-cone of bronze, preserved from old St. Peter's."23*

The Bizarre Bent Cross Crucifix Of Pope John Paul II

The crucifix, just above the pine cone on the Papal staff used by the current Vicar of Christ on Earth, Pope John Paul II, is not the traditional straight Crucifix used by other Popes, but rather the Satanic Bent, or Broken Cross, carried by all lower ranked "bishops."

This Bent Crucifix (one Catholic author writes) "... is a sinister symbol, used by Satanists in the sixth century, that had been revived at the time of Vatican Two. This was a bent or broken cross, on which was displayed a repulsive and distorted figure of Christ, which the black magicians and sorcerers of the Middle Ages had made use of to represent the Biblical term 'Mark of the Beast'. Yet, not only Paul VI, but his successors, the two John-Pauls, carried that object and held it up to be revered by crowds, who had not the slightest idea that it stood for anti-Christ."24

Therefore, Pope John Paul II is telling occultists everywhere that he is not a traditional Pope, but a Pope that is committed to carrying out the role of a World Religious Leader as called for in the New World Order Plan.

Another Roman Catholic author, Malachi Martin, makes this same claim in his book, *The Keys To This Blood* - that Pope John Paul II is committed to the New World Order Plan.25

THE LARGEST PINE CONE IN THE WORLD
seen here as an ancient bronze statue, a blatantly pagan symbol in a prominent Vatican setting.

144

In Summary

There can be no way to simply explain away the fact that the Roman Catholic Church is deeply enmeshed in pagan worship. So also, as we will later discuss in some detail, are virtually all Protestant denominational churches that have retained varying degrees of Roman Catholic tradition and practice. This almost universal apostasy is a matter that YHWH does not take lightly:

> *Behold, I set before you today a blessing and a curse: the blessing, if you obey the commandments of the LORD your God which I command you today; and the curse, if you do not obey the commandments of the LORD your God, but turn aside from the way which I command you today, to go after other gods which you have not known.* (Deut 11:26-28)

THE POPE'S BIZARRE BENT STAFF WITH A PINE CONE AT ITS BASE.
The ultimate pagan symbol. (Cutting Edge Ministries, Used by permission)

C.J. Koster summarizes the crystal clear and often repeated message of Scripture on this centrally important imperative:

"Pagan worship is forbidden to the people of the Almighty, even if mixed with True Worship. Many Scriptures testify to this: Deut. 4:13-19; 12:1-4; 12:29-32; 18:9; Lev.20:23-26; Jer. 10:2-3; Eph. 4:17-22; 2:1-4; 2 Cor. 6:7; 1 Cor. 10:14-21; 1 John 5:21 etc. Notice especially in 2 Kings 17:33 and 41 how True Worship was mixed with idol worship. Note also, that even the high priest Aaron was persuaded by his people to lead them into a mixed worship (Ex.32:5). The Almighty's wrath was kindled and he wanted to destroy everybody except Moses. Other examples of mixed worship are Ez. 23:38-39; Jer. 7:2 and 8-18."[26]

One can't help but wonder if the myriad problems being experienced by the Christian Church today might not be just such a curse resulting from its seemingly endless disobedience and apostasy beginning from the time it was founded by Constantine and continuing into the contemporary world-wide Christian Church we now see disintegrating before our very eyes.

[1] *Encyclopedia Mythica*, Article: Mithra, www.pantheon.org

[2] Pictures of San Clemente and associated mithraeum are taken from course material of Class: History 211, Lecture One, Syracuse University. Found at: www.maxwell.syr.edu

[3] *Encyclopedia Judaica*, Supplement (1982) Article: *Middle and Late Roman Period*, page 160

[4] Hislop, Alexander, *The Two Babylons*. Page 215 (First published as a pamphlet in 1853—greatly expanded in 1858)

5 Noonan , James-Charles, Jr, The Church Visible, page 189.

[6] Ask Why Publications, Article: *The Religion of Mithras*, pages 9-10   www. askwhy.co.uk

[7] Hislop, Alexander, *The Two Babylons*. Page 87 (First published as a pamphlet in 1853—greatly expanded in 1858)

[8] Rev. Jovian P. Lang, OFM, *The Dictionary of the Liturgy*, page 486

[9] *The Catholic Encyclopedia*, Article: *Altar Vessels:Ostenorium*

[10] "The Magic Square of the Sun (666):The numerical symmetries in magic squares symbolized a form of hidden knowledge to priests and mystics in many ancient cultures. The Greek Mystery Religions and the Hebrew Kabbalah both utilized magic symbols, squares, spheres, diagrams, astrology, and gematria to explain the cosmos. The Kabbalists believed that the sun and the planets were each governed by a 'spirit' whose secret name had a gematria value equal to the sum of its magic square. The Hebrew Kabbalists assigned the 6x6 magic square to the sun and of the magic squares to the various planets. The Sun's 'spirit' was named Sorath and the gematria value of his name was equal to 666. The 'magic square of the sun,' was one of the most important symbols used to represent the sun in antiquity because of all the symbolism involving the perfect number '6.' There are six sides to a cube, the numbers 1, 2, an 3, when added or multiplied together are equal to '6,' and the sum of all the numbers from 1 to 36 arranged in a 6x6 magic square are equal to the number '666.' The square was "magic" because the sum of any row, column, or diagonal was equal to the number '111.' " (From: Article: " The Sacred Geometry Stories of Jesus Christ in the New Testament." www.jesus8880.com/gematria/666.htm)

[11] "Pagan Sun Worship and Catholicism—," Article: found at www.aloha.net

[12] Ligouri Publications, *Catechism of the Catholic Church*, page 347

[13] Dr. C.J. Koster, *Come Out of Her My People*, pages 23-26, quoted by permission.

To order this excellent book, see www.isr-messianic.org, or by mail, write: The Institute for Scripture Research, PO Box 4347, 2125 Randburg, Republic of South Africa

[14] *The Catholic Encyclopedia*, Article: *Devotion to the Blessed Virgin Mary*

[15] AD CAELI REGINAM: Encyclical of Pope Pius XII on Proclaiming the Queenship of Mary, October 11, 1954

[16] *Time* Magaizine, "Handmaid or Feminist?", December 30, 1991, p. 62-66

[17] "She probably did not concoct this theory out of thin air. The promised seed of the woman who would bruise the head of the serpent was a well known prophecy from the time of Adam and Enoch." Editorial comment given to the author by Paul Jablonowski, Awareness Ministry (Director Robert Somerville).

[18] Hislop, Alexander, *The Two Babylons,* pages 58 - 83, as condensed in the article: *The Virgin Mary is Popularly and Affectionately Called the "Queen of Heaven,"* found at www.cuttingedge.org

[19] *The Catholic Encyclopedia*, Article: "The Pope."

[20] *The Catholic Encyclopedia*, Article: "Fathers of the Church.'

[21] *Encyclopedia Britannica*, Article: "Obelisks."

[22] Dr. C.J. Koster, *Come Out of Her My People*, pages 72-73

[23] The Catholic Encyclopedia, Article: *The Vatican: III. Description Of The Palace*

[24] Compton, Piers, The Broken Cross: *Hidden Hand in the Vatican*, page 72, as quoted in the article: *The Bent Cross Crucifix versus the Traditional Cross*, found at www.cuttingedge.org.

[25] ibid (Article)

[26] C. J. Koster, *Come Out of Her My People*, page 3

Chapter Four

Replacement Theology and Other Remarkable Points of Roman Catholic Teaching and Practice

As earlier noted, given the broader context and limits to the readers' indulgence, many interesting aspects of Roman Catholicism, some of which have been carried forward into Protestant practice, cannot here be included. Even so, there are several not yet discussed points of Catholic theology, remarkable enough, I believe, that they should be at least introduced. One of these, Replacement Theology, is central to my motivation for writing this book.

Replacement Theology

"Replacement Theology is a misguided systematic approach to the Bible that has not only led millions of Christians astray over the years but it has, in addition, birthed evil of the most horrific proportions. Replacement Theology played a role in the persecution of Jews by the church through the centuries, including the Holocaust." [1]

Replacement theology is the opinion, often put into practice, that Israel, having failed God, has been replaced by the Church. The Church is now seen as spiritual Israel and spiritual Jerusalem. This theology claims that all the promises and blessings, in fact Israel's entire inheritance, now belongs to the Church. (Israel, however, gets to keep the curses.)

Replacement Theology was first established at the Council of Nicea in 325 AD, but the idea was preached as early as the late first century CE by some of the "Church Fathers." During the last 1,600 years, Reformations and Revivals have come and gone, myriad new denominations have sprung up, but this root of Replacement Theology which continues to produce its anti-Semitic fruit, has not been cut off. This is a great stumbling block to the Jews as it prevents them from recognizing their own Messiah, Yeshua.

Scripture, I believe, teaches that Gentile believers in Yeshua are not supposed to be an entity outside of, or instead of Israel, but are to become a part of (an entirely spiritual, not physical part) of the *Spiritual* Commonwealth of Israel (not the modern, physical State of Israel, or the ethnic race of Jewish people). God does not have two spiritual frameworks, He has only one: Israel, His everlasting possession. He has given His Name to no other. This is the spiritual 'Framework of *Torah*', in which Yeshua was born and in which the early Jewish believers operated. The true *Torah* observant Messianic Community is within the spiritual Household of Israel.

To believe in Replacement Theology is to sever oneself from the root and to become part of another framework instituted originally by Rome. This is a false institution, founded on anti-*Torah* doctrines.[2]

The Roman Church certainly makes no bones about its position relative to the Nazarenes. They are at once disallowed as a legitimate part of the faith, much less its founding body, as they are dismissed, like the Messianic Seal of the Jerusalem Church, to an early burial in the depths of Mount Zion:

"In the writings of the New Testament the words are sharply distinguished. With them *ecclesia* denotes the Church of Christ; *synagoga*, the Jews still adhering to the worship of the Old Covenant. Occasionally, it is true, ecclesia is employed in its general significance of 'assembly' (Acts 19:32; I Cor.14:19); and *synagoga* occurs once in reference to a gathering of Christians, though apparently of a non-religious character (James 2:2.) But *ecclesia* is never used by the Apostles to denote the Jewish Church. The word as a technical expression had been transferred to the community of (Gentile) Christian believers."[3]

The Catholic Church also leaves no doubt about its position regarding the supersession of the Old Covenant by the New. The *Catholic Encyclopedia* states:

"Other doctrines, specifically Christian, are not added on to Judaism to develop, but rather to supersede it. In reality, between the New and Old Testaments there is a direct but not revolutionary succession as a superficial observer might be inclined to believe; just as in living beings, the imperfect state of yesterday must give way before the perfection of to-day although the one has normally prepared the other. If the mystery of the Trinity and the spiritual character of the Messianic Kingdom are ranked among the peculiarly Christian dogmas, it is because the Old Testament was of itself insufficient to establish the doctrine of the New Testament on this subject; and still more because, at the time of Jesus, the opinions current among the Jews went decid-

148

edly in the opposite direction."[4]

It is a sad if not tragic thing indeed that much of the Protestant Church carried along with it lingerings of this same Replacement Theology, as it was spawned by the Roman progenitor from which its reformers fled. The Baptists offer a typical main line Protestant view: "---discontinuity between Israel and the church (is) an historic Baptist emphasis."[5]

Replacement Theology is not just an abstract theological system: rather it has profound contemporary application of central importance to the State of Israel, and more specifically to Jerusalem, declared and argued by Israel to be its "eternal and undivided capital."

The Church and the "Peace Process"
A Case Study of Contemporary Replacement Theology

During Pope John Paul II's recent visit to the Galilee, he conducted a mass near the site where Yeshua presented the "Sermon on the Mount." The gathering, widely heralded as an "historical event" of great consequence, was attended by more than 100,000 "pilgrims" who had traveled to Israel from many nations. There were several large chorale groups, each, in turn, competing for the Pope's attention as they offered musical tributes to God, His "Vicar," and their Church. One such group, who had traveled only the short distance from so called, would be "Palestine" (Judea and Samaria), offered, for Papal ears and for the attention of a huge international television audience, a very pointed and sim-

YASSAR ARAFAT KISSES POPE JOHN PAUL II'S RING

ple anthem in praise of a different veneration. Joyfully, they sang passionately forth from an honored position very near the Pope, a few but many times repeated words in Arabic: "Down with Israel&Up with Palestine!"[6]

Yassar Arafat met with Pope John Paul II on February 15, 2000 to conclude an agreement pointedly against the interests of Israel that could only have been signed by a Pope who agreed with his church that Israel no longer has the slightest relevance or significance

A background article dealing with Arafat's frequent interface with the Pope is quoted in part:

YASSAR ARAFAT PRESENTS A MEDAL TO POPE JOHN PAUL II DURING THE POPE'S RECENT VISIT TO BETHLEHEM.

Their obvious mutual appreciation is aimed at establishing their joint political control over Jerusalem in place of Israel from which this control is to be wrested as a part of the "Peace Process."

POPE KISSES THE KORAN

The Koran's comments are vitriolic and threaten violence to both Christianity and Judaism. In May 1999, during an audience granted to three Muslims at the Vatican, Pope John Paul II bowed to the Muslim holy book, the Koran, and kissed it. The three Muslims were the Shiite Imam of Khadum mosque, the Sunni president of the Iraqi Islamic Bank, and a representative of the Iraqi ministry of religion. [7]

"You would think Yasser Arafat grew up as an altar boy in a Catholic parish. Nine times since the Oslo process began in September 1993, the Palestinian leader has trekked to Rome to kiss the ring of Pope John Paul II. The latest pilgrimage came in mid-February, two days after Arafat missed a critical deadline that was to have ended Oslo's interim stage and a month before the Pope is set to embark on his historic journey to the Holy Land.

"The two make a curious couple, as their recent encounter at the Vatican attested. Arafat - the Cairo-born Muslim and terrorist kingpin turned-peacemaker, donning his trademark keffiyah. The Pontiff - a former Polish priest, venerated Catholic figurehead and eyewitness of the Holocaust, robed as always in stately vestments. As they greeted one another, the Pope reiterated the Holy See's "solidarity" with the Palestinian people and then retired to quieter quarters with Arafat's entourage to preside over the signing of a new PLO-Vatican agreement. That agreement, although it touched on a number of significant topics, clarified more than anything else that the driving force between this peculiar relationship - with both men growing more visibly frail with age - is Jerusalem.

"The Pope confesses he has dreamt of making the upcoming trip to Jerusalem throughout his 21-year pontificate. The pilgrimage is billed as his very personal quest to trace "the history of salvation" - leaving behind a highly symbolic legacy for future Catholic gener-

150

ations in this Millennial year.

"Arafat too confesses his personal "destiny" is Jerusalem. In recent years, Arafat has held court routinely in Bethlehem and Ramallah... on the very doorsteps to the city. But he has yet to step inside. Nine times to Rome, but not even one morning jog to Al Quds? With both Morocco's King Hassan and Jordan's King Hussein laid to rest last year, Arafat now stands alone in claiming the prestigious title of official guardian of Islamic holy sites in Jerusalem, notably the Temple Mount mosques. He prefers to make his own highly symbolic entry into Jerusalem at the head of a triumphant Palestinian and Muslim procession to pray on the Temple Mount, without having to pass through one Israeli checkpoint.

"On the eve of the Pope's visit to Jerusalem, it appears he and Arafat have worked out an accommodation in furtherance of their respective dreams. In effect, the Vatican-PLO agreement suggests the Roman Catholic Church is looking to piggyback its interest in an expanded role in Jerusalem onto Palestinian claims to the city - which Arafat is determined to press to conclusion this year, the Jubillennium no less.

"But the new Vatican-PLO document - not to mention certain items on the Papal itinerary - have raised many sound objections. For one, the agreement upgrades their relationship without adequately addressing the PLO's long record of atrocities and persecution against Christians, particularly among the pro-Papacy Maronite community in Lebanon and the Christian minority now under Palestinian Authority rule. The PA has encouraged Muslim encroachments on Jewish and Christian holy sites and carried out a brutal campaign against Muslim converts to Christianity. Yet at the same time, Arafat has carefully maneuvered in recent years to court favor with the Vatican and Eastern Orthodox church leaders, often playing to residual anti-Semitic sentiments among these denominations. It is demeaning for the Vatican to overlook or condone this sorry mischief.

"But the most objectionable aspect of the agreement, despite Vatican disclaimers, is the politically charged language on the issue of Jerusalem.

The preamble declares that 'unilateral decisions and actions altering the specific character and status of Jerusalem are morally and legally unacceptable' It further calls for a 'special statute for Jerusalem, internationally guaranteed, which should safeguard... the proper identity

and sacred character of the City and its universally significant, religious and cultural heritage.'

"When in Jerusalem, the Pope plans to visit the Temple Mount, but has-decided not to pray there out of deference to Muslim sensitivities. Yet nowhere is his moral weight more needed on this historic visit than in challenging the exclusive Islamic claim to that site. From a Christian perspective alone, more events recorded in the New Testament occurred on the Temple Mount than any other single place. Jesus himself verified its universal significance as a 'House of prayer for all people.' Yet neither

Jew nor Christian can pray there today, and Muslim Waqf authorities are not even allowing Christians to take along their Bibles when touring the Mount. It is hollow for the Vatican to demand Israel accede to an international regime in Jerusalem to 'safeguard... its universally significant, religious and cultural heritage,' while remaining silent about the Muslim vise around the very footstool of God.

"A senior figure at the Latin Patriarchate in Jerusalem voiced concern recently that, 'all the Pope's speeches are already written, but we are nervous he won't stick to the script.' Let us hope he is brave enough to do just that - for his own conscience's sake."[8]

On the odd chance the reader still has the slightest doubt where Yassar Arafat is coming from vis-à-vis Israel in general and Jerusalem in particular, here is what he had to say to 40 Arab diplomats at Stockholm's Grand Hotel on January 30, 1996 (several years after the signing of the Oslo Accords):

"We Palestinians will take over everything including all of Jerusalem ---The compensated rich Jews will all journey to America---We of the PLO will now concentrate on splitting Israel psychologically---We will eliminate the State of Israel and establish a purely Palestinian state---I have no use for Jews: they are and remain Jews."[9]

To put a cap on the Pope's visit, he neither addressed the issue of prayer on the Temple Mount nor, as widely hoped for and expected by Israelis, did he apologize on behalf of the Church for its contributory activities during the Holocaust.

In all fairness, however, I must mention what to me is both a greatly satisfying yet perplexing aspect of the Pope's visit that went almost unnoticed in the local and world press. Here is a Pope who planned and dreamed for years that he might one day visit Israel. Surely, one would think, when finally this long awaited dream became a reality, this Vicar of Christ on earth would certainly choose one of several quite imposing Catholic Churches in which to celebrate his very first mass in this incredibly Holy City.

Not so. The first place he headed for was Mount Zion: not, mind you, to the large and ornate Cathedral *near* the Tomb of David, but rather to the very unimposing place right next door, the Upper Room (called the Holy Cenacle by the Roman Church). There in the small room, the very place where some 120 Nazarene Jews returned after the Ascension of Yeshua: there in a very Jewish setting (albeit, some new Arab language inscribed gaudy stained glass windows had been hastily installed for the occasion); inexplicably, there, to this most ancient of all Messianic Jewish Synagogues, is where Karol Wojtyla (now Pope John Paul II) came to offer his first, and very private mass in Israel.

POPE CELEBRATES MASS IN UPPER ROOM.
Pope John Paul II, without the usual pagan-rooted *mitre* on his head, holds forth the "host," not enclosed, as it is normally in a sunburst monstrance, as he celebrates a private mass in the Upper Room on March 23, 2000. Are we to be encouraged that deep within his heart, perhaps even the Pope is being drawn back to the Jewish roots of the Christian Church?)

The Doctrine of Salvation by Works

The Catholic Church teaches that salvation is a process that begins with infant baptism which is undeserved and given by grace. However, the process of justification doesn't end there. It is incumbent upon all Catholics to continue the process toward justification by doing good works. The Church's position on this matter is, stated briefly:

"No one can merit the initial grace which is at the origin of conversion. Moved by the Holy Spirit, we can then merit for ourselves and for others all the graces needed to attain eternal life, as well as necessary temporal goods."[10]

The Catholic Church teaches plainly that eternal life is something that can only be earned by observing certain laws and ceremonies. In fact, this was the central issue that led Roman Catholic priest, Martin Luther, to realize there is no Salvation through the Roman Catholic Church. The foundational Protestant doctrine is that salvation is by grace alone:

For by grace are you saved through faith; and that not of your-selves: it is the gift of God: Not of works lest any man should boast.
(Ephesians 2:8,9)

This issue is one of the major dividing points between Roman Catholicism and Protestantism, and is perhaps the central reason why Rome martyred over 8 million Protestants from 1550-1850 (*circa*).

The Doctrine of "Auricular Confession" of Sin

Roman Catholics teach the doctrine of "auricular confession," or confession made to a priest with a view to the absolution of sin. This doctrine holds that it is a duty of all Catholics to confess to a priest, at certain seasons, all their sins, secret and open, of which they have been guilty; all their improper thoughts, desires, words, and actions; and that the priest has power to declare on such confession that the sins are forgiven. The Church itself comments on the nature of this process:

"Penance (Auricular Confession) is a sacrament of the New Law instituted by Christ in which forgiveness of sins committed after baptism is granted through the priest's absolution to those who with true sorrow confess their sins and promise to satisfy for the same.--- As an outward sign it comprises the actions of the penitent in presenting himself to the priest and accusing himself of his sins, and the actions of the priest in pronouncing absolution and imposing satisfaction---the penitent is at once the accuser, the person accused, and the witness, while the priest pronounces judgment and sentence. The grace conferred is deliverance from the guilt of sin and---eternal punishment; hence also reconciliation with God, justification. Finally, the confession is made not in the secrecy of the penitent's heart nor to a layman as friend and advocate, nor to a representative of human authority, but to a duly ordained priest with requisite jurisdiction and with the 'power of the keys', i.e., the power to forgive sins which Christ granted to His Church."[11]

This doctrine, claiming that Vicar of Christ has extended his Godly power and authority to forgive sin to every ordained priest is a relatively new phenomenon that was not claimed until 1551, by the Council of Trent who declared:

"As a means of regaining grace and justice, penance was at all times necessary for those who had defiled their souls with any mortal sin. Before the coming of Christ, penance was not a sacrament, nor is it

154

since His coming a sacrament for those who are not baptized. But the Lord then principally instituted the Sacrament of Penance, when, being raised from the dead, he breathed upon His disciples saying: 'Receive ye the Holy Ghost. Whose sins you shall forgive, they are forgiven them; and whose sins you shall retain, they are retained' (John 20:22-23). By which action so signal and words so clear the consent of all the Fathers has ever understood that the power of forgiving and retaining sins was communicated to the Apostles and to their lawful successors, for the reconciling of the faithful who have fallen after Baptism."[12]

The Church finds support for this doctrine in two Scriptures, the first being:

If you forgive the sins of any, they are forgiven them; if you retain the sins of any, they are retained. (John 20:23)

There is a strong and universal consensus among Protestant commentators that the Catholics are in great error on this point. Albert Barnes provides a typical interpretation of this Scripture:

"It is worthy of remark here that Jesus confers the same power on all the apostles. He gives to no one of them any special authority. If Peter, as the Papists pretend, had been appointed to any special authority, it is wonderful that the Savior did not here hint at any such pre-eminence. This passage conclusively proves that they were invested with equal power in organizing and governing the church. The authority which he had given Peter to preach the gospel first to the Jews and the Gentiles, does not militate against this.--- This authority given them was full proof that they were inspired. The meaning of the passage is not that man can forgive sins that belongs only to God (Isa. 43:23) but that they should be inspired; that in founding the church, and in declaring the will of God, they should be taught by the Holy Spirit to declare on what terms, to what characters, and to what temper of mind God would extend forgiveness of sins. It was not authority to forgive."[13]

The second Scripture held out by the Catholics in support of "Auricular Confession" is James 5:16

Confess your trespasses to one another, and pray for one another, that you may be healed. The effective, fervent prayer of a righteous man avails much.

Albert Barnes again provides a short but to the point synopsis of the most commonly held Protestant position:

"Disease is often greatly aggravated by the trouble of mind which arises from conscious guilt; and, in such a case, nothing will contribute more directly to recovery than the restoration of peace to the soul agitated by guilt and by the dread of a judgment to come. This may be secured by confession—confession made first to God, and then to those who are wronged. It may be added, that this is a duty to which we are prompted by the very nature of our feelings when we are sick, and by the fact that no one is willing to die with guilt on his conscience; without having done everything that he can to be at peace with all the world. This passage is one on which Roman Catholics rely to demonstrate the propriety of 'auricular confession,' or confession made to a priest with a view to an absolution of sin. The doctrine which is held on that point is, that it is a duty to confess to a priest, at certain seasons, all our sins, secret and open, of which we have been guilty; all our improper thoughts, desires, words, and actions; and that the priest has power to declare on such confession that the sins are forgiven. But never was any text less pertinent to prove a doctrine than this passage to demonstrate that. Because:

(1) The confession here enjoined is not to be made by a person in health, that he may obtain salvation, but by a sick person, that he may be healed.

(2) as mutual confession is here enjoined, a priest would be as much bound to confess to the people as the people to a priest.

(3) no mention is made of a priest at all, or even of a minister of religion, as the one to whom the confession is to be made.

(4) the confession referred to is for 'faults' with reference to 'one another,' that is, where one has injured another; and nothing is said of confessing faults to those whom we have not injured at all.

(5) there is no mention here of absolution, either by a priest or any other person.

(6) if anything is meant by absolution that is Scriptural, it may as well be pronounced by one person as another; by a layman as a clergyman. All that it can mean is, that God promises pardon to those who are truly penitent, and this fact may as well be stated by one person as another. No priest, no man whatever, is empowered to say to another either that he is truly penitent, or to forgive sin. 'Who can forgive sins but God only?' None but he whose law has been violated, or who has been wronged, can pardon an offense. No third person can forgive a sin which a man has committed against a neighbor; no one but a parent can pardon the offenses of which his own children have been guilty towards him; and who can put himself in the place of God, and presume to pardon the sins which his creatures have committed against him?"

While I totally agree with the representative commentaries provided by Barnes on these (from a Catholic point of view) foundational verses, the DuTillet Matthew's original Hebrew offers a completely different understanding on just what Yeshua meant when He gave this guidance to Peter. The original Hebrew of Matt.16:19 (the same imperative as in John 20:23 and Matt. 18:18) is translated into English as:

"And to you will I give the keys of the Kingdom of Heaven, and whatever you will *prohibit* on earth has been *prohibited* in heaven; whatever you will *permit* on earth has been *permitted* in heaven."

The Hebrew word used here for "prohibit" literally means to bind, a Semitic idiomatic expression meaning to forbid or prohibit. The Hebrew word used here for "permit" literally means "loose," a Semitic idiomatic expression meaning to allow or forbid.[15]

It would seem clear, from the original Hebrew, that Yeshua had a completely different purpose here than to provide guidance on the authority to forgive sin.

A Different Ten Commandments

The Roman Catholic Church teaches a significantly altered set of ten commandments from what the Lord God of Israel carved with His finger on tablets of stone and gave to Moses on Mount Sinai, as it is recorded in the Old Covenant, and as they are understood by the rest of Christendom outside the Catholic Church. The Church's official position with respect to the Ten Commandments:

"The Ten Commandments are precepts bearing on the fundamental obligations of religion and morality and embodying the revealed expression of the Creator's will in relation to man's whole duty to God and to his fellow-creatures. They are found twice recorded in the Pentateuch, in Exodus 20 and Deuteronomy 5, but are given in an *abridged form* in the catechisms. Written by the finger of God on two tables of stone, this Divine code was received from the Almighty by Moses amid the thunders of Mount Sinai, and by him made the ground-work of the Mosaic Law. Christ resumed these Commandments in the double precept of charity—love of God and of the neighbor; He proclaimed them as *binding under the New Law* in Matthew 19 and in the Sermon on the Mount (Matthew 5). He also simplified or interpreted them, e.g. by declaring unnecessary oaths equally unlawful with false, by condemning hatred and calumny as well as murder, by enjoining even love of enemies, and by condemning indulgence of evil desires as fraught with the same malice as adultery (Matthew 5). *The Church, on the other hand, after changing the day of rest from the Jewish Sabbath, or seventh day of the week, to the first, made the* **Third Commandment refer to Sunday** as the day to be kept holy as the Lord's Day. The Council of Trent condemns those who deny that the Ten Commandments (as thus abridged and changed by the Church) are binding on Christians."[16]

The Ten Commandments, as abridged and edited by the Church, offer a remarkable example of just how deep and wide the Pope's authority is interpreted to reach. On one hand, the Church acknowledges that these commandments as given to Moses and twice stated in the Old Covenant are, by command of the original Christ, binding on all Catholics.

Then, presumably, in part because the Church otherwise holds that the Old Covenant has been replaced by the New, and because the Pope as Vicar of Christ on earth has every power and authority to change the very word of YHWH as he sees fit, does indeed make some sweeping alterations.

The Roman Catholic Ten Commandments:[17]

1. I, the Lord am your God ...You shall have no other gods beside me
2. You shall not take the name of the Lord your God in vain
3. Remember to keep holy the Sabbath Day[18]
4. Honor your father and your mother
5. You shall not kill

6. You shall not commit adultery
7. You shall not steal
8. You shall not bear false witness against your neighbor
9. You shall not covet your neighbor's wife
10. You shall not covet your neighbor's house

The first major alteration made by the Church was to totally omit the second commandment as it was given to Moses:

> *"You shall not make for yourself a carved image, or any likeness of anything that is in heaven above, or that is in the earth beneath, or that is in the water under the earth; you shall not bow down to them nor serve them. For I, the LORD your God, am a jealous God, visiting the iniquity of the fathers on the children to the third and fourth generations of those who hate Me,---."* (Exod 20:4-5)

When the Church eliminated this commandment, they eliminated three whole verses of Scripture, including the only verse which talks about how jealous God is whenever anyone makes a graven image of anything, being human or animal or natural object, and then prays to and/or worships that graven image.

It certainly seems obvious why this particular commandment had to be written out of the *Torah* by the Church. Much of Catholic worship includes veneration of graven images. As a matter of everyday practice, Catholics pray to and worship statues and carved figures of the various saints, not the least of which is their "Queen of Heaven," the "Mother of God."

The Catholic crucifix (both the traditional straight variety in wide use throughout the world, and the strange bent version carried about by Pope John Paul II) features a carving of Yeshua Himself, suffering on the cross. How could this be categorized in any other way but as an idol?

Then, consider the countless medals, paintings, and all manner of other artists' interpretations: adored, worshipped, bowed down to, venerated, worshipped, all of this in direct violation of the second commandment given by God to Moses.

The second major alteration, one openly admitted by the Church, was to arbitrarily and with absolutely no authority (other than the Pope's exercised through a council of men) desecrate the Fourth Commandment by changing the Sabbath from *Shabbat* (Saturday) to Sunday. God gave Moses the commandment:

> *Remember the Sabbath day, to keep it holy. Six days you shall labor and do all your work, but the seventh day is the Sabbath of the LORD your God. In it you shall do no work: you, nor your son, nor your daughter, nor your male servant, nor your female servant, nor your cattle, nor your stranger who is within your gates.* (Exod 20:8-10)

The Church offers no explanation why they made this seemingly arbitrary change. There is certainly no need for any further interpretation here. The seventh day of the week (Saturday) is an absolute. It can in no way be construed to be the first day (Sunday).

While there is no explanation of substance, there is a very real reason why the Church made this change. *Shabbat* is a "Jewish thing" and from the very beginning of Christianity, the Church made every conceivable effort to distance itself from everything Jewish. If they felt it appropriate to destroy the Hebrew Scriptures, and to subscribe the Messianic Seal to oblivion, it isn't a far reach to suggest that they would feel equally licensed to change the Sabbath from *Shabbat* to Sunday. Why would a Church, largely founded on pagan doc-

Mithra.[19]

C.J. Koster provides the following additional insight:

"The Council of Trent in 1562 set all hesitation aside by openly declaring that tradition stood above Scripture! (Archbishop Reggio's) words were, "The authority of the Church could therefore not be bound to the authority of the Scriptures, because the Church had changed... the Sabbath into Sunday, not by the command of Christ, but by its own authority." (*Canon and Tradition*, p.263). Similar confessions as to the un-Scriptural origin of this change are to be found in the theological works of all the major denominations."[20]

The third major alteration made to the Law of Moses as it was carved by the finger of God was one driven by mathematical necessity. If the Church were to stay with the scheme of simply dropping the Second Commandment, they would have ended up with nine instead of ten commandments, a seeming hard sell to the Church itself, much less to its many detractors.

The solution was simple, however. The Church obviously took a look at the commandments as they were given to Moses and fixed upon the Tenth Commandment which seemed a likely candidate to divide into two separate commandments, thus making up for the discarded original Second Commandment.

The Tenth Commandment, dealing with covetousness, as given by God to Moses was written:

You shall not covet your neighbor's house; you shall not covet your neighbor's wife, nor his male servant, nor his female servant, nor his ox, nor his donkey, nor anything that is your neighbor's. (Exodus 20:17)

As noted above, this original Tenth Commandment became the Ninth and Tenth in The Roman Catholic listing:

9. You shall not covet your neighbor's wife

10.You shall not covet your neighbor's house

160

[1] Malcolm Hedding, as quoted in "What is Replacement Theology?" Article, found at: www.fannet.au

[2] Ibid., (Article)

[3] *The Catholic Encyclopedia*, Article: "The Church."

[4] Ibid., Article: "The New Testament."

[5] Kenneth Good, *Are Baptists Reformed*, pp. 278-279

[6] Related to the author by a personal friend , a member of the Israeli Defense Force, who was a part of the huge security force dispatched to protect the Pope and all there assembled. One forecast concerning the visit: "The upcoming visit of Pope John Paul II next month will cost the taxpayers no less than NIS 30 million ($7.5 million). Over 20,000 soldiers and police persons will be involved in providing security during the visit, with at least 5,000 troops being deployed each day while the Pope is in Israel. The visit is set for March 21-26, 2000. Details of the visit and massive security undertaking were approved during the weekly cabinet meeting held on Sunday (Feb. 6)." *Israel Wire* www.israel.com

[7] *Christian News*, October 18, 1999, page 16

[8] "Jerusalem Bound," *The Middle East Digest*, March 2000, as quoted by ICEJ News Service, March 15 , 2000

[9] Sarah Honig, "Puddle-Ducks of a feather," *The Jerusalem Post*, Friday, April 14, 2000

[10] *Catechism of the Roman Catholic Church*, page 490, para # 2027, found at www.cuttingedge.org

[11] *The Catholic Encyclopedia*, Article: *"Confession."*

[12] Ibid

[13] Barnes, Albert, *Notes on the New Testament, Luke and John*, Commentary on John 20:23, page 378-379

[14] Ibid, *James, Peter, John and Jude*, Commentary on James 5:16, pages 95-96

[15] James Trimm, translator of *"DuTillet" Hebrew Matthew*, Society for the Advancement of Nazarene Judaism, footnotes 4 and 5, Chapter 16, page 2

[16] *The Catholic Encyclopedia*, Article: *The Ten Commandments*

[17] Ibid: "Adapted from Exodus 20:2-17, and placed in this order by St. Augustine"

[18] The Catholic meaning here is Sunday, not Saturday *(Shabbat)*

[19] Article: *The Cult of Sol Invictus; The Sun-Gods of Ancient Europe;*
Christian worship of the Sun; Man and the Sun; Roman festivals; Christmas; found at: www.christianism.com

According to the hypothesis suggested by H. Usener [1834 - 1905], developed by B. Botte (Les Origines), and accepted by most scholars today, the Birth Of Christ was assigned

The date of the Winter Solstice (December 25 In the Julian Calendar, January 6 In The Egyptian), because on this day, as the sun began its return to northern skies, the pagan devotees of Mithra celebrated the dies natalis Solis Invicti (birthday of the invincible sun). On Dec. 25, 274, Aurelian had proclaimed the sun-god principal patron of the empire and dedicated a temple to him in the Campus Martius. Christmas originated at a time when the cult of the sun was particularly strong at Rome. This theory finds support in some of the Church Fathers' contrasting the birth of Christ and the winter solstice; indeed, from the beginning of the 3d [sic] century "Sun of Justice" appears as a title of Christ (Botte, Les origines 63). Though the substitution of Christmas for the pagan festival cannot be proved with certainty, it remains the most plausible explanation for the dating of Christmas.

[20] C.J. Koster, *Come Out of Her My People*, page 12

Chapter Five

Martin Luther and the Beginning of Protestantism

Almost immediately after I was born again into the Kingdom of God, I began to hunger for a better understanding of the teachings and history of my new faith. Like many new Protestant believers I was taught, or at the very least simply took for granted, that while the Roman Catholic Church was steeped in all manner of error, Martin Luther and the rest of the "reformers" had set everything aright and the faith into which I had just entered had been made free of all heresies. Of course, I understood that there were many doctrinal disagreements within Protestantism itself, thus accounting for its many (by some accounts as many as 2,600) different denominations. "Not to worry," I was taught, and unhesitatingly accepted: the differences are slight, and even constructive since they in the end promote church growth.

STATUE OF MARTIN LUTHER IN WORMS, GERMANY MEMORIALIZING HIS FAMOUS PROCLAMATION THAT BEGAN THE REFORMATION.

I, like many others, had been greatly misled. The supposed sweeping away of all heresies by the Protestant Reformation was, at best, a very serious overstatement. The fact is, while at first some, then later even many errors were set

163

right by Martin Luther, John Calvin and others, there remained within Protestantism, much of the same potpourri of error that was first introduced by Constantine, then fostered by Rome.

Even further to this point, Martin Luther made it clear that he never intended his separation from the Roman Catholic Church to be permanent—he fully intended to reunite his followers to the one true church just as soon as it responded properly, as he knew it would, to what he felt were sure to be quickly resolved differences.[1]

This, reunification, as history has shown, did not occur, at least not in Luther's time or in the following centuries, up to time present. However, one could make a good case that the progressive liberalization of the Lutheran Church, as well as the other "high" liturgical churches (Anglican/Episcopal, Orthodox) along with several very earnest recent past and still ongoing attempts of these bodies to reunite with the Roman Catholic Church may yet prove out Luther's original thinking. If this should occur, however, it won't be primarily because the Roman church has at last changed, but rather because these lost sheep from the "high" churches have at last returned to the fold.

Martin Luther, the 95 Theses and "Papal Indulgences"

Martin Luther was born November 10, 1483 in Eisleben, Thuringia (central Germany). He was brought up in the strict religious atmosphere of the Roman Catholic Church. After attending the Latin Schools at Mansfeld, Magdeburg, and Eisenach, he entered the University of Erfurt in 1501 from which he received a Bachelor's degree in 1502 and a Master's degree in 1505. During his student years, Luther was terrified by thoughts of the wrath of God. He continually sought a means of finding inward peace. To achieve this goal, he entered an Augustinian Monastery on July 17, 1505 where he became a monk. Two years later, he was ordained as a priest. In 1508, Luther was appointed Professor of Philosophy at Wittenberg University, and he also studied there subsequently to receive the Doctor of Theology degree in 1512. In 1515, Luther was appointed Augustinian Vicar for Meissen and Thuringia.

During the period of his appointment as Vicar, Luther underwent a modification in his views and beliefs. He was still devoted to the church, but in his continued quest for inner peace, he turned from religious philosophy to the Bible as the basis of his theological conclusions. These conclusions ultimately led Luther to combat some doctrines and practices of the church. He was eventually branded a heretic and was excommunicated for his radical defiance of attack on the church, and Luther did not want it to be circulated. Never-the-less, the news spread throughout Germany within a period of just two weeks and Luther was soon to be branded a heretic.[2]

For a number of years, I had surmised, quite mistakenly, that these Ninety-five Theses were a detailed shopping list of Luther's specific exceptions to various Roman Catholic theological positions and practices that collectively formed a general catalog of the new Protestant approach to Christianity.

Surprisingly, all of Luther's 95 Theses addressed only one and the same issue: the sale of Papal Indulgences. In short, the doctrine that Luther objected to was the widespread practice of the Church to sell, for various large sums of money, "Papal Indulgences," which would extricate the souls of specific dearly departed from the jaws of "Purgatory," and, thus, with their Church punched ticket in hand, speed them on their way to heaven.

Martin Luther was not in any way objecting to the doctrine of Purgatory, but rather to the idea that the Church was preying upon its believers to fill its coffers, rather than to grant such dispensations out of love.

As stated in a quite unclear manner by the Church itself, the still held Roman Catholic doctrine of Purgatory is:

"Purgatory (Lat., 'purgare', to make clean, to purify) in accordance with Catholic teaching is a place or condition of temporal punishment for those who, departing this life in God's grace, are, not entirely free from venial faults, or have not fully paid the satisfaction due to their transgressions. The faith of the Church concerning purgatory is clearly expressed in the Decree of Union drawn up by the Council of Florence (1031), and in the decree of the Council of Trent as defined: 'Whereas the Catholic Church, instructed by the Holy Ghost, has from the Sacred Scriptures and the ancient tradition of the Fathers taught in Councils and very recently in this Ecumenical synod that there is a purgatory, and that the souls therein are helped by the suffrages of the faithful, but principally by the acceptable Sacrifice of the Altar; the Holy Synod enjoins on the Bishops that they diligently endeavor to have the sound doctrine of the Fathers in Councils regarding purgatory everywhere taught and preached, held and believed by the faithful'. Further than this the definitions of the Church do not go, but the tradition of the Fathers and the Schoolmen must be consulted to explain the teachings of the councils, and to make clear the belief and the practices of the faithful."[3]

While it was the sale of indulgences for sins that initially incited Luther into action; later, in 1518, he publicly professed his implicit obedience to the church. Simultaneously, however, he boldly denied the absolute power of the Pope.

The events that followed this act took place within several years. There was not an immediate conflict with the hierarchy of the church. However, on April 16, 1521, Luther was brought before the august meeting of the Holy Roman Empire, known as the Diet, at Worms, Germany. He was asked whether he acknowledged his writings and public statements.

Luther requested a day for consideration of his answer. The next day, he replied that he would retract nothing written or said unless he could be shown through Scripture that his writings and statements were in error. He ended his brief speech with the now famous pronouncement: "Here I stand, I can not do otherwise, God help me!" Luther left Worms on May 25 having been declared an outlaw of the church. He was seized by the Elector Frederick and taken to Wartburg Castle.

There he remained in hiding under the assumed name, "Squire George." It was during his long stay at Wartburg Castle that Luther began his work as a reformer. One of his first projects was to translate the Bible into German. A New Testament translation was printed in 1522. Meanwhile, the Wittenberg Augustinians had begun to change the worship service and to do away with the Mass. This displeased Luther greatly, who after all, was still in his heart a Roman Catholic priest. He returned to Wittenberg and spent most of his remaining lifetime carrying out a gradual change in the form of the worship service. The Protestant Reformation was now fully underway. In spirit and inwardness, it had not been conceived as anti-Catholic, but ultimately a separate and distinct Protestant Church was formed.[4]

[1] Alister E. McGrath, *Christian Theology*, page 66

[2] Charles K. Moss, "The Musical Reforms of Martin Luther," Article: www.classicalmusic.hispeed.com

[3] *The Catholic Encyclopedia*, "Purgatory"

[4] Charles K. Moss, "The Musical Reforms of Martin Luther," Article: www.classicalmusic.hispeed.com

Chapter Six

The Continuing Reformation after Martin Luther

While Martin Luther may have begun what many consider to be the most remarkable and important revolution in the history of man, other reformers and their movements were soon to follow him in what became a sweeping and continuing challenge to the Roman Church. Principal among these, chronologically, were:

Ulrich Zwingli and the "Anabaptists" (1519)

Ulrich Zwingli is known in Church history as the "Second Great Reformer." Leading a group of German speaking Protestants that arose in Zurich, just two years after Luther began his own revolt, Zwingli dubbed his followers the "Anabaptists." "Ana-baptist," means, literally, "re-baptism."

Doctrinally, Zwingli moved Protestant Christianity significantly further away from Luther's benchmark. His principal additions were:

- In keeping with their name, the Anabaptists held that Luther hadn't gone far enough by simply retaining infant baptism. Therefore, they began the practice of "re-baptizing" all the children by immersion at older age, as a matter of their own election.

- Zwingli held that the Roman Catholic understanding of the Sacrament of the Eucharist (The Lord's Supper) as yet unchanged by Luther was in error. He strongly disagreed with the idea that the Lord became physically present: with the bread becoming his very flesh and the wine his holy blood. Instead, Zwingli's Eucharistic concept was that the sacrament was a symbolic memorial of the suffering and death of

Christ: although Zwingli does not deny that Christ is present to the "eye of faith." On the contrary, the Lord's presence is to be enjoyed through the word and through faith, "in a spiritual way."[1]

Anabaptists hold to a "congregational" approach wherein each local church is autonomous. Some of the more well known groups that have followed in this tradition are: (1) the Mennonites, in Holland, then later in Pennsylvania, (2) the Hutterine Brethren of Pennsylvania, (3) the Amish of Ohio and Illinois, (4) the American Baptists, and, (5) the United Brethren Church.[2]

King Henry VIII and The Church of England (1534)

While King Henry VIII, at the age of 40, may have had some secondary genuinely ecclesiastical motivation for founding the Church of England, it is hard to otherwise conclude that his primary interest in disavowing Papal authority was to justify shedding Catherine of Aragon, the first of his six wives, so that he could legally marry Anne Boleyn, the second: whom, by and by, he ultimately be-headed so that he could marry Jane Seymour, the third of the six, *etcetera*.

Not surprisingly then, the "Anglican Church" regards itself derived not from Reformation influences but from the renunciation of Papal jurisdiction by Henry VIII in 1534, when, with the "Act of Supremacy," the King declared himself to be the supreme head of the English Church, with fullness of authority and jurisdiction.

While Henry VIII ultimately denied all Papal authority, he did not reject substantially other principal articles of the Roman Catholic faith. It was later, under James VI and Elizabeth that the Church of England was further reformed, with respect to such matters as Scripture as the rule of faith, the sacraments, the nature of the Mass, and the constitution of the hierarchy.

In general, the Church of England (In the United States, the Episcopal Church) struck a compromise between Catholics and Protestants. Its basic tenets of beliefs, as stated in the "Book of Common Prayer," recognize three sacraments: Baptism, the Eucharist, and

Penance. Among other identical holdings, the Anglicans teach that salvation is to be found in having faith in God's grace and doing good works.[3]

Movements that sprang from roots in the Church of England were:

- ● Episcopalians (in both England and America)
- ● Methodists (Formed by John and Charles Wesley as a prayer group, the "Holy Club", nicknamed "Methodists", because they were so faith-

ful and disciplined in the performance of their religion studies and moral lifestyle). Later, the Pentecostals ultimately sprang from the Holiness Movement which itself was founded in Methodism.

● Evangelicalism (the movement, in general, as it developed in England and America).

John Calvin and the "Calvinists" (1536)

John Calvin, was the third, and by any account the most radical of the great reformers. Calvin, a Frenchman, established his movement in French-speaking Switzerland. While he rejected the Pope, in some thinking he himself then became even more than a Pope: The virtual religious and political dictator of Geneva, the capital of the non-Lutheran Reformation in Europe.

In 1536, he established a theocratic government in Geneva in which the affairs of the city were controlled by Calvin's new church. Geneva became a model of Puritan sobriety in which the lives of all citizens were closely policed and all offenses punished severely... all people were expected to live the life of a monastic, with no alcohol, no dancing and singing.

Calvin's intolerance for Catholics, Jews, or Muslims, was proverbial. For example, Servetus, the Roman Catholic doctor who discovered the pulmonary circulation of the blood, was executed for the heresy of believing in infant baptism, and disagreements on the Trinity.

Calvin's most controversial tenets remain the absolute predestination of some persons to Heaven and others to Hell; the certitude of salvation for the elect, and the incapability of the elect to lose grace.

However, Calvin, did agree with Luther on the issues of biblical authority and justification by faith alone.

With respect to the Lord's Supper, Calvin, like Luther eventually reached a centrist position between the Catholic view that the communion elements became the actual flesh and blood of the Lord, and Zwingli's view that the elements were only memorial symbols. Called consubstantiation, this centrist view is that the body and blood of Christ are received in Communion, but in a "spiritual" not material manner.

Calvin published the "Institutes of the Christian Religion," which became and remains the classic textbook of Reformed, as distinguished from Lutheran, theology. Calvinistic theology opened the way for what some would consider the more radical forms of Protestantism which exist today as worldwide churches:[4]

- Presbyterians (In Scotland and America)
- Dutch (and other) Reformed Churches (Europe and America)
- Huguenots (France)
- Puritans (England and America)
- Separatists and Congregationalists (not entirely Calvinistic but many Calvinist tenets)

John Smith and the Baptists (1605)

The Baptists are the largest of all American Protestant denominations, with more than 37 million members, in 30 bodies in the United States; the largest being the Southern Baptist Convention. There are 310 separate and independent Baptist denominations in the world.[5]

The movement was founded by John Smith in 1605 in England. In America, Roger Williams founded the first Baptist church in Providence, Rhode Island in 1639.

Baptist theology is a distinctive mix of Luther, Calvin and Zwigilian tenets. In essence, this broad Baptist theological understanding might best be described as a "moderated Calvinism" although some baptists, Southern Baptists in particular, would insist that they have always been strictly Calvinists.

Adherents are called "Baptists" because of their doctrine concerning "Baptism"— called an "ordinance," they reject "infant baptism," and consider only baptism by immersion as valid, to persons who can decide to receive it, and can accept the personalexperience of being "born again."

Baptists are strong advocates of the separation of church and state. They also hold that no authority can stand between the believer and God.

While Baptists do not have a formal creed, they subscribe to two professions of faith formulated in 1689 and 1832, and they are in general agreement with classical Protestantism theology regarding Scripture as the sole rule of faith, original sin, justification through faith in Christ, and the nature of the Church.

With respect to the Lord's Supper, Baptists take the Zwinglian view that the elements "---are sometimes called by the names of the things they represent; i.e., the body and the blood of Christ, albeit, in substance and nature, they still remain truly and only bread and wine, as they were before."[6]

The Latest Chapters of a Continuing Reformation:
Pentecostalism (1896-1906) and the Charismatic Renewal (1960)

Pentecostalism, from its beginning in the 19th Century United States, remains today far and away the fastest growing worldwide Christian movement.

The name, Pentecostal, is taken from the Christian Feast of Pentecost (Jewish Feast of Weeks - *Succoth*) which celebrates the coming of the Holy Spirit in tongues of fire upon the 120 Nazarene Jewish believers who were waiting in the Upper Room on Mount Zion (or as some hold, in the Temple Courts) as they had been instructed by the Lord.[7]

Pentecostalism emphasizes a post-conversion experience of spiritual purification and empowering for Christian witness, entry into which is most often, but not necessarily signaled by utterance in unknown tongues (*Glossolalia*). The movement, while emphasizing speaking in tongues, more importantly points to a profound Holy Spirit generated "renewal" that takes in any or all of the other "gifts of the Spirit," enumerated in Scripture.[8]

Although Pentecostalism generally aligns itself with Fundamentalism and Evangelism, its distinguishing tenet (speaking in tongues) reflects roots in the Methodist originated American Holiness movement, which believed in the post-conversion experience (Baptism with the Holy Spirit) as entire sanctification.

The Assemblies of God, formed in 1914, soon became the largest Pentecostal denomination in the world. Most of the Pentecostal groups that began after 1914 were based on the model of the Assemblies of God. They include the Pentecostal Church of God, the International Church of the Foursquare Gospel and the Open Bible Standard Church.

The greatest growth for Pentecostal churches came after World War II. With more mobility and greater prosperity, Pentecostals began to move into the middle class and to lose their image of being disinherited members of the lower classes.

The emergence of healing evangelists such as Oral Roberts and Jack Coe in the 1950s brought greater interest and acceptance to the movement. The TV ministry of Oral Roberts also brought Pentecostalism into the homes of the average American.

The founding of the Full Gospel Business Men in 1948 brought the
Pentecostal message to a wider audience of middle class business leaders

fessional and business men, helping further to change the image of the movement.

Pentecostalism entered a new phase in 1960 with the appearance of "the Charismatic Renewal" or "Neo-Pentecostalism" in the traditional churches in the United States.

The first well-known person to openly experience *glossolalia* and remain within his church was Dennis Bennett, an Episcopal priest in Van Nuys, California. Although forced to leave his parish in Van Nuys because of controversy over his experience, Bennett was invited to pastor a small and nearly defunct inner-city Episcopal parish in Seattle, Washington. Bennett's new church experienced explosive growth after the introduction of Pentecostal worship, becoming a center of neo-Pentecostalism in the northwestern United States, then later the focus of the entire world-wide movement.

This new wave of Pentecostalism soon spread to all other major Protestant denominations in the United States and also to many other nations.

Most notably, in 1966, Pentecostalism entered the Roman Catholic Church as the result of a weekend retreat at Duquesne University. As *glossolalia* and other charismatic gifts were experienced, other Catholic prayer groups were formed at Notre Dame University and the University of Michigan. By 1973 the movement had spread so rapidly that thirty thousand Catholic Pentecostals gathered at Notre Dame for a national conference. The movement had spread to Catholic churches in over a hundred nations by 1980. Today, it has been estimated that as many as 31% of Roman Catholics have been "born again" and "baptized with the Holy Spirit" as a result of the "Charismatic Movement" within their church.

Unlike the rejection of the earlier Pentecostals, the Charismatic Renewal was generally allowed to remain within the mainline churches. Favorable study reports by the Episcopalians (1963), Roman Catholics (1969, 1974), and the Presbyterians (1970), while sometimes pointing out possible excesses, generally were tolerant and open to the existence of a Pentecostal spirituality as a renewal movement within the traditional churches.

By 1980, the denominational Pentecostals had grown to be the largest family of Protestants in the world, according to *The World Christian Encyclopedia*. The 51 million figure attributed to the traditional Pentecostals did not include the 11 million charismatic Pentecostals in the traditional mainline churches. Thus, only seventy-five years after the movement began in Los Angeles, there were 62 million Pentecostals in over a hundred nations of the world.[9]

To further illustrate this explosive growth, amazingly, by 1997, the number of Pentecostals and Charismatics worldwide had grown to an astounding 497 million. Just one year later, in 1998, "More than 25% of the world's Christians are (were) charismatic or Pentecostal--- there are close to 2 billion people [of] the Christian faith worldwide--- of that number, 540 million are charismatic or Pentecostal." [10]

[1] *International Standard Bible Encylopaedia*, Electronic Database Copyright (C) 1996 by Biblesoft), Article: "The Lord's Supper."

[2] "Protestant Denominations and Sects," Article: www. Religion-cults.com

[3] Ibid

[4] Ibid

[5] www.Adherents.com (Taken from my own survey of all listed worldwide denominations)

[6] Reformed Baptist Church, *The Baptist Confession of Faith*, Chapter 30, "Of the Lord's Supper." www.bible.ca

[7] Acts 1:4-5

[8] 1 Cor 12: 7-11

[9] M.C. Tenney, "Pentecostalism, General Information," Article: www.mb-soft.com

[10] "1998 Pentecostal/Charismatic world membership 540,000,000," (Statistic from Table) www.adherents.com

Chapter Seven

What Did the Protestant Reformation Actually Change?

"We on our part confess that there is much that is Christian and good under the Papacy; indeed everything that is Christian and good is to be found there and has come to us from this source. For instance, we confess that in the Papal church there are the true Holy Scriptures, true baptism, the true sacrament of the altar, the true keys to the forgiveness of sins, the true office of the ministry, the true catechism in the form of the Lord's Prayer, the Ten Commandments and the articles of the Creed." (Martin Luther)[1]

Some years ago, when for the first time I visited the imposing Cathedral in Worms, Germany, then later strolled through the lovely adjacent City park, I stood, almost reverently, beneath the huge, bigger than life bronze statue of Martin Luther and with awe read his famous words etched into the marble foundation: "Here I stand. I cannot do otherwise. God help me." But now, from the perspective of some thirty ensuing years I find myself asking, as well should ask every other believer who is even in the least way concerned about the condition of the Body, just what, precisely did this great reformer and the other architects of the Reformation actually change?

The "Good News"— The Major Revisions of Martin Luther and other Reformers

The Papacy: Within Protestantism, that may be best characterized by its many disagreements, there is one thing with which all non-Roman Catholic denominations can perfectly agree: The Vicar of Christ has been removed from his earthly throne.

Even the much smaller Eastern Church (Orthodox), in most other ways nearly identical with Roman Catholicism, even they from the very beginning, have denied Papal Authority. The Eastern Church (Orthodox) instead governs their Body through four nationally specific Ancient Patriarchates: namely, that of Constantinople or the Ecumenical, and those of Alexandria, Antioch and Jerusalem; as well as through three new Patriarchates of Russia, Serbia, and Romania, the Autocephalous Churches of Cyprus, Greece, Georgia (Iberia) and Poland; and the autonomous Churches of Czechoslovakia, Esthonia, Lithuania, Finland, North and South America, Northwestern and Central Europe, Australia and Mount Sinai.

While the Pope has thus been universally deposed from all but the Roman Catholic Church, in his place the denominations have variously erected governing hierarchies ranging from those who stringently "control" their memberships (such as the Eastern Church (Orthodox) who, for example, continue to encourage, although not demand auricular confession) to the more congregational churches that have no governing body at all, beyond that imposed by the local church.

The Doctrine of Purgatory: All major Protestant denominations have joined Martin Luther in rejecting the Doctrine of Purgatory. The Anglicans, for example hold, in their official statement of belief: "The Romish Doctrine concerning Purgatory, Pardons, Worshipping and Adoration, as well of Images as of Reliques, and also invocation of Saints, is a fond thing vainly invented, and grounded upon no warranty of Scripture, but rather repugnant to the Word of God."

The Lord's Supper: While all of the changes were not immediate, today, all but the Eastern Orthodox Churches, reject the Roman Catholic doctrine of transubstantiation—the belief that the communion elements are transformed to be the physical body and blood of Yeshua. Generally, all of the "high" liturgical groups hold to the doctrine of consubstantiation which teaches that Yeshua is spiritually present during the partaking of the elements, and that His "spiritualized" body and blood are partaken. However, the elements remain materially bread and wine and are not physically changed. The great majority of other Protestant denominations take the Zwingli view that the communion elements are merely symbols of the Lord's sacrifice and that taking them is a remembrance of this sacrifice.

Veneration of Mary: Only the Orthodox Churches venerate Mary in the same way as the Roman Catholics, with the exception that they reject the doctrine that Mary herself was miraculously conceived. The Anglicans, along with the two catholic groups, hold to Mary's continuing virginity after the birth of Yeshua. All other major denominations completely reject Mary worship.

Salvation by Faith and Works: Only the Roman Catholics and the Eastern Orthodox Churches retain the belief that works, together with faith, are *required* for justification (salvation). There is, generally, universal agreement among Protestants that salvation is through faith made possible by the grace of God.

Auricular Confession: While the Eastern Orthodox Churches encourage confession of sins to a priest, they hold that such confession is not required for God's forgiveness. Other Protestants universally agree that confession and forgiveness is a private communication between man and God without the need for any third party intervention.

The Ten Commandments: Only the Roman Catholics have perverted the Ten Commandments as they were originally given to Moses. Even the "Catholic" Eastern Orthodox Churches hold "—- all the ten commandments in the law of Moses are obligatory for Christians. Christianity has not altered them."[2] While some might question the Orthodox emphasis on icons, the Church is emphatic that its many icons (pictures of Biblical characters) are used only for teaching and are in no way to be worshipped.[3] Generally, all Protestants hold to the Ten Commandments as they were given to Moses and are recorded in the Old Testament.

The "Bad News": The Yeast in the Dough— What the Reformers left Unchanged!

Your glorying is not good. Do you not know that a little leaven leavens the whole lump?

Christian Anti-Semitism: The pervasive spirit and tangible program of anti-Semitism put in place by the Roman Catholic Church continues on today in much of Protestantism. If anything, the reformers fanned these evil flames rather than quenching them. It is no small coincidence, for example, that Adolf Hitler chose the celebration of Martin Luther's birthday upon which to hold the infamous "Kristallnacht, in November 1938—the beginning of the Holocaust when the synagogues were burned in Germany.[4]

Replacement Theology: Much of Protestantism continues to teach, in varying degrees, that the Old Covenant has been replaced by the New Covenant; that the *Torah* of Moses is therefore abolished; that the Land and Nation of Israel have been replaced by the Church which has become the "New Israel," and therefore, Gentile Christian believers have replaced ethnic Jews as "Spiritual Jews," and/or the "True Israel," and that the State of Israel and the Jewish people no longer have any Biblical or spiritual relevance.

by YHWH. In all of Christendom, only the Seventh Day Adventists, a seemingly solid Bible based, fundamentalist group that is widely scorned and often labeled a cult, primarily because of its position on the Sabbath, is the only credible and well known Protestant denomination that holds to the Jewish *Shabbat*.

With respect to the trans-denominational view that Sunday is the universally accepted Sabbath, having, replaced the Jewish *Shabbat* (Saturday), the Reformed Baptist's are the only denomination whom I have discovered that were bold enough to state their rationale for this greatly significant and otherwise unexplained change. The Baptist's position:

"As it is the law of nature, that in general a portion of time, by God's appointment, be set apart for the worship of God, so by his Word, in a positive moral, and perpetual commandment, binding all men, in all ages, he has particularly appointed one day in seven for a Sabbath day to be kept holy unto him, which from the beginning of the world to the resurrection of Christ was changed into the first day of the week, which is called the Lord's day; and it is to be continued to the end of the world as the Christian Sabbath, the observation of the last day of the week being abolished. (Exod 20:8; 1 Cor. 16:1, 2; Acts 20:7; Rev. 1:10)

"The Sabbath is then kept holy unto the Lord, when men, after a due preparing of their hearts, and ordering their common affairs aforehand, do not only observe an holy rest all day, from their own works, words and thoughts, about their worldly employment and recreations, but also taken up the whole time in the public and private exercises of his worship, and in the duties of necessity and mercy. (Isa 58:13; Neh 13:15-22; Matt. 12:1-13) "[5]

It is interesting to review the Scriptures cited here as proof text:

● *Remember the Sabbath day, to keep it holy.* (Exod 20:8):

This command was written by the finger of God on a tablet of stone and given to Moses some 1,500 years before Constantine was born. All commonly accepted translations of "Sabbath" here are rendered in Hebrew, *Shabbat*, the last day of the week, Saturday. It is simply irrational to translate Sabbath here to mean Sunday, or the first day of the week.

● *Now concerning the collection for the saints, as I have given orders to the churches of Galatia, so you must do also: On the first day of the week let each one of you lay something aside, storing up as he may prosper, that there be no collections when I come.*
(1 Cor 16:1-2):

The Jewish *Shabbat* begins at sundown on Friday and ends when the third star is visible on Saturday evening. Nazarene Jews and the Gentiles among them would have surely spent this time in worship and prayer. Then, they would have joined together for a meal at the end of *Shabbat*, on Saturday evening. By Jewish reckoning (and Paul's), this evening time would have been the beginning of the "first day of the week." Since Sunday, the next morning was a work day, it seems very reasonable that they would have conducted the "business" of collecting tithes and offerings at this gathering on Saturday evening. However, even if they had waited until Sunday morning to collect these financial gifts (which makes no sense since the men would have been off to work and the women about their regular business) there still is no basis whatsoever for taking this use of "the first day of the week" to mean that the Sabbath had been changed from *Shabbat* to Sunday.

● *Now on the first day of the week, when the disciples came together to break bread, Paul, ready to depart the next day, spoke to them and continued his message until midnight.* (Acts 20:7)

Viewed in the above light that "the first day of the week" began after darkness on Saturday night, it makes every sense that their meeting would have begun with the beginning of the new day, and continued on until midnight.

They not only met on this particular first day—Scripture informs us further that they met together *daily*. (See Acts 2:46-47).

● *I was in the Spirit on the Lord's Day, and I heard behind me a loud voice, as of a trumpet,* (Rev 1:10)

There is no indication whatsoever that "Lord's Day" here means either *Shabbat* or Sunday. In either case it would be irrelevant to the argument that *Shabbat* had been replaced by Sunday.

● *"If you turn away your foot from the Sabbath, from doing your pleasure on My holy day, and call the Sabbath a delight, the holy day of the LORD honorable, and shall honor Him, not doing your own ways, nor finding your own pleasure, nor speaking your own words, Then you shall delight yourself in the LORD; and I will cause you to ride on the high hills of the earth, and feed you with the heritage of Jacob your father. The mouth of the LORD has spoken."* (Isa 58:13-14).

The Lord gave this prophecy to Isaiah some 1,000 years before Constantine replaced the Lord's Holy *Shabbat* with the pagan "Sun-Day." Again, there seems absolutely no possibility that the Lord could have been referring here to the first day of the week, rather than literally to the Hebrew *Shabbat* (Saturday).

● *In those days I saw people in Judah treading wine presses on the Sabbath, and bringing in sheaves, and loading donkeys with wine, grapes, figs, and all kinds of burdens, which they brought into Jerusalem on the Sabbath day. And I warned them about the day on which they were selling provisions. Men of Tyre dwelt there also, who brought in fish and all kinds of goods, and sold them on the Sabbath to the children of Judah, and in Jerusalem. Then I contended with the nobles of Judah, and said to them, "What evil thing is this that you do, by which you profane the Sabbath day? "Did not your fathers do thus, and did not our God bring all this disaster on us and on this city? Yet you bring added wrath on Israel by profaning the Sabbath." So it was, at the gates of Jerusalem, as it began to be dark before the Sabbath, that I commanded the gates to be shut, and charged that they must not be opened till after the Sabbath. Then I posted some of my servants at the gates, so that no burdens would be brought in on the Sabbath day. Now the merchants and sellers of all kinds of wares lodged outside Jerusalem once or twice. So I warned them, and said to them, "Why do you spend the night around the wall? If you do so again, I will lay hands on you!" From that time on they came no more on the Sabbath. And I commanded the Levites that they should cleanse themselves, and that they should go and guard the gates, to sanctify the Sabbath day. Remember me, O my God, concerning this also, and spare me according to the greatness of Your mercy!* (Neh 13:15-22)

Nehemiah, like Isaiah, lived many centuries before Constantine. Most certainly, this Scripture is a very clear prohibition from YHWH through the prophet, spoken to His Jewish people in Hebrew, admonishing them to honor *Shabbat* (not Sunday) by refraining from work, etc. Again, to the Jews in Israel, Sunday was then and remains today the first work day of the week.

● *At that time Jesus went through the grainfields on the Sabbath. And His disciples were hungry, and began to pluck heads of grain and to eat. And when the Pharisees saw it, they said to Him, "Look, Your disciples are doing what is not lawful to do on the Sabbath!" But He said to them, "Have you not read what David did when he was hungry, he and those who were with him: "how he entered the house of God and ate the showbread which was not lawful for him to eat, nor for those who were with him, but only for the priests? "Or have you not read in the law that on the Sabbath the priests in the temple profane the Sabbath, and are blameless? "Yet I say to you that in this place there is One greater than the temple." But if you had known what this means, 'I desire mercy and not sacrifice,' you would not have condemned the guiltless. "For the Son of Man is Lord even of the Sabbath." Now when He had departed from there, He went into their synagogue. And behold, there was a man who had a withered hand. And they asked Him, saying, "Is it lawful to heal on the Sabbath?"—that they might accuse Him. Then He said to them, "What man is there among you who has one sheep, and if it falls into a pit on the Sabbath, will not lay hold of it and lift it out? "Of how much more value then is a man than a sheep? Therefore it is lawful to do good on the Sabbath." Then He said to the man, "Stretch out your hand." And he stretched it out, and it was restored as whole as the other.* (Matt 12:1-13)

The Pharisees were religious Jews who in this instance were chastising Yeshua because He had, in their view, violated Scripture by "working" on *Shabbat*. If Yeshua had been doing these things on Sunday, the first work day of the week, the Pharisees would have found no reason to challenge Him in this manner since working on Sunday was then, and still is, a perfectly normal thing to do. Further, there can be no argument that the Greek *Sabbaton* used here is taken directly from the Hebrew *Shabbat*, meaning the seventh day of the week, not the first. Finally, current scholarship holds that Matthew was originally written in Hebrew,[6] hence the word *Shabbat* (Saturday) here was the original usage.

In summary, none of these several "proof texts" offered by the Baptists, offers even one single shred of evidence, or for that matter even one reasonable suggestion, that anyone other than Constantine abolished YHWH's Holy *Shabbat* in favor of the satanic rooted Mithratic "Sun-Day." Is it any wonder that none of the other denominations have come forward with their own attempts to justify this obviously heretical change?

The Advent and Resurrection of Yeshua: While I find *all* the spiritual baggage brought into Protestantism from Roman Catholicism troubling, the universal celebration of Yeshua's birth on Christmas, and His resurrection on Easter, both, satanic, pagan rooted festivals selected by a Roman king in utter defiance of all things I hold most sacred, genuinely breaks my heart. I take this error more personally than the host of other issues, since I grew up in the Church doing the very same thing: worse still, this is how I raised my own three daughters. We must, all of us, repent and turn to what the Scriptures reveal.

an excellent witness to celebrate the reality of the Advent of Yeshua on or about Chanukah when all of Judaism and Christianity are focused on this joyous season.

Resurrection day is entirely another matter. By all means, every believer, Jew and Gentile alike should focus first on Passover (the 14th of Nissan) and then look to the morning of the third day thereafter to rejoice in the empty tomb and the incredible thing He has done for us all.

Since the Southern Baptist Convention is perhaps the most staunchly conservative of all Protestant denominations, and seemingly least likely to allow itself to drift into doctrinal error, I was honestly shocked to discover that Baptist Book Stores, and the Sunday School Board of the Southern Baptist Convention, are, at the time of this current writing, urging its people to buy "Resurrection Eggs" to aid them in celebrating Easter! This mixes paganism with the most beloved Christian celebration. This new product was advertised:

"**NEWS BRIEF:** Great For Family Devotions: Resurrection Eggs. What Advent calendars are to Christmas, these colorful eggs are to Easter. Comes with companion guide to help you turn each enclosed object into a fun, family learning experience." [7]

"Resurrection Eggs" as a new "Easter tradition" is by no means an exclusively Baptist phenomenon. There were numerous other endorsements of the new product idea, one for example posted by www. Gospelcom.net who calls itself *"The most popular Christian site in the world!":*

"You'll love this easy, Easter-time tradition! Colorful "Resurrection Eggs" teach about Christ's death, burial and resurrection. Here's a fun way to teach your kids valuable truths about Easter. This 'new tradition' is built upon a simple array of easy-to-locate materials - colorful plastic Easter eggs, a cardboard or Styrofoam egg container,

BAPTIST BOOKSTORES' ADVERTISEMENT FOR "RESURRECTION EGGS"

and miscellaneous household items like toothpicks and a small piece of cloth. Sure, you can purchase a pre-made version of this Easter 'kit,' but making it yourself is a wonderful family time activity, too! This craft is so easy and inexpensive that parents usually wonder why it took them so long to discover and introduce this faith-affirming tradition for the Easter holiday. Whether you buy or build your tray of twelve Resurrection Eggs, be sure to watch your child's face as he/she opens each plastic egg, discovers the hidden surprise and reads about its symbolic relationship to Easter."[8]

[1] Martin Luther, Quoted by Alister E, McGrath,: *Christian Theology*, "The Doctrine of the Church," page 411

[2] Greek Orthodox Archdiocese of America, Article: "The Ten Commmandments," www.goarch.org

[3] Article: "Some Straight Answers about the Orthodox Church," www.ocf.org

[4] Elizabeth Moll Stalcup, "Hidden from the Holocaust," *Charisma*, May 2000, page 65

[5] Reformed Baptist Church, "The Baptist Confession of Faith," www.bible.ca/cr-baptist

[6] The "DuTillet" Matthew uses the Hebrew "Shabbat," in these verses.

[7] "Protestant Church Apostacy Reaches New Proportions," Article: www.cuttingedge.org

[8] Article: "Resurrection Eggs," www. Gospelcom.net The most popular Christian site in the world!

Chapter Eight

The State of the Christian Church in the Year 2000

"If the mildew reappears in the house after the stones have been torn out and the house scraped and plastered, the priest is to go and examine it and, if the mildew has spread in the house, it is a destructive mildew; the house is unclean. It must be torn down—its stones, timbers and all the plaster—and taken out of the town to an unclean place. (Lev 14:43-45)

I am a Messianic Jew who was led to my blessed salvation in Yeshua through the loving care, teaching and ministry of a succession of non-Jewish Christian pastors (mostly U.S. Air Force Chaplains). Ever since, under such never failing care and guidance, I have struggled along the continuing upward pathway of sanctification. Along the way, I was so very privileged to sit under the devoted care and feeding of the greatly anointed faculty of a wonderful conservative Christian seminary. So great is my love, so deep is my appreciation, I could never begin to repay the enormous debt I owe the Christian Church for all it has done to bring me to this point in my already long life.

It is thus exceedingly difficult and painful for me to offer, you, my brothers and sisters in Yeshua, an open and honest assessment of the deplorable state in which I see the Christian Church standing today. Yeshua said, *And you shall know the truth, and the truth shall make you free*.[1] May we all come to better understand the true condition of the Church so that working and praying together, we might be able to shore up its crumbling foundation before it collapses altogether before our very eyes.

The Various Bodies that Constitute the Worldwide Church

The total number of independent denominational Christian bodies vary according to the different measurement parameters used. Even by the most conservative estimates, there are more than 500 such independent denominations: according to some reports, there are as many as 2,600. From either of these extremes, or from any place between them, the Body is incredibly divided, unable to speak with anything that remotely resembles a common voice, and, from all appearances, almost totally disinterested in attempting to do so.

There are 23 independent and separate Christian bodies (denominations) worldwide, with memberships greater than one million:

Christian Body	Year Reported	Membership[2]
All Christians (world)	1998	2,200,000,000
All Pentecostal/Charismatic (world)[3]	1998	540,000,000
	1995	60,280,454
Assemblies of God (world)	1997	30,000,000
Southern Baptist Convention	1995	15,663,296
The United Methodist Church	1995	8,538,662
	1998	8,500,000
	1997	8,000,000
	1996	7,000,000
	1995	5,190,489
	1995	4,711,500
	1995	3,669,489
	1996	3,500,000
	1995	2,594,555
	1995	2,536,550
	1996	2,500,000
	1995	2,500,000
	1998	2,000,000
	1997	1,900,000
	1995	1,655,000
	1995	1,517,400
	1995	1,500,000
	1995	1,472,213
	1996	1,230,842
Christian Churches & Churches of Christ	1998	1,070,600

In the past thirty years there have been great declines in the membership of the liberal mainline Protestant denominations. This deeply saddening reality would seem to be a Divine response to the sweeping apostasy that has spread throughout this very heart of the Church and which now seems to be threatening its very life. According to a recent article in *Charisma* magazine, the following declines have occurred:

Change in Membership in Seven (Liberal) Denominations During the Last 30 Years[5]

1967	Denomination	1997	% Change
1,600,000	American Baptist Churches	1,200,000	-25
5.8	Evangelical Lutheran Church in America	5,200,000	-10
1.8	Disciples of Christ	879,436	-51
3.4	Episcopal	2,300,000	-32
10.2	United Methodist	8,400,000	-18
4.2	Presbyterian (USA)	3,600,000	-14
2.0	United Church of Christ	1,400,000	-30
29,000,000	Totals	22,900,000	-21

The Liberal Denominations' Clergy and the Seminaries that produce them have turned abruptly away from God

Following, are just a few of seemingly countless examples of apostasies committed by these liberal denominations that surely, at least in part, must account for their perilous and continuing demise.

● Well known evangelical leader Harold Lindsell reports:

"It is not unfair to allege that among denominations like Episcopal, United Methodist, United Presbyterian, United Church of Christ, the Lutheran Church in America, and the Presbyterian Church, U.S.A. there is not a single theological seminary that takes a stand in favor of biblical infallibility. And there is not a single seminary where there are

189

not faculty members who disavow one or more of the major teachings of the Christian faith."[6]

● The Episcopal leadership seems to be in a contest with their Anglican mother church to see which can depart faster and further from the fundamental precepts of Christianity.

"In the first half of the 20th century, Episcopal Bishop James Pike denied all of the major tenants of the Christian faith. He said 'Religious myth is one of the avenues of faith and has an important place in the communication of the Gospel' and he spoke of the 'myth' of the Garden of Eden and the 'myth' of the virgin birth. Pike said, 'I have abandoned ship on the doctrine of the Trinity. I have jettisoned the doctrine of the virgin birth of Jesus Christ.'[7]

"John Spong, another Episcopal Bishop, has gone to the outer limits in radical theology. After worshiping in a Buddhist temple in 1988, Spong said 'As the smell of incense filled the air, I knelt before three images of Buddha, feeling that the smoke could carry my prayers heavenward. It was for me a holy moment for I was certain that I was kneeling on holy ground. ...My conviction is that the true God, the divine mystery, the essence of holiness, is within and beyond all of these ancient worship traditions. ...when I visit a Buddhist temple it is not for me a pagan place...It is rather a holy place where human beings different from me have felt the presence of God. ...I will not make any further attempt to convert the Buddhist, the Jew, the Hindu or the Moslem. I am content to learn from them and to walk with them side by side toward God who lives, I believe, beyond the images that bind and blind us all.'"[8]

"In his book *Rescuing the Bible from Fundamentalism*, Spong states, 'Am I suggesting that these stories of the virgin birth are not literally true? The answer is a simple and direct 'Yes.' Of course these narratives are not literally true. Stars do not wander, angels do not sing, virgins do not give birth, magi do not travel to a distant land to present gifts to a baby, and shepherds do not go in search of a newborn savior.'"[9]

● In 1985, Lutheran theologian and pastor J. Kincaid Smith who claims to have been "converted back to the orthodox Lutheran faith" testified of his experiences with Modernism in Lutheran seminaries:

'When I graduated in 1973 (from a Lutheran Seminary) to the best of my knowledge, none of my classmates, nor I, believed in any of the miraculous elements in the Bible, in anything supernatural, no six day creation, that Adam and Eve were real historical people, that God really spoke to people, the flood with Noah and the Ark, the Red Sea parting. We believed that no Old Testament Scriptures foretold of Jesus of Nazareth, that Jesus was not anticipated in the Old Testament. No virgin birth. One of my New Testament professors was moved to write a poem for the occasion of his receiving tenure. It was read at the service at Wittenberg University Chapel. In it he speculated that Jesus' father was an itinerant Roman soldier. He flatly denied the real deity of Christ.'[10]

● The prevailing theological climate in the United Methodist Church is equally disturbing:

"Bishop James Thomas stated at the UMC Quadrennial General Conference in 1976: 'We do not believe...in rigid doctrinal concepts to hold us steady in a wavering world.' This is an understatement; the fact is that most UMC pastors don't believe in the Bible. Polls have shown that at least 30 percent of UMC ministers do not believe Jesus Christ is God, and 82% say they do not believe the Bible is the perfect Word of God. As early as 1968 a widely publicized scientific survey by Jeffrey Hadden which was published by Washington University showed that about 60% of the Methodist clergy did not believe in the virgin birth and at least 50% did not believe in the bodily resurrection of Christ."[11]

● The gospel promoted in the Presbyterian Church (USA) is primarily a false social gospel. Emphasis is toward social-political causes in the world, with little attention to traditional Christian evangelism. David W. Cloud reports:

"A survey taken in 1986 revealed that only 5% of the clergy and 16% of the membership in the PC-USA believe the Bible is to be taken literally. More than 75% of those polled rejected the idea that those who had not heard of Jesus Christ will be damned. In 1987 the PC-USA adopted a report which says that Christians and Jews worship the same God and that Jews are already in a covenant relationship with God and do not therefore need to be born again through faith in Jesus Christ to enjoy such a covenant. In 1982 the United Presbyterian Church ordained Mansfield Kaseman in spite of the fact that he denied Jesus Christ is God, that He was sinless, and that Christ rose bodily from the dead. In a typical neo-orthodox doublespeak Kaseman said, 'I believe in the resurrection without necessarily believing in the bodily resurrection.' When asked if Jesus is God, he replied, 'No, God is God.' Yet the presbytery voted 165-59 to admit Kaseman to the Presbyterian ministry.---The 'Brief Statement of Faith' approved at the 1991 General Assembly of the PC-USA contained no clear affirmation of the Trinity; made no reference to Heaven, Hell, or the bodily resurrection of Jesus Christ, but it affirmed sexual equality and environmental concerns."[12]

● The United Church of Christ, formed in 1957, has, according to David W. Cloud,"---been on the cutting edge of ecumenical/modernistic weirdness from its inception." Theologically, the UCC has taken a decidedly Unitarian and Gnostic position, having, in 1959, adopted a non-Trinitarian "Statement of Faith." Dr. Donald Bloesch, professor of Theology at Dubuque Seminary and one of the most widely known and read UCC theologians, made this assessment:

"The theological trend in the UCC is toward a new gnosticism. It could be called post modern theology with its strong emphasis on relativism. Its primary drive is a need for immediate knowledge of God through experience. The role of the Bible in this theology is simply to provide a textbook of spiritual experiences from another age. ...the UCC seems to be following the path of the United Church in Canada which has become a Unitarian church because it sees three persons of the trinity as metaphors rather than distinct entities."[13]

The Liberal Denominations have almost universally legitimized Immorality, Homosexuality and Abortion

● After a three-year study, an Episcopal Church commission in 1991 recommended that bishops be allowed to ordain homosexuals to the priesthood. In his book, *Living in sin: A Bishop Rethinks Human Sexuality*, Episcopal Bishop John Spong said:

"I have known too many non-marital relationships marked by the qualities of holiness to suggest that they are immoral because they are not within the narrow bands of legal marriage. ...I regard the blessing of gay or lesbian couples by the church to be inevitable, right, and a positive good."

This immoral thinking has, apparently, now penetrated the entire Episcopal denomination. In a 1993 study, 70% of nearly 20,000 Episcopalians surveyed said it is possible for sexually active homosexuals to be faithful Christians, and 75% of those surveyed said a faithful Christian can live with someone of the opposite sex without being married.[14]

● The Evangelical Lutheran Church in America head Bishop, Herbert Chilstrom supports the ordination of homosexuals as members of the clergy

192

and publicly pronounced his agreement with President Clinton's call for allowing homosexuals in the U.S. military. In 1992 the ELCA distributed a report on human sexuality which claims that homosexuals were created by God and that sexual relations outside of marriage are not always wrong. An ELCA youth program guide entitled "Let Justice Roll Down Like Waters," teaches young people that the Bible does not condemn homosexuality.[15]

● While officially the United Methodist Church took a stand against homosexuality in 1984, this position is almost universally ignored throughout the denomination. For example, immediately after the anti-homosexual position was published, UMC bishops defiantly ordained homosexuals in Colorado and California. UMC Bishop Melvin Wheatly said in 1983, "I clearly do not believe that homosexuality is a sin. ...Homosexuality, quite like heterosexuality, is neither a virtue nor an accomplishment. It is a mysterious gift of God's grace...His or her homosexuality is a gift...neither a virtue nor a sin. Many UMC churches have performed wedding ceremonies for homosexuals, and a number of homosexuals have been ordained into the UMC ministry.

The UMC, at its General Conference in 1972, called for the legalization of abortion. The UMC was a founding member of the Religious Coalition for Abortion Rights, which sought "to encourage and coordinate support for safeguarding the legal option of abortion." In one year the UMC contributed more than $400,000 to the abortion rights coalition. The UMC came out in support of the 1973 Roe v. Wade Supreme Court decision which legalized abortion in the United States.[16]

● The Presbyterian Church (USA) has a formal policy that allows for homosexuals to be received as members, and even allows for their ordination as long as they do not engage in same-sex relationships. In practice, homosexuals within the PC-USA carry on with their homosexual lifestyles without being disciplined by the church.

The PCA-USA is also a member of the Religious Coalition for Abortion Rights, which seeks "to encourage and coordinate support for safeguarding the legal option for abortion." In 1985 the denomination reaffirmed its support for the right to abortion and determined, in a move to silence any opposition within the denomination, proclaimed that no new studies on abortion were to be undertaken by the church.[17]

● The United Church of Christ is also a strong supporter of homosexuals and openly embraces them in both their membership and ordained clergy. For example, the UCC has declared opposition to all laws criminalizing homosexual activity; opposed the exclusion of gays from the military; became the first mainline denomination to openly ordain homosexuals to the clergy; and in 1977, ordained the first of now many lesbians.[18]

● Even the traditionally more centrist Disciples of Christ, in 1997, urged the enactment of "legislation on local, state and national levels which would end the denial of civil rights and the violation of civil liberties for reasons of sexual orientation. The Disciples of Christ's resolution in this regard specifically recognized that "the church, among other elements in society, has contributed to the persecution and suffering of homosexuals, and it is its culpability in this regard which provides one reason for seeking a more enlightened understanding."[19]

This denomination has experienced, by far, the greatest membership decline in the past thirty years, although, its public position on homosexuality is very recent. Obviously, there must be other reasons beyond my understanding that would account for this otherwise unexplained dramatic decline.

The "Flip Side": The Larger, Conservative Fundamentalist Denominations Have Enjoyed Remarkable Growth

Christian Body	1960	1995	Change
Southern Baptist Convention	9,732,000	15,399,000	+58.2%
National Baptist Convention USA	5,256,000	8,200,000	+56.0%
National Baptist Convention of America	2,669,000	3,500,000	+31.1%
African Methodist Episcopal Church	1,166,000	3,500,000	+200.2%
Lutheran Church-Missouri Synod	2,391,000	2,599,000	+8.7%
African Methodist Episcopal Church Zion	770,000	1,200,000	+55.8%
Totals	21,984,000	34,398,000	+56.5%

The very large differences in membership changes experienced by these two groupings of denominations seems remarkable, if not puzzling. One could speculate that God has shined upon the more conservative denominations (as well as the explosively growing Pentecostals/Charismatics) simply because they have, for the most part, renounced the doctrinal and social apostasies universally embraced by the liberal denominations.

Even so, all of these denominations, conservative and liberal alike, continue to embrace at least much of the pagan rooted legacy inherited from the Roman Catholic Church from which they commonly sprang. All celebrate

Christmas and Easter—all disregard the Shabbat mandated by YHWH in favor of Sunday substituted in its place by Constantine. Will our Lord finally grow weary of all this?

Then he said, "Hear now, O house of David! Is it a small thing for you to weary men, but will you weary my God also?" (Isa 7:3)

An Even More Frightening Phenomenon:
The "Catholic" Churches and Pagan Cults are also Experiencing Rapid Growth

For we do not wrestle against flesh and blood, but against princi-palities, against powers, against the rulers of the darkness of this age, against spiritual hosts of wickedness in the heavenly places.
(Eph 6:12)

Christian Body	1960	1995	Change
The Roman Catholic Church	42,105,000	59,858,000	+42.2%
Church of Jesus Christ (LDS) Mormon	1,487,000	4,520,000	+204.0%
The Orthodox Church in America	755,000	2,000,000	+164.9%
Greek Orthodox Diocese N.& S. America	1,200,000	1,950,000	+62.5%
Jehovah's Witnesses	273,000	927,000	+239.6%
Totals	45,820,000	69,255,000	+51.1%

In Search of Ecumenism

In recent years there have been several ecumenist attempts to bring various denominations into some sense of unity. However, for the most part these initiatives have involved the various "High" (liturgical) denominations: Anglican, Episcopal, Lutheran, in concert with other "liberal" groups: Methodist, United Church of Christ, and others, who have sought to return ever closer to the Roman Catholic Church. Like Martin Luther planned at the outset of the Reformation, these denominations evidently envision an ultimate return to the Roman fold, and the Roman Catholic Church from all appearances is most receptive to this eventuality.

If these denominations can be considered the "liberal" end of the Protestant spectrum, then many would agree that the Southern Baptists[20] stand in juxta-position, in the opposite most "conservative" position. When, in 1996, the ecumenically oriented "Promise Keepers" organized a Clergy Conference in Atlanta, the more than 39,000 pastors who attended were urged to embrace what was named the "Atlanta Covenant," calling in part for them to reach out beyond racial and denominational barriers.

The Baptist's response to this call for ecumenism was, in part, to cite numerous instances of apostasy in the various denominations with which they were being called into some form of unity. This strong Baptist rejection is summarized by David W. Cloud:

"Promise Keepers is calling for denominations to come together. When examined in the light of the character of today's mainline denomina-tions, it is clear that this is a call for fellowship with apostasy. Either Promise Keepers leaders are ignorant of the facts or they simply don't care. Either way, they demonstrate that they are unqualified to lead God's people. When confronted with these facts, many respond, 'Yes, there is much apostasy in the denominations, but we must stay in them and be the salt and light.' This is unscriptural nonsense. The Bible says a little leaven leavens the whole lump. Leaven in Scripture is a symbol for evil and error. A little error, if left alone, will quickly permeate an entire church or denomination. This is precisely what has happened. God does not instruct His people to stay in the midst of apostasy; He instructs them to come out and be separate."[21]

[1] John 8:32

[2] All data is from www.Adherents.com unless otherwise stated

[3] Assemblies of God News, quoted in "Salt Lake City Tribune," 3 October 1998, Article: "25% of World Christians are Pentecostal." www.Adherents.com

[4] The Mormon Church is elsewhere often identified as a non-Christian cult. My inclusion of it here is not to imply that I hold otherwise.

[5] *Charisma*, "The Decline of the Mainline Church," March 2000, page 61

[6] Harold Lindsell, *Battle for the Bible*, pp. 145-146

[7] *Christian Beacon*, March 17, 1995, as quoted by David W. Cloud in an Article: "The Denominations Today," www.whidbey.net   This reference, and all following references to, and quotations from this article are used with permission and were originally published in David W. Cloud's *Way of Life Encyclopedia of the Bible & Christianity*, copyright 1996, Way of Life Literature, 1701 Harns Rd., Oak Harbor, WA 98277.

[8] Ibid, quoted from John Spong, Bishop of Newark, "A dialouge in a Buddhist temple," *The Voice*, January 1989.

[9] Ibid

[10] Ibid, quoted by David W. Cloud from *Christian News*, April 29, 1985

[11] Ibid

[12] Ibid

[13] Ibid

[14] Ibid

[15] Ibid

[16] Ibid

[17] Ibid

[18] Ibid

[19] Ontario Consultants on Religious Tolerance, "The Disciples of Christ and Homosexuality," www.religioustolerance.org

[20] There are 310 different "Baptist" denominations world-wide, most but not all of which are "fundamental' (conservative) in most of their positions. The Southern Baptists are by far the largest of these denominations with 15.7 million members at the end of 1998, making it second in size to only the Roman Catholic Church.

[21] David W. Cloud, Fundamental Baptist News Service, Article: "Denominations Today," page 16, www.whidbey.net (See: 2 Cor 6:14-18; Rev 18:4)

Chapter Nine

Who is a Gentile?
(What is the Christian Church?)

Summing Up

"Now everyone who hears these sayings of Mine, and does not do them, will be like a foolish man who built his house on the sand: "and the rain descended, the floods came, and the winds blew and beat on that house; and it fell. And great was its fall" (Matt 7:26-27)

Part One of this book: "Who is a Jew?" begs a question long asked by many and not easily answered. The first question posed by Part Two: "Who is a Gentile?" is much more easily answered. The American Heritage Dictionary defines "Gentile" quite simply as "One who is not of the Jewish faith, or is of a non-Jewish nation."

Beyond this important but obvious definition, the real substance of Part Two is to be found in the not at all simple multi-faceted answer posed by its sub-title: "What is the Christian Church?" This is a much more vital matter, and certainly the central question I have done my best to address. In summary, following are the main points I have endeavored to convey:

● There is only one, not two, much less three, "great monotheistic faiths." That faith is Judaism.

● Those Jews who originally accepted Yeshua as their Messiah and subscribe to His divinity, death, resurrection and promised return were the exclusive members of a Sect of Essene Jews who called themselves Nazarenes. Today, Jews with a like confession of faith in Yeshua are most accurately called Messianic Jews. While most Messianic Jews worship Yeshua from a more Jewish perspective within the Messianic Jewish movement, some believing Jews worship Him from within the mostly Gentile context of the Christian Church.

● For approximately the first 10 years of the Nazarene Sect's existence, its membership remained almost exclusively Jewish. Some suggest, I believe accurately, that there were as many as 400,000 Nazarene Jews (100,000 of whom were in Jerusalem) at the height of the movement before the Second Revolt against Rome in 135 CE.

● There were, as a result of the 120 original Nazarene's faithful response to Yeshua's "Great Commission," an ever increasing number of pagan rooted Gentiles coming to faith in Yeshua. Up until the Council of Jerusalem in 49 CE, those Gentile converts who were physically in Jerusalem, where they would have been under the supervision of the more conservative Nazarene's, most likely would have been "fully converted" to Judaism, including circumcision of the flesh, as a prerequisite to their becoming fully accepted by the Nazarenes. These Jerusalem converts would have, most likely, been called *Gerim* (literally converts to Judaism)[1]

Such converts who came to faith in Yeshua outside of Jerusalem, particularly as a result of the early international missionary activities of Paul and others, would most likely not have been "fully converted" to Judaism and therefore remained uncircumcised. Those who did "fully convert" would also have been known as *Gerim*. Those Gentiles[2] who did not convert, were first called "Christians" at Antioch in 43 CE.[3] From this time forward, except for the relatively few converts in Jerusalem and even fewer outside of Jerusalem who continued to "fully convert" to Judaism, thus becoming *Gerim*, all other Gentile believers would, most assuredly, have been known as "Christians."

● Nazarene Jews then, and Messianic Jews now, would not properly have been called (at least among themselves) "Christians" which in their thinking has always been and remains an appellation exclusively descriptive of Gentile believers. On the other hand, Gentile believers, then and now, would *properly* not have been called "Jews," or any other appellation derived therefrom. Even those Jews who now worship from within the context of the Gentile Christian Church, generally identify themselves as Messianic Jews, "complete Jews," or with some other appellation denoting their Jewish ethnicity.

● Nazarene Judaism, as a cohesive and viable sect, for all intents and purposes, disappeared soon after 135 CE, although there remained isolated communities of Nazarene believers in Israel and elsewhere in the Middle east until about the end of the 5th Century. This demise was brought about, principally, by the combined pressures of the emerging Christian Church, and the other "traditional" Jewish sects.

● Bound only by the four *Torah* imperatives legislated by the Council of Jerusalem,[4] from the outset, the emerging Christian Church made a concerted effort to distance itself from all things Jewish. For example, I believe (in our earlier work, *The Messianic Seal of the Jerusalem Church*) we have made a convincing case that the early Gentile Church dismantled the three-part Messianic Seal, stripping away its very Jewish Menorah and Star of David: keeping only the fish, which became the Christian symbol for both Yeshua and the Church. Also, most notably, many Nazarene sacred writings, including several "gospels" and other "epistles" were destroyed or suppressed. Only a few of these have survived in tact, others only in fragments, and some only by later reference to their existence by the "Church fathers."

● Hence, with its Jewish *Torah* and worship roots suppressed, and/or otherwise ignored, an enormous spiritual/foundational vacuum existed in explosively expanding Christianity. YHWH had permitted an open door to the newly emerged Church, and satan wasted no time to rush in, bringing along the many pagan roots, traditions and practices most notably contributed by Constantine, but added to over the centuries by many others as well.

● These same pagan roots, traditions and practices are still with the Christian Church today: they are all around us. The Church almost uniformly rejects the Sabbath as it was instituted by YHWH, embracing instead, with not a shred of scriptural authority, the pagan "Sun-Day," instituted by Constantine. Obelisks are considered national treasures in Washington D.C. and Paris, and they appear even on America's printed currency. The clergy of many of our liturgical churches continue to adorn themselves in robes right out of Mithratic paganism, while we persist in addressing Anglican and Episcopal priests "Father," a title reserved by YHWH for himself alone. We cherish evergreen trees, pine cones, Yule logs and the like as sacred traditions: all of them pagan rooted symbols we choose to adore right along with our precious Lord Himself as we celebrate His birth. The current President of the United States manages to find time away from his many "affairs," some of them wholesome, some not, to supervise a traditional annual Easter "egg roll' on the White House lawn: all of this while we teach our children that rabbits lay eggs and all things signifying fertility are to be treasured. Is it any wonder our young people are growing up well founded in promis-

201

cuity? Is it any greater wonder that an estimated 50 percent of Christians are addicted to pornography?[5]

● Thank God that the sickness introduced by this satanic blend of Christianity and Paganism has not yet totally penetrated and consumed the entire Christian Church. While the enormous "liberal" component of Protestantism would seem to be terminally ill and is disappearing before our very eyes, the Lord has seen fit, at least for the time, to continue to prosper the "Fundamental" and "Pentecostal/Charistmatic" branches of the Church which are growing, even remarkably.

● Even so, not nearly all of the many who are fleeing the liberal denominations in droves are rushing into "Fundamental," "Pentecostal/Charismatic," the great variety of "Community," or other "non-denominational churches. Many, especially those who flatly reject the lingering replacement theology generated teachings, such as Sunday worship, etc., and refuse to keep pagan rooted feasts of Christmas and Easter, they are looking elsewhere. Many of them are just now discovering the Jewish roots of their faith and they are rushing in ever increasing numbers to find an appropriate way to respond to this wonderful realization.

[1] These Gentile converts to Judaism were, scriptually, "the strangers who dwelt among us" For example, see Lev. 19:33

[2] There were also Jewish believers at Antioch. Conceivably, these too could have been included in the group called "Christians."

[3] Acts 11:26

[4] Acts 15:29

[5] Rick Joyner, "From A Gate of Hell to a Door of Heaven," *The Morning Star Journal*, Volume 10, Number 2, page 83

Part Three

Removing the Thorns of Disunity
Discovering and Embracing the Jewish Roots of Christianity

There shall come forth a Rod from the stem of Jesse, and a Branch shall grow out of his roots. (Isa 11:1)

Introduction

Parts One and Two of this book have been my attempt to lay a foundation for Part Three. My heartfelt purpose and prayerful hope is that what follows will provide a "road map" for my Christian brothers and sisters who are already leaving the mainline Christian Churches, and the legions of others who will surely follow them, to discover and embrace their divinely appointed and unique places in the Body of Yeshua. For, not only are you all greatly treasured members: Without each of you, the Body is unable to function properly and there can be no real unity.

Chapter One

The Confused Offspring of Replacement Theology Recognizing and Coping with an Identity Crises

Indeed I will make those of the synagogue of Satan, who say they are Jews and are not, but lie—indeed I will make them come and worship before your feet, and to know that I have loved you. (Rev 3:9)

On a spiritual level, Replacement Theology, the notion that the Church has somehow replaced Israel, and therefore that all believers (Jews and Gentiles) alike have replaced the non-believing ethnic Jewish people, is upsetting enough. However, the matter goes from being simply upsetting to potentially tragic when some Gentile Christians, quite literally, have come to believe that they, through their faith alone, have become Jewish in *every* respect.

Therefore, having been so transformed, these "Jews," who were formerly Gentiles, genuinely believe that they have become the only and true benefactor's of the Abrahamic Covenant in which YHWH, among other things, gave the Land of Israel to His Chosen people as an ever lasting inheritance. These now "True Jews" then take a giant leap by declaring and genuinely believing that they have inherited the physical Land of Israel, and have replaced ethnic Jews as God's chosen people. They further believe that they are now the subject of the many Old Covenant imperatives calling *them*, the "Jews," home: that they have thus come to Israel, fully enfranchised by the Word of God to stay here forever, or at least for as long it may please them to do so.

While many of these so transformed "True Jews," are coming to Israel with the intention, come what may, of staying, the problem goes beyond the State of

Israel. There are those former members of failing Protestant denominations who, having come to think of themselves as genuinely and completely "Jewish," for a variety of reasons, have postponed making "*Aliyah*," and instead put into practice their new Jewish identities by attempting to become totally integrated, identical in every way, with their ethnically Jewish brothers and sisters in the rapidly expanding Messianic Jewish communities elsewhere, mostly in the United States.

This pretense of ethnic Jewishness is potentially very dangerous. It has created a genuine *Identity Crisis* of the worst sort: a growing mass confusion that arises primarily from two sources.

The first source of this *Identity Crisis* is the deep and abiding longing of those Christians, who, having understandably given up on the Church, have come to believe that the answer they are seeking is through some supernatural metamorphosis that has miraculously transformed them from Gentile into Jew.

The second source of this growing Church-wide *Identity Crisis* is the widespread hermeneutical error in interpreting the very words of Yeshua regarding the continuing validity of the *Torah*, as well the flawed exegeses of several related Pauline Scriptures.

Let me quickly add, perhaps not quickly enough for some, I am in no way disputing the perfectly sound Scriptural exegeses that believing Gentiles can and should be considered, individually, as "*spiritually* grafted in,"[1] "*spiritual* Jews,"[2] and collectively, in their Christian Church, as "co-members of the *spiritual* Commonwealth of Israel."[3] Together with their born again ethnically Jewish brothers and sisters, they completely share in absolutely every *spiritual* way, the same salvation, through the same blessed Messiah, Yeshua. This entirely *spiritual* sharing is elaborated in a later chapter.

For now, I earnestly pray that my central point be clearly understood: *ethnic* Jews are and ever will remain, *ethnic* Jews, whether they are believers in Yeshua or not. *Ethnic* Gentile Christians are *ethnically* Gentile and so, in this dispensation, they will forever be. Absolutely nothing mandated by Scripture, or made possible through any person's desire or faith, however strong, sincere or motivated, can change these realities of nature, the flesh and genealogical inheritance. Nor should we, either Jew or Gentile, try to change them. To do so is to slap our blessed Creator in the face for having made us who and what we are. We should instead continuously praise Him for making us precisely who and what He chose us to be—all the while prayerfully and humbly trying to discern just what it is, exactly, He has for us to do in order that we might get into the very center of His Will for us, and remain there, in that Holy place, for all the remaining days of our lives.

Those Who Say They Are Jews And Are Not

David Stern, the eminent Messianic Jewish translator, theologian and commentator offers:

"In the first century, the Jewish religion was highly regarded; many Gentiles became Jewish proselytes. It is not surprising that other Gentiles preferred a short-cut, reaping the advantage of Jewish identification without the burden of adherence to *Torah*. Sha'ul (Paul) had already encountered such types in Galatia (see Ga 6:12-13).

"Should it nevertheless be thought improbable that Gentiles would call themselves Jews, Hebrews or Israelites, consider the following modern examples. The '"British Israel"ites' regard the British as the Ten Lost Tribes. The Mormons not only consider themselves to be the Ten Lost Tribes but regard themselves as Jews and everyone else (real Jews included) as Gentiles! A sect of mostly American-born blacks consider themselves the true Hebrews; several thousand of them are living in Israel. "All of these are outside the pale of Christianity. In addition, scattered about are well-meaning Gentile Christians whose strong identification with and love for the Jewish people has made them believe—without a shred of evidence—that they are actually Jewish themselves...In fact, some years ago a congregation was expelled from the American Lutheran Church because, along with a general drift into weirdness, its pastor and dozens of its members claimed to have heard from God that they were really Jews; many even said they knew which tribe they belonged to.

"Without exception, this phenomenon of Gentiles imagining and asserting they are Jewish when they are not leads to strange patterns of doctrine and practice." [4]

The Jerusalem Syndrome

The Jerusalem Syndrome is a very real, usually temporary psychiatric condition that manifests itself in an alarming number of Christians who visit Israel. Dr. Yair Barel, the doctor responsible for Jerusalem's mental health portfolio predicted that as many as 40,000 pilgrims who visit Jerusalem in the year 2000 may come down with the syndrome, with nearly 600-800 requiring hospitalization, and that some of these patients could possibly pose a danger to the public.

The Jerusalem Syndrome, characterized by otherwise normal Christian "pilgrims" believing that they are biblical figures such as Jesus, John the Baptist, the "two witnesses" of Revelation 11:3, or Moses, has long been known to Israeli psychiatrists. The phenomenon was identified in the 1930s by Dr. Heinz Herman, the father of Israeli psychiatry, but was only labeled as the Jerusalem Syndrome in the last two decades.

Typically, a Christian "pilgrim" who is overcome by this condition, occasionally wrapped in no more than a hotel sheet, will envision him/herself as a biblical character and begin singing praise songs and preaching to all who pass by. The "Messiah," "King David," the "Two Witnesses" and "Deborah the Prophetess" have not infrequently been found singing, guitar-playing, and prophesizing the approaching Day of Judgment in the labyrinth of alleyways in Jerusalem's Old City, and at other popular tourist sites scattered throughout the country.

Some examples of the Jerusalem Syndrome phenomenon that have appeared in recent years are:

"Brother David:" Originally a businessman from New York, Brother David rented out lodgings in Jerusalem to visiting Christians to await the return of Jesus on the Mount of Olives. He was deported from Israel in November, 1999 by Israeli officials.

"Elijah:" An American tourist turned Biblical prophet who resides in Jerusalem. He sports a long white beard and white robe and is usually found preaching God's word to passersby in the Old City.

"Jim and David:" Disciples of "Elijah." As yet, they haven't taken on a Biblical *persona* but are preparing for the momentous occasion by ritual bathings and fasts. David, a former Hollywood film star, can be found in Jerusalem laying his hands on people's heads and praying for them.

"King David:" Usually found at the Zion Gate, "King David" dresses in a white robe and a gold crown. He strums a out-of-tune harp and accompanies his playing with a warbling singing voice. 'King David," age 56, hailed originally from Brisbane, Australia until his call from God beckoned him to Jerusalem.

"Brother Solomon:" A former New York City school teacher and native of Jamaica, "Brother Solomon" can be found preaching God's word in the vicinity of the Mount of Olives. He preaches that Christ's return will take place between April 2000 and July 2001. He has a group of disciples that followed him to Jerusalem from Brooklyn, N.Y.

"John the Baptist:" Usually seen on Ben-Yehuda Street preaching to anyone who will listen.

"Name Unknown:" The American Consultate in Jerusalem was visited by a man who was adamant that he was Jesus Himself. Feeling the consulate officials may need to reach him, he left them with his cell-phone number.

"Messiah and Messiah:" Dr. Yair Bar-El recalls, "There was one case where two different patients insisted they were the Messiah, so I decided to put them in a room together to see if they would come to their senses. It didn't work. Each thought the other was an impostor. . .." [5]

Some of these many "pilgrims" who suffer from the Jerusalem Syndrome have a previous history of mental disturbance. Some have just forsaken their prescribed medical regime, and the symptoms they show during their Israeli visit are easily dissipated by returning to their prescribed drugs. Others have had no prior problems at all. In many cases, the patients have no recollection afterwards of their street corner preaching, and are quite embarrassed by the attention they have drawn. [6]

Even before we made a*liyah* to Israel some eight years ago, I had my first personal encounter with a closely related manifestation of this bizarre condition. Since then, while I certainly make no claim to offer qualified medical opinion, I have had many other personal experiences that have, collectively, absolutely convinced me that their common root is the essence of what David Stern has offered above: "--- these well-meaning Christians whose strong identification with and love for the Jewish people has made them believe—without a shred of evidence—that they are actually Jewish themselves." Some examples:

A "Jewish Heart:" One of the people most responsible for leading me back to my Jewish roots is a dear non-Jewish Christian brother who worshipped with us in our first Messianic congregation in the United States.

During one of our first *Shabbat* services together, this dear brother, clad in a *keepah* (skull cap) struggled haltingly to read the *Torah* portion in rudimentary Hebrew.

After the service, I quite sincerely asked him: "How is it that you cover your head when Paul teaches us (1 Cor.11:7) that men are not to do so?"

He unhesitatingly replied: "I cover my head because I am Jewish. All Jews, including you, should cover their heads out of respect and tradition."

Quite taken aback, I further inquired: "I had no idea you were Jewish. Were both your parents Jewish?"

He replied: "No, neither of my parents were Jewish, and before you ask, no, I have not converted to Judaism."

"Then," I responded, quite perplexed, "if neither of your parents were Jewish and you are not a convert, how is it that you reckon you are Jewish?"

He hesitated for a moment, then spoke slowly and with great emotion as his eyes filled with tears: "I have a Jewish heartæand since I have a Jewish heart, it must be Jewish blood that flows through my Jewish heartætherefore, since I have a Jewish heart through which flows Jewish blood, surely you must see that I, like you, am Jewish."

Two "*Hasidim*" Visitors: Some years after we had planted roots in Tiberias, one of our friends from the United States who was touring Israel, called to say he was in Tiberias and would be bringing two other visitors from his congregation to meet us. We were, as usual, quite excited to have some much needed fellowship with brothers from America, and we eagerly awaited their arrival.

A short time later, I tried very hard to conceal my genuine surprise, even shock, at what I beheld standing before me when I opened the door to our home. There with my causally dressed old friend were two impeccably dressed young men who in every detail appeared to be the most orthodox *Hasidim*. Formal black suits, starched white shirts, *keepahs* over which sat broad brimmed black fedoras, full beards and ear locksænothing was missing.

My mind raced with all manner of imaginations as I tried to make casual conversation. Why would two *Hasidim* from the United States want to visit us despised Messianics? Had we somehow been "found out" by the local Anti-Missionary organization and had these two been sent to investigate us?

Our friend, enjoying the moment, kept a straight face as long as he could, then introduced the two visitors by their full names, both of which sounded not at all Jewish.

As we shook hands, I framed several candidate questions, then thought better of it and boldy inquired: "Are you Jewish?"

The two laughed at my obvious distress, as one of them recovered long enough to reply, "No, we are Messianic Gentiles."

"Pardon me for asking," I replied, "but why is it you dress like *Hasidim*?"

"Because it makes us *feel* more Jewish," one of them responded. "And it helps us to relate better to other Jews to whom we have come to witness," the other added.

"Is the Pope Catholic?": We attended a fiftieth wedding anniversary about a year ago, celebrating the long marriage of a lovely local Messianic couple.

While most of our fellow guests were Messianic believers, a minority of other secular and traditional Jews had been invited. One very orthodox looking young couple stood out from the others: both were dressed in every detail as *Hasisdim*, he in the traditional black suit with all accouterments, she in a full length very conservative dress with a traditional bejeweled cloth sack that entirely covered her hair.

Since I did not know them, I made a point to introduce myself. Both were quite rigidly formal, and seemed a bit uncomfortable in these strange, very unorthodox and informal surroundings. He shook hands quite stiffly, and she, in keeping with orthodox Jewish tradition, did not enter into our short, perfunctory conversation.

A short time later, Donna and I were discussing these newcomers with another Messianic couple who had also made it a point to introduce themselves.

"They are very orthodox," our lady friend reported, "I offered my hand to him and he pulled back, quite offended. I was so embarrassed."

Still later, I inquired of our host how it was that he happened to know and invite this orthodox couple. He laughed, then replied, "They aren't orthodox: they aren't even Jewish. They are new in town and we wanted to make them feel at home, so we invited them."

Now, totally intrigued by my host's revelation, I engaged the new couple in further conversation. "Will you live in Tiberias," I inquired. "What are your plans?"

The man responded as his wife stood traditionally, rigid and silent by his side and one pace behind, "We hope to start a Messianic congregation here as soon as our citizenship is approved."

Since Israeli citizenship is only awarded to immigrants who are certifiably Jewish, I wanted to be certain that my host had not misunderstood the ethnicity of the newcomers. "Are you Jewish?" I inquired quite boldly.

"Is the Pope Catholic?" he responded rhetorically, in a feigned Yiddish accent.

This couple left Tiberias soon after we met, and from what we can determine they are no longer in Israel.

The "Jewish" Pastor: We had for a number of years been praying that the Lord would send a Messianic pastor to Tiberias who would meet the very special needs of the many local English speaking Jewish believers. When a major American Church group sent out a young pastor about two years ago to plant a church in our city, for a time, I felt quite certain that he had come in a direct answer to our prayers.

I was genuinely drawn to this relatively young man and his family. We soon became good friends. His love for the Lord was obvious, and his call to Israel, by his own report was the product of many years of seeking and preparation.

While we and another Messianic couple faithfully attended his meetings for a time, he was, for a variety of reasons, unable to attract other local interest, and his congregation from the outset was largely transitory with a new assortment of mostly American tourists each week.

Soon after his arrival, the pastor became a regular and faithful member of the intercessory prayer group that meets in our home each week. He is a delightful prayer warrior who fit in well as we prayed for the unreached in the "10-40 Window" and for the various needs of Israel.

At one such meeting, when we were praying for the protection of the Land from being given away to our enemies, I asserted, while praying, that the Land had been given to the Jewish people as an ever lasting inheritance. The pastor seemed to take a somewhat different position, implying that the Land had been given to *all* believers, including himself. Finally, when other members of the group intervened with their disagreement, the entirely Gentile Christian pastor blurted out: "I am just as Jewish as you are Bob Fischer, and I can prove it to you from the Bible!"

Later, he offered the traditional eisegesis of several Pauline Scriptures in support of his assertion that although, ethnically Gentile, he was nevertheless a "Spiritual Jew" and therefore the same in every respect as all other Jews.

It truly broke my heart and still greatly saddens me that this ministry failed a short time later and the pastor and his family returned to the United States.

"Circumcised Hearts" do not Residents of Israel Make: Some dear friends, a Christian couple, operate a Bed & Breakfast in a suburb of Jerusalem. We stay with them during our overnight and longer visits to the City.

Another Christian couple from the United States had been staying with them for about a year, and we had come to know them during our various visits. They had been in Israel on tourist visas which they had regularly renewed every 90 days during mandatory exits, followed by immediate reentry into the country.

This couple had determined to remain permanently in Israel and believed they had a God given right and call to do so. In response to this conviction, they recently applied to the Ministry of Interior for the more permanent and infrequently granted status of "temporary residency." "Temporary residency," is usually granted only after a stay in Israel of many years that has been maintained by various work and/or volunteer visas.

Since this particular couple was here on already several times renewed tourist visas, and since they had no secularly recognizable reason to remain in the Land, they were well advised by our mutual friends that their chances of approval were slim and that only supernatural intervention on their behalf could bring success. They were further advised, by all means, not to mention their Christian orientation during their official interview since the Ministry of Interior is hyper sensitive to potential "missionaries" and if found out, they would surely be rejected on that basis alone.

Never-the-less, during their official interview in support of their application, they asserted words to the effect: "We are Jewish because we have circumcised hearts, and we are therefore entitled to remain in Israel forever!"

Their application was denied on the spot, but this did not dissuade them. They further asserted words to the effect: "It doesn't matter! We will immediately return as tourists and keep returning!"

The government official responded by stamping their passports with a permanent: "Do not admit."

Each of the foregoing examples are the bitter fruit of this "Intra-Body" *Identity Crisis:* each in itself a needlessly endured and faith shattering tragedy for those whose agony it was to live through them.

It can, without a doubt, be edifying, satisfying and instructive for a non-Jewish Christian to embrace and practice Jewish social, cultural and religious traditions. However, for such a non-Jewish brother or sister to embrace even the slightest notion that by adopting such exclusively Jewish life-style traditions and practices is, or ever can be, in and of itself a certification or in any way whatsoever lend credence that the person so participating is therefore a Jew, is a profound and very dangerous error, and not in keeping with a correct interpretation of Scripture. To better drive home this vitally important point, please consider this final, very painful example.

Of Lost Hope and Shattered Dreams: Some fifteen years ago, a young couple, from the same English speaking country, who had not yet met, came separately to Israel. Both have entirely Gentile Christian backgrounds, although she has "strong feelings" that she is Jewish but can find absolutely no proof to this effect.

He came to Israel to accept employment with an Israel company; she came as a volunteer worker on a kibbutz. They met, fell in love and married. From the very beginning of their marriage, they determined that they would remain in Israel for the rest of their lives: both felt called by the Lord to do so.

They both became members of a mostly non-Jewish Congregation founded, led and supported by the company for whom he worked. This particular congregation, although it identifies itself as "Messianic," is more accurately, by its own description, Evangelical Baptist with some Messianic Jewish trappings.

The young couple soon had two children, neither of whom, like their parents, had any claim to Israeli citizenship. Even so, the family persisted in maintaining that they (entirely on the basis of her continued conviction) were Jewish, had been called to Israel, and come what may, would remain in the Land.

The pressure of their dependence upon his work visa, as the sole basis for the family to remain in Israel, began to take a toll upon his health. This insecurity was compounded by their assessment that their congregation was not nearly Jewish enough to meet their needs or expectations. However, although never stated directly, they "understood" that his continued employment was largely conditioned by their continued worship with the company supported and led congregation.

Looking for something "more Jewish" to augment the family worship situation, they began attending an independent Bible Study offered by a person who was not affiliated with the company congregation. They found this new association to be satisfying enough that when the congregation outlawed both the teacher and the teachings of the separate group, they persisted in their attendance.

It is not surprising that the mounting pressures of this situation led to his near fatal heart attack, followed by emergency by-pass surgery. Although they desperately needed both prayer and material support, he was instead terminated by the company and they both were excommunicated by the company supported and led congregation, the members of which, former close friends and prayer partners included, were directed by the pastor not to communicate with or to pray for this family, and that any one who did so would also be subject to excommunication.

Out of work, out of fellowship, in extremely poor health, cut off entirely from the great majority of their former friends and now with no legal basis to remain in Israel, it would have seemed reasonable for them to return to the place from whence they had come. However, this was not their decision. Instead, they applied to the Ministry of Interior for "temporary residency," a process that can take many years, and which they undertook knowing that there was very little hope of a favorable outcome. They quite openly confessed that they had undertaken this long process just to buy more time in Israel, (as it turned out in this case with several legal appeals, what amounted to several years) until the notoriously slow Ministry of Interior, wading through its mountain of paperwork, finally got to their application.

While it is not a published policy, or one that would ever be admitted, the Ministry of Interior has a way of putting applications they don't want to approve, and eventually will disapprove in a seemingly "ignore" status, assuming , it would seem, that the applicant will eventually run out of funds or patience or both and simply give up without the benefit of an official decision.

So it would seem was the application in point being handled, or better stated "not handled." While they waited, all the while ever trying to convince themselves and all those around them that they would be remaining in Israel permanently, they moved to a Jewish Settlement in Samaria where they could live relatively inexpensively while waiting for an offical answer, the inevitable substance of which they already knew, unofficially, in their hearts.

Still out of any regular fellowship with other believers, they frequently attended a traditional Jewish synagogue and became totally integrated members of the local Israeli community. They and their children were by now fluently bi-lingual.

Even though they lived at a bare survival level, an originally generous financial inheritance he had earlier received slowly but surely began to vanish. After a period of several years, to their great disappointment but no surprise, their application for temporary residency was finally officially disapproved. Even so, they were still not deterred. They reapplied, and hired an attorney to represent them in the matter.

Finally, after another period of years with one disappointment following another, they ran out of money and, however reluctantly, returned to their native land, broken in spirit, their marriage in a shambles, virtually penniless and with him in ever worsening health.

In our most recent contact, they report that they are still living at a low poverty level, on welfare, and attending a local traditional Jewish synagogue. Although they have returned to an entirely English speaking environment, they continue to speak Hebrew at home and otherwise hold to their Jewish self-identification with the expectation that the Lord will one day make a way for them to fulfill their dreams by returning them to Israel.

The "Flip Side"- Jews Who Would be Gentiles

As incredible as it may seem, there are those Jews, some believers and some not who, for a number of greatly different reasons, overtly attempt to "pass" as Gentiles. Of this I am certain. For a number of years I was a Jew who wore this very tragic and all too transparent, Gentile mask: so did my father before me, and his father before him.

In my grandfather's case, his Gentile facade was borne out of necessity. He ran a small business in New York which was patronized by mostly anti-Semitic Christians.

My father learned well from his father, and when, in the midst of the "Great

Depression" of 1929 he had an opportunity to get a good starting executive position with a major American corporation, who at the time had firm, but unwritten anti-Semitic hiring practices, naturally my father was miraculously "transformed" into a "Protestant" which he dutifully entered into the space on the employment application asking for "religious preference."

In my own case, it wasn't just the example of my immediate progenitors who led me into donning my own false identity: it went much deeper. Incredulously, my first few years were spent in a distinctly Anti-Semitic environment, and, even as a young boy I had unwittingly begun to take on these horrible sentiments as my own. Then, once I discovered my own ethnic Jewishness, I was anything but eager to take upon myself this burden of my true identity when I had absolutely no interest or thought, at least in a positive way, about *anything* Jewish.

When, years later, I was led to my own salvation in an entirely Christian Church setting, my temporary mask, in a manner of my own thinking, became a form of spiritual plastic surgery. I had indeed *become* a Gentile Christian: never mind the physical realities to the contrary.

I offer this personal testimony for two reasons. First, because I know first hand what it is to live such a self delusion and how glorious it is to be restored to one's own true identity, whatever it may be.

Second, I offer this personal glimpse into my own soul, because I know most assuredly there are other Jews, perhaps many, who have given their hearts to *Yeshua*, but who still think of Him as *Jesus* from their reverse grafted-in false identities as members of the Christian Church. I am not meaning to imply that there is anything whatsoever superior about one name or the other for our precious Messiah, or for that matter, from a salvational point of view, that Messianic Judaism is in anyway superior to the Christian Church: what I am trying to point out is a matter of ethnic and traditional identity.

Remember the "Hebrew Christian" progenitors of contemporary Messianic Judaism: they quite deliberately and consciously threw off every aspect of their Jewishness and fully convertedæreligiously, culturally, socially, even traditionallyæto denominational Christianity.

After all, just look at the evangelistic focus, vis-à-vis Jews, of some contemporary Christian denominations, exemplified by the on going missionary focus of the Southern Baptists who have set a goal of converting *all* Jews from their Jewishness into their own special Baptist fold.

God made each member of the Body of Yeshua just the way He wanted them to be. He didn't make any Gentile with the understanding this precious being of His creation was supposed to later transform himself into a Jew. Nor did He ever create any Jew to later change himself into a Gentile. He made us

218

all, each one of us just the way we were born: the very special, wonderful way we each are; the way we ever more shall be. He made us each to hear the Good news about His Son: His wonderful plan of redemption, paid for in His own precious blood. And, having heard, He made us each to respond from within the ethnic, social, cultural and traditional framework wherein we were originally made, nurtured, then called.

[1] Rom 11:17 vf

[2] Rom 2:28-29

[3] Eph 2:14

[4] David Stern, *Jewish New Testament Commentary*, (Rev. 1:18) page 796

[5] "Examples of the Jerusalem Syndrome," Article: found at: www.jerusalemsyndrome.com/jscas.htm#top

[6] Ellis Shuman, "The Jerusalem Syndrome- Dateline: 11/22/99," www. About.com

Chapter Two

The Body of Yeshua: A Body with Many Members or "One New Man?" The Distinctly Different Scriptural Roles of Jewish and Gentile Believers

For in fact the body is not one member but many. If the foot should say, "Because I am not a hand, I am not of the body," is it therefore not of the body? And if the ear should say, "Because I am not an eye, I am not of the body," is it therefore not of the body? If the whole body were an eye, where would be the hearing? If the whole body were hearing, where would be the smelling? But now God has set the members, each one of them, in the body just as He pleased. And if they were all one member, where would the body be? But now indeed there are many members, yet one body. (1 Cor 12:14-20)

But now in Christ Jesus you (Gentiles) who once were far off have been brought near by the blood of Christ. For He Himself is our peace, who has made both (Jew and Gentile) one,--- so as to create in Himself one new man from the two, thus making peace, (Eph 2:13, 14a, 15b)

For as many of you as were baptized into Christ have put on Christ. There is neither Jew nor Greek, there is neither slave nor free, there is neither male nor female; for you are all one in Christ Jesus. And if you are Christ's, then you are Abraham's seed, and heirs according to the promise. (Gal 3:27-29)

If you are confused by Paul's apparent self contradiction in these vitally important yet often misinterpreted and misused Scriptures, then you (and I) are in very good company. Paul was even unclear to Peter, his fellow Apostle. [1]

For our present focused purpose, the central question begged by these three Pauline Scriptures is: Are Jewish and Gentile believers, as equal members of the Body of Yeshua, because of their shared faith, in any way (substantively, functionally, traditionally) different from one another as suggested by Paul in 1 Cor 12, or, have they, because of their shared faith, become as "one flesh," indistinguishable from one another in any way (substantively, functionally, traditionally) as suggested by Paul in Eph 2 and Gal. 3?

The answer, I believe, is both intuitively and hermeneutically clear. First, intuitively, despite contemporary social pressures to the contrary, there are both obvious and essential differences between male and female. There are other obvious differences, such as race, culture, language, etc., between members of the Body of Yeshua. We enter the Body as wonderfully unique members: each a very specific blend of physical, social, cultural and traditional components. Each one of us is absolutely distinguishable, even beyond our one of a kind DNA, from every other human being who ever was or who ever will be created. There is absolute truth in the idiom that "God made each one of us, then threw away the mold."

In the same way, there are very clear physical, social, cultural and traditional differences between groups of peoples. Collectively, Jewish believers and Gentile believers, although members of the same Body of Yeshua, are, as groups, clearly distinguishable, one group from the other.

A widely understood principle of hermeneutics is that Scripture itself is the best interpreter of itself. The Scriptures abound with testimony that Jews and Gentiles, saved and unsaved alike, have, by their mutual Creator, been called as two distinctive groups of people to very different callings and for distinctly different purposes.

The Unique Scriptural Roles and Imperatives God Gave to His Jewish People

A People Chosen By God: For reasons known only to Himself, YHWH chose the ethnic Jewish people to be the earthly vessels through which He would bring forth and fulfill His plan of redemption for all people. This election was implemented in the unconditional and everlasting covenant He made, then later ratified, with Abraham, guaranteeing among other things that the Messiah would be Jewish and that He would ultimately have to pay the price for man's disobedience,[2] and that the Land of Israel would be an ever lasting possession of Abraham's physical descendants.[3] This covenant was later repeated, and narrowed, to Abraham's son, Isaac,[4] and then to his grandson, Jacob[5] (whom he later named Israel) making all of these everlasting promises and the election of the Jewish people inarguable. Confirmation of God's election of the Jewish people is not confined to the Old Covenant. His sacred promises are clearly confirmed in the New Covenant.[6]

Custodians of the Word of God: All of the Old Covenant was given by God to His Jewish people. Moses, the Psalmists, and all of the major and minor prophets were Jewish. With the one exception of Luke, the Gentile author of the Gospel of Luke and the Book of Acts,[7] all of the canonized New Covenant was given by God through Jews. Moreover, the great wealth of Nazarene Jewish apocryphal writings, including several Gospels, were either destroyed or suppressed by the Christian Church fathers in their zeal to de-Judaize Christianity.

A Light unto the Nations: God made it abundantly clear in His Word, in both the Old Covenant[8] and New Covenant,[9] that He has called His Jewish people to bring the Gospel of Yeshua to the Gentiles. He gave His "Great Commission" first to eleven Jewish disciples. [10] Gentile believers, who, only after they were later grafted in to the Jewish root, came to share with the Jews, along with their salvation, Yeshua's "Great Commission" imperatives.

There is a, perhaps unwitting, understanding and practice among some Christians that they are called by God to convert Jews to Gentile Christianity and in the process to deliver them from their Jewish roots and traditions. Said differently, these are they who can't easily accept or understand the idea that a Jew can be saved through belief in Yeshua and at the same time remain distinctively Jewish. It is this sort of insensitivity that drives Jews away from their Messiah, not toward Him. The Southern Baptists have been particularly aggressive in this outreach. As reported in *U.S News Online*, September 20, 1999:

> "A Southern Baptist campaign to pray for the conversion of Jews during Judaism's high holy days has set off a furor that threatens to further fray already tattered relations between U.S. Jewish groups and the nation's largest Protestant denomination.

> "In a booklet published to coincide with the Jewish observance of Rosh Hashanah and Yom Kippur, Baptist leaders are urging the church's 15.9 million members to "pray each day for Jewish individuals you know by name that they will find the spiritual wholeness available through the Messiah [Jesus].

> "Jewish leaders expressed outrage. B'nai B'rith President Richard D. Heideman called the initiative 'not merely insensitive but hostile. It contradicts the legitimacy of Judaism and its continuity.' Abraham H. Foxman, director of the Anti-Defamation League, said the campaign 'projects a message of spiritual narrowness that invites theological

hatred.'

"The Baptists stirred a similar reaction in 1996 when they launched a special effort to proselytize Jews. 'We mean no offense,' explains Louis Moore, a Baptist associate vice president. As evangelical Christians, he says, 'we are obligated to pray for anyone who does not know Jesus Christ as Lord and Savior.'"

That such Christian evangelistic outreach, however well intentioned, is considered inappropriate and offensive by most Jews, believers and unbelievers, was well expressed by British author, Benjamin Disraeli: "The Jews are a nervous people. Nineteen centuries of Christian love have taken a toll."

A Continuing Guide and Foundational Presence: The Jewish role as spiritual guides and pillars of the Body of Yeshua continues even into the 1,000 years of Yeshua's reign in the new millennium. Scripture teaches:

Then I looked, and behold, a Lamb standing on Mount Zion, and with Him one hundred and forty-four thousand (Jews), having His Father's name written on their foreheads. (Rev. 14:1)

Also she (the New Jerusalem) had a great and high wall with twelve gates, and twelve angels at the gates, and names written on them, which are the names of the twelve tribes of the children of Israel.
(Rev. 21:12)

Now the wall of the city had twelve foundations, and on them were the names of the twelve (Jewish) apostles of the Lamb. (Rev. 21:14)

In "the end" it isn't the Jews who will turn to the Gentiles to guide them home, but quite to the contrary:

This is what the LORD Almighty says: "In those days ten men from all languages and nations will take firm hold of one Jew by the hem of his robe and say, 'Let us go with you, because we have heard that God is with you.'" (Zech 8:23, NIV)

The Unique Scriptural Roles and Imperatives God Gave to His Gentile People

The Lord gave Gentile Christians one very clear and overriding imperative with respect to the Jews:

"Comfort, yes, comfort My people!" Says your God. "Speak comfort to Jerusalem, and cry out to her, that her warfare is ended, that her iniquity is pardoned; for she has received from the LORD'S hand double for all her sins." (Isa 40:1-2)

This, I believe, is God's call to individual Christians and the Christian Church for the comforting of Israel and the Jewish people after years of their persecution. There are those who would have us believe that this is God asking the Church to bless itself or asking us to bless and comfort each other. According to Robert S. Somerville, Director of Awareness Ministry:

"The 'You' being addressed in this verse is speaking most specifically to the body of Christ because it is the Church who has the spirit of the Comforter (John 14:26). 'My people' is a direct reference to the Jewish people and the nation of Israel. Through the prophet Isaiah, God Himself is giving a directive for someone to be His love extended and to be a comforter to the downtrodden remnant of Israel. The Church and Israel are the only two bodies of people in the earth who have been referred to as the people of God. The statement 'her iniquity is pardoned' is not so much a redemptive word for Israel as a word of conclusion. This is the time when God says enough is enough and He will no longer permit their continual persecution and dispersion. This is a national forgiveness:

'For I will set mine eyes upon them for good, and I will bring them AGAIN to this land: and I will build them, and not pull them down; and I will plant them, and not pluck them up.'

(Jer. 24:6)

"Concerning the commission to comfort, the following New Testament passage has been identified by theologians as the 'Great Commission,' meaning the phrase encapsulates the mission of the Church upon the earth:

'Go ye therefore, and teach all nations, baptizing them in the name of the Father, and of the Son, and of the Holy Ghost: Teaching them to observe all things whatsoever I have commanded you...' (Matt 28:19-20)

"Unfortunately this commission has too often been limited in scope to include only the redemptive gospel or just those things which have been set forth in the New Testament. However it is important that we also hear the words of Jesus as He spoke through the Old Testament writers. The 'I AM' who spoke unto Moses from the burning bush (Exodus 3:14) is the same as He who said unto the disciple: '...I AM the way, the truth and the life...' (John 14:6). Jesus is the eternal embodiment of the word of God to mankind. Therefore, the commissions which Jesus has delivered to the Church include those that are set forth in the Old Testament as well as those in the New Testament. One of those commissions was heard through the prophet Isaiah: "COMFORT ye, comfort ye my people, saith your God" (Isaiah 40:1). This is

225

not an option but a command and a mandate to the body of Christ. We must obey it and teach all nations to be obedient. Every minister of the Lord Jesus Christ is therefore duty bound to make the comforting of Israel a vital part of his ministry. Every church should make this a vital part of its agenda and teach all nations that blessing Israel is a significant aspect of the "all things" which are to be observed by the Church. Once the remnant of Israel are gathered and restored to their land it will be a permanent restoration. It will also be a prelude to their spiritual restoration and redemption as is indicated by the following verse:

> 'And I will give them an heart to know me, that I am theLORD: and they shall be my people, and I will be their God: for they shal l return unto me with their whole heart' (Jer 24:7).'

"We see clearly the prophetic order of events. They must be restored to their land before their national day of salvation occurs. The individual Jew may be saved at anytime he accepts Messiah. But the great national revival that awaits them is a specific appointment and it is the comforting efforts of the Church that will contribute to the preparations that are necessary for this great event to occur."[11]

At this point, Christians may well be asking, just how, specifically they might meet God's calling upon them with respect to the Jews. May I offer the following for consideration. Christians may:

● **Respond to the call materially:** Steve Lightle, has for a number of years stood at the forefront of an active ministry, now shared by several other ministries that are dedicated to physically transporting Jewish immigrants to Israel from the former Soviet Union. There are opportunities for Christians to physically participate in this "Operation Exodus II," as crew members and staff, etc. And/or, the number of Jews that can be thus brought to Israel is a direct function of the level of financial support which has come mainly from Christians. For those interested in finding out more about this very real ministry opportunity, please contact:

Ebenezer Emergency Fund
Ebenezer House
5a Poole Road, Bournemouth BH25QJ, England
Tel: 44-1202-294455 e-mail: eef@btinternet.com

● **Intercede through focused prayer for individual, congregational and national situations within the Israeli Body**: Some take this opportunity very seriously and even come to Israel for cloistered prayer vigils. There are several "prayer houses" scattered throughout the Land that have been set up by various, mostly American, ministries to accommodate this need. Certainly, there is no need to be here in the Land to pray for its people and their many situations.

In order to uplift focused prayer, obviously one has to be informed about the situations needing prayer. There are several free inter-net news services. I highly recommend the three following services to provide such focus for prayer:

ICEJ NEWS SERVICE
Editor: David Parsons
To subscribe (free), please email a blank message to:
icej-news-service-subscribe@icej.org.il

FOR ZION'S SAKE MINISTRY
P.O.B. 1429 Jerusalem, Israel 91013
Tel/Fax: (972)-(2)-648-2056
To subscribe: type subscribe in the subject box
and send to: newslist@netvision.net.il

ARUTZ SHEVA
Phone: 972-2-997-2425
To subscribe for English version, view
http://www.a7.org (select English Home page)

Provide direct financial support to help new immigrants start new businesses in the Land of Israel: There are two excellent non-profit foundations to which you can contribute. Both focus their support on new immigrants who are members of the Israeli Body. For more Information contact either or both:

The Nehemiah Trustees Covenant Fund
P.O. Box 64
Ma'aleh Adumim, 98100
Israel
Tel: (972-2) 590-3070
Fax: (972-2) 535-7806
e-mail: ntcf@netvision.net.il

The Joseph Project
International Alliance of Messianic
Congregations & Synagogues
e-mail iamcs@mjaa.org

Exercise your political clout: Write to your respective governmental representatives to solicit their support for various contemporary Israeli issues. This kind of activity is especially needed as pressure is mounting on Israel from the United States, England and virtually all other Western nations to cede its precious God given Land in exchange for "Peace." At least one agency, VIPAC, offers draft letters on various contemporary issues as guidance. You may subscribe to receive these regularly at: www.vipac.org

Getting Back to Paul-What Did He Mean by "One New Man?"

I have attempted to show, from the three Scriptures cited at the beginning of this chapter, that the Body of Yeshua is best illustrated according to the model Paul provides in 1Cor.12:14-20. The Body has many different members, each of them entirely unique at several different material and spiritual levels. One of many physical distinctions has to do with the ethnicity of its individual members or groups of members who share the same ethnicity. Hence there are separate ethnic groups of Jewish and Gentile believers, each in turn comprised of a myriad of uniquely different individuals, made so by a whole host of other physical characteristics beyond their ethnic distinctiveness, such as physical height, hair and eye coloration, etc.

At another physical level, one branch of Jews can now be *scientifically* identified by a shared genetic characteristic. The American Society for Technion, Israel Institute of Technology announced on 10 July 1998:

Priestly Gene Shared By Widely Dispersed Jews

"The finding last year of genetic links among Jewish men thought to be descendants of the Biblical high priest Aaron was greeted with tremendous interest and clamoring for more information. A team of British and Israeli scientists have now found additional information that links the priestly cast, the Cohanim, which includes men with last names that are variations on 'Cohen.'

"Using a combination of molecular genetics and mathematical analysis, the scientists arrived an estimated date for the most recent common ancestor of contemporary Cohanim. According to this analysis, the common ancestor lived between the Exodus (approx. 1000 BCE) and the destruction of the first Temple (586 BCE), consistent with the biblical account. Similar results were obtained based on analysis of either Sephardi or Ashkenzi communities, confirming the ancestral link of the two communities which had been separated for more than 500 years.

"The study by Prof. Karl Skorecki of the Technion-Israel Institute of Technology and Rambam Medical Center in Haifa, and colleagues at the Rambam Medical Center Oxford University, University College London and University of London is published in the July 9 *Nature*.

"The findings received an added boost when the researchers discovered that by contrast, the Y chromosome of many contemporary Levites, descended from the tribe of Levi of which Moses was a member, display distinct sets of genetic markers, suggesting a heterogeneous pattern of descent which does not reflect a single pattern of direct paterilineal lineage."

As interesting as this scientifically identifiable "Jewish Gene" and all the rest of the other less scientific, albeit still observable physical Jewish distinctions may be, there is another entirely separate spiritual level of distinctiveness that must be considered, and this is where Paul's "One New Man" model becomes pertinent.

As already demonstrated, there are many different Jews and many different Gentiles who are physically distinguishable from one another. On a spiritual level there is absolutely no distinction between them with respect to their shared salvation by faith through grace. There are spiritual differences, but none that have anything whatsoever to do with ethnicity. Instead this individual spiritual distinctiveness has to do with sanctification.

When we are born again, in a theological reference we have become "justified." Immediately after we have become "justified" we begin the polishing process called "sanctification" that will continue for all the remaining days of our lives until we finally meet Yeshua face to face and are "glorified" with Him.

The polishing process of sanctification is often difficult. Each member of the Body of Yeshua stands at any given moment in a distinctly different place along the upward climb to glorification.

This is the one and only spiritual distinction between members of the Body of Yeshua, and no member can be aware of precisely where he or any other believer stands along the way: this is only known to the Holy One of Israel who awaits us at the end of our journey.

I believe that Paul's "One New man," model can be viewed in two different spiritual ways. First, in this "dispensation," I believe that Paul was making the simple statement that all believers, Jewish and Gentile alike, are saved in the same way. Second, I believe that in the next "dispensation," after we have become glorified with Yeshua, that there will no longer be any physical distinctiveness between believers and indeed we will finally be, in every respect, "One New Man."

[1] 2 Pet 3:15-16

[2] Gen 15:1-17 (the covenant ratified)

[3] Gen 12:7; 13:15; 15:18; 17:4-8; 22:18; 24:7; Psalm 105:6-10

[4] Gen 26:3-4

[5] Gen 28:13-14

[6] Acts 3:25; 7:7; Gal 3:8; 3:16

[7] Col 4:14

[8] Isa 2:3; 42:6; 49:6; 51:4-5; 60:3; Ps 110:2

[9] Luke 2:32; 24:47; Rom 10:18; Acts 1:8; 13:47

[10] Matt 28:16-20

[11] Robert S. Somerville, *The Seed of Abraham*, quoted by permission from the author, Article: "The Seed of Abraham," pp 16-17 www. awareness.org

Chapter Three

The Continuing Divisive Barriers of Replacement Theology The First Barrier: Christian Anti-Semitism

Author's Note: My research for this chapter has been a life changing experience. I find it difficult to come to grips with the unbelievable depths of the Church's Anti-Semitic perversity that I have thus come to understand. What follows is only a summary of Christian Anti-Semitism. The several examples of the Church's "teachings" on this subject are only a smattering. To share them all would require a separate volume of considerable length. Thus forewarned, let us embark on this sad journey with the words of the great reformer, Martin Luther.

"What then shall we Christians do with this damned, rejected race of Jews? Since they live among us and we know about their lying and blasphemy and cursing, we cannot tolerate them if we do not wish to share in their lies, curses, and blasphemy. ...We must prayerfully and reverentially practice a merciful severity. ... Let me give you my honest advice: First, to set fire to their synagogues or schools and to bury and cover with dirt whatever will not burn, so that no man will ever again see a stone or cinder of them. This is to be done in honor of our LORD and of Christendom. Second, I advise that their houses also be razed and destroyed. Third, I advise that all their prayer books and *Talmudic* writings, in which such idolatry, lies, cursing, and blasphemy are taught, be taken from them. Fourth, I advise that their rabbis be forbidden to teach henceforth on pain of loss of life and limb. Fifth, I advise that safe conduct on the highways be abolished completely for the Jews. For they have no business in the countryside, since they are not lords, officials, tradesmen, or the like. Let them stay at home. Sixth, I advise that usury be prohibited to them, and that all cash and treasure of silver and gold be taken from them, and put aside for safe keeping. Seventh, I recommend putting a flail, an ax, a hoe, a spade, a distaff, or a spindle into the hand of young, strong Jews and Jewesses and letting them earn their bread in the sweat of their brow. (Martin Luther)"[1]

Yeshua was a meticulously *Torah* observant Jew, born of a Jewish family, and raised in an entirely Jewish tradition. During His physical walk among us, His ministry was entirely to Jews. Virtually all of His teachings, except those real-time revelations He received directly from His Father, came from or were rooted in the *Tanach*, Rabbinical Oral Law, Apocryphal literature, Essene writings, or in other entirely Jewish sources. He was recognized, by other Jews, as the promised Jewish Messiah, and He acknowledged that He was indeed the fulfillment of the Messianic promise of the Old Covenant. Even so, through all this there isn't the slightest hint that He ever intended to start a new religion with Himself as its Head and focus. He continued in this theme even after His resurrection: on the road to Emmaus, He taught two of His disciples "---beginning at Moses and all the Prophets, He expounded to them in all the Scriptures the things concerning Himself."[2]

Soon after His Ascension, His small band of disciples grew dramatically into an Essene rooted Jewish Sect who called themselves Nazarenes. There was absolutely nothing in the Nazarene's teachings that constituted heresy from the point of view of the other major Jewish Sects of the time. Quite to the contrary, the Nazarenes, who even proclaimed that Yeshua was the promised Messiah, were openly accepted by other Jewish sects, and were most welcome to worship their arisen Messiah, Yeshua, in the very courts of the Temple.

According to the Book of Acts, and as later recorded by Church and secular historians, thousands of Jews joined the Nazarenes each day, until at their height, they numbered as many as 400,000 within Israel, of whom as many as 100,000 were in Jerusalem.

One can only speculate what would have happened had the Nazarene Apostles, principally Paul, not been so zealously obedient to Yeshua's "Great Commission" and so successful in bringing legions of pagan Gentiles into the Kingdom of God. One might reasonably ask: Would Nazarene Judaism eventually have become the one universal Jewish Sect with Yeshua accepted as Messiah? It certainly seemed to be heading that way, even quickly so.

One can also only speculate: What would have happened had Peter and other leaders in Jerusalem prevailed rather than Paul thus requiring Gentiles to first fully convert to Judaism, including circumcision, before being allowed to join what had been, up to then, an exclusively Jewish Sect? Would there have been far fewer such *Gerim*: but, would they, as well founded *Torah* observant followers of Yeshua, ever dreamed of turning upon and ultimately consuming the Jewish foundation from which they had sprung? Or, more poignantly, would their contemporary 2.2 billion Gentile Christian descendants, even now still be relentlessly spewing forth their vitriolic anti-Semitism, born in the early Roman Catholic Church and further inflamed by Martin Luther and the other "Reformers?"

Speculation, not withstanding, history unfolded otherwise. In 49 CE the Council of Jerusalem yielded to Paul's way of thinking and established the legitimacy of Gentile Christianity, freed from the principle requirements of the *Torah*. From that time forward, there was a new religion called "Christianity" that would develop its own vocabulary in Greek and Latin, dramatically new doctrine and worship practices, and in many other ways that would make it increasingly divergent from Judaism in general and Nazarene Judaism in particular. In short, Paul did far more than to simply prevail in a passing argument with Peter and the other more conservative Jerusalem based Nazarene elders: the success of his crucial position to exempt Gentile converts to Nazarene Judaism from the requirements of the *Torah*, not the least of which was circumcision, did, in a very profound and abrupt way forever change the history of the world.

The newly emerging Christian Church, so freed from the requirements of the *Torah*, quickly distanced itself from all other things Jewish, thus creating a spiritual, social, cultural and traditional vacuum into which rushed the myriad pagan practices and traditions that Constantine ultimately blended with basic Nazarene doctrine of redemption into the newly emerging "Christian" religion.

"Replacement" was the culmination of this de-Judaizing process: Christian anti-Semitism was given birth as the very heart and soul of this new satanically inspired theology. The Church had now become the "True Israel" and "True Israel," quickly launched a campaign of sorrows to totally discredit the "other" Israel from which it had sprung.

"The Church Fathers turned out volumes of literature to prove that they were the true people of God, and that Judaism had only been a prelude to or in preparation for Christianity. Justin Martyr along with Hippolytus (170-236 CE) was obsessed with the belief that the Jews were receiving and would continue to receive God's punishment for having murdered Jesus."[3]

It is difficult to believe how universal is this false understanding, shared by many Christians who, as a matter of doctrine, proclaim that the Jews, single-handedly, killed Christ. The label "Christ Killer," thus assigned to all Jews, has surely been validated by history as the blindly followed rallying point used by the likes of Adolf Hitler to justify such anti-Semitic tragedies as the Crusades, the Holocaust, etc.

Martin Luther wrote a 58 page "textbook" for Hitler, from which the quote at the beginning of this chapter is taken: why and how the German people should hate and ultimately eliminate the Jews, principally because the Jews allegedly, single handily, had killed Christ.

Even before His death, Yeshua seemed to go out of His way to prevent this terrible barrier of hatred from being erected. He made certain, through the power of the Holy Spirit, its author, that the Word would clearly characterize His sacrificial journey to the Cross as first an unavoidable fulfillment of His Father's and His own plan for the world's redemption, a plan to which He willingly submitted Himself.[4] Yeshua also made it clear that His Crucifixion should only be seen as a joint act of Jews and Gentiles. All three synoptic Gospels give the same account: the Sanhedrin, under the supervision of Caiaphas the High Priest, who was a Sadducee, unanimously condemned Yeshua to death, and it was the Gentiles who did the actual killing.[5]

Even so, the litany that spewed forth from the founders of the Church embraced far more than just the matter of culpability for Yeshua's death. Following are representative positions uttered by the "Church Fathers":

Ignatius Bishop of Antioch (98-117 CE) – Epistle to the Magnesians

"For if we are still practicing Judaism, we admit that we have not received God's favor...it is wrong to talk about Jesus Christ and live like Jews. For Christianity did not believe in Judaism, but Judaism in Christianity."[6]

Justin Martyr - Dialogue with Trypho (Between 138 and 161CE)

"We too, would observe your circumcision of the flesh, your Sabbath days, and in a word, all your festivals, if we were not aware of the reason why they were imposed upon you, namely, because of your sins and the hardness of heart. The custom of circumcising the flesh, handed down from Abraham, was given to you as a distinguishing mark, to set you off from other nations and from us Christians. The purpose of this was that you and only you might suffer the afflictions that are now justly yours; that only your land be desolated, and your cities ruined by fire, that the fruits of your land be eaten by strangers before your very eyes; that not one of you be permitted to enter your city of Jerusalem. Your circumcision of the flesh is the only mark by which you can certainly be distinguished from other men...as I stated before it was by reason of your sins and the sins of your fathers that, among other precepts, God imposed upon you the observance of the Sabbath as a mark."[7]

Origen of Alexandria (185-254 CE) – A ecclesiastical writer and teacher who contributed to the early formation of Christian doctrines

"We may thus assert in utter confidence that the Jews will not return to their earlier situation for they have committed the most abominable of crimes, in forming this conspiracy against the Savior of the human race...hence the city where Jesus suffered was necessarily destroyed, the Jewish nation was driven from its country, and another people was called by God to the blessed election."[8]

Saint John Chrysostom (344-407 CE)

Saint John Chrysostom was one of the "greatest" of church fathers; known as "The Golden Mouthed." A missionary preacher famous for his sermons and addresses, he is considered a "doctor of the Church," and among the greatest of the Greek Fathers. He was Bishop of Antioch toward the end of the 4th Century when he wrote eight famous lengthy anti-Semitic sermons, one more vitrolic than the next, entiltled "Homilies Against the Jews." Following is a brief "sample" from "Homily 1":

"Many, I know, respect the Jews and think that their present way of life is a venerable one. This is why I hasten to uproot and tear out this deadly opinion. I said that the synagogue is no better than a theater and I bring forward a prophet as my witness. Surely the Jews are not more deserving of belief than their prophets. 'You had a harlot's brow; you became shameless before all.' Where a harlot has set herself up, that place is a brothel. But the synagogue is not only a brothel and a theater; it also is a den of robbers and a lodging for wild beasts. Jeremiah said: 'Your house has become for me the den of a hyena.' He does not simply say 'of wild beast,' but 'of a filthy wild beast,' and again: 'I have abandoned my house, I have cast off my inheritance.' But when God forsakes a people, what hope of salvation is left? When God forsakes a place, that place becomes the dwelling of demons.

"But at any rate the Jews say that they, too, adore God. God forbid that

I say that. No Jew adores God! Who say so? The Son of God say so. For he said: 'If you were to know my Father, you would also know me. But you neither know me nor do you know my Father.' Could I produce a witness more trustworthy than the Son of God?

"If, then, the Jews fail to know the Father, if they crucified the Son, if they thrust off the help of the Spirit, who should not make bold to declare plainly that the synagogue is a dwelling of demons? God is not worshipped there. Heaven forbid! From now on it remains a place of idolatry. But still some people pay it honor as a holy place."[9]

St. Augustine (c. 354-430 CE), Confessions, 12.14

"How hateful to me are the enemies of your Scripture! How I wish that you would slay them (the Jews) with your two-edged sword, so that there should be none to oppose your word! Gladly would I have them die to themselves and live to you!" [10]

Peter the Venerable – known as "the meekest of men, a model of Christian charity" (1120 CE)

"Yes, you Jews. I say, do I address you; you, who till this very day, deny the Son of God. How long, poor wretches, will ye not believe the truth? Truly I doubt whether a Jew can be really human… I lead out from its den a monstrous animal, and show it as a laughing stock in the amphitheater of the world, in the sight of all the people. I bring thee forward, thou Jew, thou brute beast, in the sight of all men."[11]

The Great Crusades (1096-1291 CE)

The first of nine "Great Crusades" in 1096 was born out of strife and political necessity in the Roman Church. There had been not one, but two Popes, and when one of them died, Urban II the survivor, needed a cause around which the Church might rally. The result was an ill conceived plan to send forth a huge army into the "Holy Land" to either convert or kill Moslems who were known to be persecuting Christians and desecrating the holy places and Jerusalem.

It was thus, in the summer of 1096, an undisciplined rabble of 200,000 peasants and artisans had assembled in France with the intention of undertaking the long march to Jerusalem where they might do the Lord's work of being

His instrument of annihilation on earth. Since there were no Moslems on hand in this part of France where they had gathered, and since the "Army of the Lord" was untrained, these champions of the cross turned their attention to the formidable local population of Jews, who, in their eyes, were just as much "infidels" and enemies of Christianity as the Moslems. They found they could not only hone their skills of annihilation on the spot, but in effect they could commence the Great Crusade in France. Clarence H. Wagner, Jr, Director of Bridges for Peace in Jerusalem summarizes:

"Cruelty, instead of charity, began at home. As the Crusaders marched through Europe on their way to the Hold Land, they literally raped, pillaged, and plundered. Faced with the wild cries of the Crusaders, 'The Jews crucified our Savior, and they must return to Him or die,' the Jews had the alternative of baptism or death. Thousands preferred the death of martyrs. While the Church did not officially sanction this activity, it nevertheless took place. Many local clergymen and bishops gave the Jews protection and refuge from the rabbles. Unfortunately, others actually participated in the executions. To share with you just one example: at Mayence, the Archbishop invited 1,300 Jews into his palace for refuge. This proved to be an invitation to slaughter, for under his supervision, they were all killed, and he even shared in the spoils confiscated from the corpses.---When the Crusaders finally arrived in Jerusalem, they were 600,000 strong. They besieged the city and on July 15, 1099 broke through the walls. They killed the Moslems in the city and herded the Jews into the synagogue. Crusaders with shields decorated with large crosses placed wood around the synagogue and burned alive all inside as they sang, 'Christ, We Adore Thee!' Is it any wonder that the cross is a symbol of hatred and death for the Jewish people, not love, reconciliation, and salvation? The cross has literally been taken and used as a sword against the Jewish people."[12]

The Spanish Inquisition (1481-1820)

The next in the long series of infamous historical events perpetrated upon the Jewish people was the so called "Inquisition" that began in Italy, but later moved to Spain where it ultimately led to the death or severe suffering of some 350,000 Sephardic Jews.

According to Canon Law, the Inquisition was not authorized to interfere in the internal affairs of the Jews, but rather to seek out Christian heretics. However, this law was rescinded by the Church on the ground that the presence of Jews caused heresy to develop in the "Christian" communities.

It was thus in Spain that tens of thousands of Jews were forced to be baptized. Because of this, they were considered Christians and expected to behave as Christians. These baptized Jews were known as *Converos* or New Christians. However, these Jews had only submitted to baptism so that they might go on practicing Judaism in the privacy of their own homes. Forced baptism does not a Christian make!

These *Converos* were thus still practicing many Jewish customs, such as lighting candles on Friday evening, changing the linen on the Sabbath, keeping kosher, observing the Feast Days, etc. To be caught practicing any one of 37 such Jewish customs, as defined by the Church, was grounds to be brought before the Inquisition court. "Christians" were to spy on their newly converted *Converos* neighbors and to report any such infractions. Once before the court, there was no way out of punishment: [13]

● If you confessed and did not repent, you were burned alive.

● If you confessed and repented, you were publicly humiliated. Any subsequent slip-ups resulted in certain death.

● If you did not confess, even if you were innocent, you were tortured until you confessed and then burned.

"The Church was not allowed to execute the victim, so they passed them to a secular arm of the Inquisition Court. Blood was not allowed to be shed, thus the burning. This they justified by a text from John 15:6, 'If a man abide not in me, he is cast forth as a branch, and is withered, and men gather them, and cast them into the fire, and they are burned.'

"Incidentally, all property was confiscated, enriching the Inquisition Court.

Practicing Jews (not *Converos*) were ultimately brought to the Inquisition Courts, as it was believed that they were Judaizers, and a bad influence on the *Converos*. They too were tried and burned." [14]

The Protestant Reformation

While Martin Luther at first criticized the Roman Catholics for having been too zealous in their pursuit and systematic destruction of the Jews, he soon grew weary himself when his evangelistic efforts toward these "stiff-necked" people bore little fruit.

In fact, inflamed and frustrated, his own brand of Anti-Semitism ultimately at least matched the intensity of the Catholics, as recorded in "His Little

Book," in 1543.

Another example, in addition to this chapter's opening quote taken from this same source, clearly shows the seeds of hate against the Jews which has worked its way into the very fabric of the Christian Church.

"But your [God's] judgment is right, *justus es Dominie.* Yes, so shall Jews, but no one else be punished, who held your word and miracles in contempt and ridiculed, insulted and damned it for such a long time without interruption, so that they will not fall, like other humans, heathens and all the others, into sin and death, not up in Hell, nor in the middle of Hell but in the pit of Hell, as one cannot fall deeper...Even if they were punished in the most gruesome manner that the streets ran with their blood, that their dead would be counted, not in the hundred thousands, but in the millions, as happened under Vespasian in Jerusalem and for evil under Hadrian, still they must insist on being right even if after these 1,500 years they were in misery another 1,500 years, still God must be a liar and they must be correct. In sum, they are the devil's children, damned to Hell... The Jews too got what they deserved. They had been called and elected to be God's mouth as Jeremiah says...Open your mouth wide and I will fill it; they however, kept tightly closed their muzzles, eyes, ears, nose, whole heart and all senses, so he polluted and squirted them so full that it oozes from them in all places and devil's filth comes from them. Yes, that tastes good to them, into their hearts, they smack their lips like swine. That is how they want it. Call more: 'Crucify him, crucify him.' Scream more: 'His blood come upon us and our children.' (Matthew 27:25) I mean it came and found you...Perhaps, one of the merciful Saints among us Christians may think I am behaving too crude and disdainfully against the poor, miserable Jews in that I deal with them so sarcastically and insulting. But, good God, I am much too mild in insulting such devils..."[15]

Martin Luther was by no means the only "reformer" who held strong anti-Semitic views. John Calvin was also notorious for his inflammatory position:

"Their [the Jews] rotten and unbending stiffneckedness deserves that they be oppressed unendingly and without measure or end and that they die in their misery without the pity of anyone"[16]

During Calvin's reign in Geneva, between 1542 and 1546, "58 persons were put to death for heresy." While he did not directly recommend the use of the death penalty for blasphemy, he defended its use among the Jews.[17]

The Pogroms

The Pogroms occurred in Russia from 1881 to1921. They were a series of attacks perpetrated against the Jews which involved wanton destruction, the looting of property, murder, and rape, all perpetrated by Russian "Christians."

While this living hell for the Jews erupted in Mother Russia, the civil and military authorities stood by and watched. The Church was, at best, silent, and even endorsed some of the attacks.

It was during this period that the infamous, *The Illuminati's Protocols Of The Learned Elders Of Zion*, appeared. The protocols were first printed in Russia in 1905 to represent an imagined conversation between Jewish leaders on the details of how they were planning to take over the world. The original publication was printed under the auspices of the secret police on the press of Czar Nicolas II of Russia. The Czar made no secret of his personal member-ship in the anti-Semitic organization, the "Black Hundreds." Even though this booklet has been proven over and over again to be an utter fabrication, it can still be found in print throughout the world, and is offered for sale on the Internet (at amazon.com, among others) even to this day.

It is difficult to assess the scope of the pogroms during the civil war years and the number of victims they claimed. Partial data are available for 530 com-munities in which 887 major pogroms and 349 minor pogroms occurred; there were 60,000 dead and several times that number of wounded.[18]

The Holocaust

I will not burden the reader with yet another detailed account of the horror perpetrated against the Jewish people by the Nazis whose purpose was to sys-tematically eliminate all Jews from the face of this earth. Any adult Christian or Jew who is alive and breathing is surely already intimately aware of the details of the horrendous evil of the Holocaust of Annihilation. The fact that this horror actually succeeded in eliminating some six million innocent people, about one third of all Jewry, is an infamy beyond all imagination

The important lesson here is that at least some major responsibility for this horror can legitimately be assigned to the anti-Semitic teachings of Martin Luther and others within the Christian Church. The Holocaust represents the very culmination of some 1,900 years of endorsed and widely promulgated teaching whose poisonous roots are firmly planted in Replacement Theology, as it was originally stated by the Roman Catholic Church and as it was carried forward, intact, by virtually all of Protestantism.

The Church had replaced Israel. Christians had become the "True Jews."

Hence, eliminating the Jews made every sense to the likes of Adolf Hitler, so greatly encouraged and justified by Martin Luther, John Calvin and others from history, and even so by the entire "Christian" infrastructure of his day, which, as personified by the Pope, *once again* sat quietly by and did nothing. Germany was the most enlightened, intellectual, cultured society in the world at that time. Yet, this so-called "Christian" society stood by and watched: many even participated.

The Holocaust in all of its severity is unique to the Jewish people. While others were killed during the war for political reasons, or social reasons, such as being prostitutes or homosexuals. The Jewish people, mothers, children, peasants, doctors, musicians, rabbis, professors, were all exterminated *just because* they were Jews.[19]

Contemporary Anti-Semitism

One would think, by all reason, that the people of the world would have learned something from the horrendous history and venomous fruit of Christian Anti-Semitism. Not for a moment it would seem: the engines of blind, murderous, and unconscionable hatred against all the Jews, simply because they are Jews, rush relentlessly on!

The Stephen Roth Institute for the Study of Contemporary Anti-Semitism and Racism at Tel Aviv University continuously studies, then publishes an annual report of the major incidents of contemporary Anti-Semitism throughout the world. Following are a few extracts from their most recent report (1998-1999):

Denmark: On 15 August, the birthday of Rudolf Hess, over 100 neo-Nazis, including several from Sweden, Belgium and Germany, marched to the Greve town hall where they heard speeches by their leaders. Greve, about 40 km south of Copenhagen is the location of the Danish Nazi headquarters. Some of the marchers wore T-shirts with the slogans "Smash the Jews" and "Kill 'em all!" For security reasons, the neo-Nazis were not allowed to march in Copenhagen and in Koege, and the demonstration took place in the very early hours of the morning. Moreover, a relatively small number of neo-Nazis participated in the march because police at the border detained 150 neo-Nazis when they attempted to cross into Denmark from Germany.

France: In early 1999 a serious incident was recorded: in January a Molotov cocktail was thrown into the parking lot of the Yavné Jewish school in Paris. According to witnesses, the perpetrators were youngsters aged between 12 and 15. The 50th anniversary of the State of Israel was marked by a bomb threat to the Jewish community in Nancy. There were three desecrations of Jewish graves—in Troyes, Dammarie les Lys and Vitry sur Seine. Anti-Semitic graffiti was found on the walls of synagogues in Ris-Orangis, Evry and Creil (near Paris) and in Toulouse, and of the Jewish school at Colmar (Alsace).

Germany: The total number of extreme right-wing crimes in 1998 remained very high.

For example, in Bavaria xenophobic violence increased by more than 50 percent (33 people were injured, 21 more than in 1997.) In Sachsen-Anhalt violent incidents increased drastically, from 166 in 1997 to 290 in 1998. Violent acts against foreigners and members of ethnic minorities have become daily occurrences in many places. Special police units have helped somewhat to control violence in the streets. Since 1990 at least 16 people have been killed by right-wing extremists, motivated by xenophobia and/or anti-Semitism. A representative poll examining German opinions on Jews, commissioned by *Die Woche*, a news magazine, and published at the end of December 1998 by the Forsa Institute, showed that one in five Germans is a latent anti-Semite. In 1998 there were 991 anti-Semitically-motivated crimes, an increase of 1.5 percent. In Berlin alone, the number of anti-Semitic incidents increased by 20 percent. Most of the incidents were propaganda and defamation offenses, but desecration of Jewish cemeteries and sites (synagogues, museums and memorials) continued in 1998 at the same level as in previous years. Noteworthy examples were the vandalization of the memorial to deported Jews in Berlin, on the eve of the 60th anniversary of the Reichsprogromnacht, and the release of a pig painted with a Star of David and the name Ignatz Bubis, in October 1998, on the famous Berlin Alexanderplatz. The most serious violent anti-Semitic incidents were the two arson attacks (in September and December), which destroyed the grave of Heinz Galinski, an important leader of the Jewish community in Germany after World War II. In another violent incident in August, a rabbi was attacked on the streets of Berlin.

United Kingdom: Recorded anti-Semitic activities and incidents increased in 1998, to 232, compared to 219 in 1997. As in previous years the largest numbers of incidents were acts of abusive behavior against members of the Jewish community (133 incidents in 1998; 86 in 1997).

Russia: Anti-Semitism has become one of the chief political and ideological weapons of the nationalist and communist opposition in the struggle for power in Russia; in comparison, the varied and open activities of ultra-nationalist groups, including Russian Nazis, seem relatively secondary. The indecisive reaction of the Russian authorities, the government, the parliament and law enforcement officers to this intensification of anti-Semitism appears to signify that, for the first time in the history of modern Russia, anti-Semitism has become an integral component of the political life of the country. During 1998 and the beginning of 1999 there were 17 anti-Semitic incidents, involving violence or threats of violence, in eight Russian cities, the most serious of which was the bombing of a synagogue in the Maryina Roshcha section of Moscow on 14 May 1998. In Krasnodar placards were posted in December 1998 calling on the local population to burn and destroy Jewish homes in order to convince the Jews to leave the city. There were four cemetery desecrations, in March and May in Irkutsk, and in June and July in Moscow. Moreover, the synagogue in Novosibirsk was destroyed and the prayer house at a Jewish cemetery in Irkutsk was set alight, both in March 1999; and on 2 and 3 May 1999 the synagogue in Birobidzhan was desecrated. Rabbis were attacked by ruffians in Nizhni Novgorod and Rostow-on-Don in September and October 1998 and an Israeli teacher was attacked in Moscow in November. There were attempts to damage a Jewish school in Nalchik in January 1998 and students were threatened in Moscow in March 1999.

The United States: In 1998, forty-two states and the District of Columbia reported 1,611 anti-Semitic incidents to the ADL, marking an increase of 40 incidents over the 1997 total. This represents a 2.4 percent rise in anti-Jewish activity. Anti-Semitic activity reported in 1998 consisted of acts of harassment (intimidation, threats and assaults) and vandalism (light property damage as well as arson, bombings and cemetery desecrations). As in the past, anti-Semitic acts of harassment, threats or assaults against Jewish individuals or institutions made up more than half of all anti-Jewish activity reported. Over 80 percent of these incidents were directed against individuals, while Jewish institutions were the targets of the remainder. Acts of anti-Semitic vandalism showed a small rise in 1998. ADL recorded a total of 715 incidents of vandalism, compared to 673 in 1997 — an increase of 6 percent. An example was the defacement of two synagogues in California's San Fernando Valley on 30 July, apparently the work of the National Alliance, whose website address was scrawled in red spray paint across an outside wall of the synagogues, along with the words, "Stop murdering the White race." New York, the state with the largest Jewish population, once again recorded the highest number of anti-Semitic acts of any state. New Jersey registered the second highest rate of anti-Semitic activity with 229, a 14 percent increase from the year before. California had 223, up 19 percent from 1997; and Massachusetts recorded 107 incidents, an increase of 7.5 percent.[20]

International: Collectively, "the nations" have been historically anti-Israel. In recent times the almost universal vehemence against the Jewish people and the State of Israel has been inescapably obvious. For example, as previously noted, in the past several years, more than half of the resolutions passed by the United Nations have been pointedly against Israel. Considering the minuscule size of the country and the tiny minority represented by even all 15 million Jews of the world, this truly out of balance world attention is absolutely amazing from any point of view.[21]

Even the International Red Cross has turned against Israel. Following is a synopsis of two recent press releases:

"Red Cross Might *"Include" Israel's Magen David Adom"*

"The United States is urging the inclusion of Israel's humanitarian aid organization Magen David Adom (Red Star of David) into the International Red Cross-Red Crescent movement. With the changing political situation in the Middle East, moves are afoot to enable Israel to join - but not with its choice of symbol.

"Israel has never been officially accepted into the international movement because it did not meet the criteria for its symbol. The symbol of the MDA is the six-pointed star, known as the Star of David. The star also appears on the blue-and-white Israeli flag.

"The State Department announced Monday that the US supports the 'prompt admission' of what it called 'Israel's outstanding national society, the Magen David Adom, into the Red Cross Movement.

" 'We welcome the decision of the Red Cross Movement, to complete the necessary actions by November,' spokesman Richard Boucher told a press briefing, in reaction to last week's decision by the movement to convene a special conference to amend its statutes.

"The conference will follow a scheduled meeting of signatories to the 1949 Geneva Convention, which established the cross and the crescent as sole symbols for the humanitarian aid society worldwide.

"The boycott to date was the result of objections of Moslem nations, as is seen in the United Nations. Israel, for example, is the only UN member nation that can't sit on the Security Council. It's the only nation that belongs to no regional (geographical) grouping at the UN.

"Chris Bowers, spokesman for the International Committee of the Red Cross in Geneva, Switzerland told the media the convention's signatories have proposed a solution to adding a third emblem - probably a red diamond - to the accepted symbols.

"Bowers said it was unlikely that the signatories to the Geneva convention would be willing to accept Israel's red star as a symbol - it requires a two-thirds majority to amend the 1949 convention and the movement's charter.

"'The Red Cross, first adopted in 1863, and the Red Crescent, added in 1876 by the Ottoman Turks, are important emblems enabling humanitarian relief to reach victims while offering the legal protection of the

Geneva Convention to the workers, Bowers said. Adding too many additional symbols, he said, would reduce the symbol's influence and recognition worldwide, he said. However, the ICRC has now "recognized that situation [regarding Israel] is unsatisfactory.'

"Bowers of the ICRC stressed that not being part of the movement had not kept Israel out of the international humanitarian field. 'There has been a lot of close cooperation. MDA is seen as part of the movement [and it does] top notch humanitarian work,' he said.

"Israel is usually among the first countries to offer aid to countries suffering from natural or man-made disasters, and has even been known to offer help to countries like Iran, which considers Israel an archenemy." [22]

In Conclusion: The Super-Natural Root of Christian Anti-Semitism

As earlier noted, there have been a number of "God-incidences" as I have researched and prepared this manuscript. Not the least of these occurred when I found myself tortured over the history and continuing reality of anti-Semitism and was searching for some way to come to grips with the deep set feelings that were beginning to take a serious toll on my Jewish soul with all of its inbred sensitivities.

I don't normally spend much time watching "Christian" television, especially, on Sunday, which is normally a very busy work day. On a recent Sunday, however, it was a different matter. I just happened to take a break from my writing in time to catch the very end of a message being delivered by the well known Pastor Jack Hayford, of the Church on the Way in California. I was so touched by what little I was able to hear that day that I made a major effort to acquire a video tape of the entire message. I offer a brief excerpt to conclude this chapter.

"Israel is God's chosen delivery system for the message of His life, truth and love, and for the gift of His Messiah to mankind: Israel has thus been the focus of Satan's animosity throughout the ages. There is the age long conflict: Satan hates the Jews. He hates mankind in general, but he hates the Jews in particular simply because they were the delivery system of blessing to mankind through which the Messiah came. Three quarters of the Bible came through Jewish agency: as a matter of fact, all but two books of the New Testament were written by men of Jewish heritage.

"Satan hates the Jewish people whether they worship God or not. Anywhere you go on the planet you will find pockets of people hating other people. But there is a common denominator across the planet: there is a global feature of anti-Semitism. Why is it there are people everywhere who hate Jews simply because they are Jews?

"There is a trail of human achievement to the benefit of mankind that has come through the Jews that is staggering in its dimensions if you take the time to assess it all, Jews have been scattered throughout the world in a Diaspora as one of the ways God has blessed humanity! Why do people hate Jews? People everywhere are taught not to like Jews. Hatred of the Jews is woven into the very fabric of mankind. Why?

"There can be no other explanation. Hatred of the Jews is something that is woven into the world's mind by the *deceiver*, the arch enemy, the dragon himself. Anti-Semitism is a supernatural horror, the most terrible manifestation of which occurred during this century in the Holocaust. Nazi hatred transcended ordinary human animosity: it was supernatural.

"Consider the world-wide passivity of the nations who knew what was taking place and who did nothing. No other people on the planet have such a uniform animosity against them. Anti-Semitism is more than a human hatred: it is a *hellish* hatred!"[23]

While Pastor Hayford did not end his message this way, I feel certain he would agree. So deeply is this hellish blind super-natural hatred of the Jews embedded into the collective human mind, that it will not be greatly diminished until at long last the final victory is won: until satan is hurled into the lake of fire, and Yeshua, the Prince of Peace, returns once again to His beloved Israel.

[1] Martin Luther, "On Jews and Their Lies," from the *Luther's Works*, Vol. 47, translated by Martin H. Bertram

[2] Luke 24:27

[3] Sandra S. Williams, "The Origins of Christian Anti-Semitism," Judaic Studies Program, University of Florida, page 11 www.ddi.digital.net

[4] John 10:17-18

[5] Matt. 20:17-19; Mark 10:33; Luke 18:31-33

[6] Article: "Anti-Semitism of the "Church Fathers," www.yashanet.com

[7] Ibid

[8] Ibid

[9] Saint John Chrysostom, "Medieval Sourcebook: Homilies Against the Jews," page 4 of 73, www.fordam.edu

[10] Article: "Anti-Semitism of the "Church Fathers," www.yashanet.com

[11] Ibid

[12] Clarence H. Wagner, Jr., "Christian Anti-Semitism, " *Jerusalem Courier*, Volume 10, No. 4, 1992

[13] Ibid

[14] Ibid

[15] Martin Luther, "On Jews and Their Lies," from the *Luther's Works*, Vol. 47, translated by Martin H. Bertram

[16] Excerpt from "Ad Quaelstiones et Objecta Juaei Cuiusdam Responsio," by John Calvin; The Jew in Christian Theology, Gerhard Falk, McFarland and Company, Inc., Jefferson, NC and London, found at www.yashanet.com

[17] Article: "The Protestant Inquisition ("Reformation" Intolerance and Persecution)" www.ic.net

[18] Semen Markovich, Dubnov , *History of the Jews in Russia and Poland from the Earliest Times Until the Present Day*, quoted by Clarence H. Wagner, Jr., "Christian Anti-Semitism, " *Jerusalem Courier*, Volume 10, No. 4, 1992

[19] Clarence H. Wagner, Jr., "Christian Anti-Semitism, " *Jerusalem Courier*, Volume 10, No. 4, 1992

[20] The Stephen Roth Institute for the Study of Contemporary Anti-Semitism and Racism at Tel Aviv University, "Anti-Semitism Worldwide 1998/9" www.tau.ac.il/Anti-Semitism/annual-report.html

[21] Editorial comment given to the author by Paul Jablonowski, Awareness Ministry (Director Robert Somerville

[22] Two typically anti-Israel "main line" press releases made no mention of the conference in November, nor of the proposed new "red triangle" symbol that would replace the Star of David. They implied that Israel's admission was a "done deal" with no exceptions. The " minor details" to the contrary were taken from the International Christian Embassy Jerusalem News Summary, dated May 19, 2000

[23] Dr. Jack Hayford, The Church on the Way, from a sermon: "The Conflict of the Ages," originally presented in October, 1999 and rebroadcast in the Middle east in April 2000.

Chapter Four

The Continuing Divisive Barriers
The Second Barrier: An Incorrect Understanding of the meaning and continuing applicability of the *Torah*

"Think not that I have come to abolish the Law or the Prophets. I have not come to abolish, but to fulfill. "Amen, I say to you, until heaven and earth pass away, not one yud or one hook will pass away from the Torah, until they all be fulfilled. "And whoever shall abolish one of these least commandments, and shall teach the sons of men so, the same will be called least in the Kingdom of Heaven.
(Matthew 5:15-17- As originally written in Hebrew, from the "Du Tillet Hebrew Matthew")[1]

The misinterpretation of Yeshua's direction regarding the *Torah,* compounded by the misunderstanding of several related Scriptures (Pauline epistles and Hebrews) has been and remains today one of the most highly divisive elements in the Body of Yeshua. These misinterpretations are almost universally embraced by Christendom. They are applied and taught throughout much of the Christian Church, and have even spilled over into the thinking of some sadly misled Messianic Jews. These are the very heart and soul of Replacement Theology and the pernicious substance upon which it feeds.

Before there can be progress in establishing genuine unity within the Body of Yeshua, first, this confusion about the meaning and continuing applicability of the *Torah* must be set right.

Yeshua's teaching on this point is crystal clear, as is the overwhelming body of testimony from all of Scripture. The *Torah* not only continues: Yeshua is its very essence. He is embodied on every page of the Written *Torah*. He is the Living *Torah*.

There is one great and central paradox operating in the very heart of the Body of Yeshua today. It is tearing its members asunder: On one side, the eyes of the Jewish people remain blinded to the Living *Torah*. Only a tiny remnant of Jews have, so far, beheld Him and believed. On the other side, the eyes of Gentile Christians remain blinded to the Written *Torah*. Only a precious few have been able to see Him come to life in the *Elohim* of Genesis 1:1; then move from page to page; from chapter to chapter; from book to book; from Old Covenant to New Covenant, until His great promise at the end: "He who testifies to these things says, "Yes, I am coming soon."

The *Torah*—a Working Definition

Brown-Driver-Briggs, a reliable and authoritative source on Hebrew words used in Scripture, defines *Torah* in two broad categories. Quite significantly the first (preferred meaning) is "instruction, direction (human or divine)." The second is "law." The last listed (least preferred) sub-definition of "law" is the meaning most commonly assigned by the Christian Church: "the Deuteronomic or Mosaic Law."

From the scholarly perspective, as it is widely understood by Christian Church commentators, *Torah* is defined as "the name of the first of the three divisions of the Hebrew canon: *Torah* (Instruction, Direction, Teaching, Law), *Neviim* (Prophets), and *Kethuvim* (Writings). The *Torah*, is comprised of the five books of Moses, which are the mainstay of Judaism.[2]

According to Merrill F. Unger, a highly respected Christian scholar, "The *Torah*, however, came to have a wider meaning among Jews and embraced the whole body of religious literature of Judaism inherited from their prophets, priests, and wise men; i.e., the entire *Tanach* (Old Covenant)."

Many Jewish sources would argue against Unger's inclusion of any sacred writings, other than the "Law" (both the first five books of the Old Covenant and the recorded oral traditions of the rabbis). Specifically, many would not include the *Kethuvim* (writings).

Most however would agree with the Pharisees and rabbis, who recognized an Oral *Torah*, composed of specific applications of the general principles of the written *Torah*."[3] The Oral *Torah*, is still recognized today and embraced as a part of *Torah* by traditional Judaism. Oral *Torah* is, in some sense, a Jewish parallel to the Christian commentators, such as Barnes, Clarke, Wycliffe and a myriad of others who offer their own written interpretations on the meaning of Scripture. The notable difference is that while Christians regard the interpretations of their commentators as advisory and instructive, traditional Judaism regards the Oral *Torah* as having nearly the same weight of authority as the written *Torah*—moreover, Oral *Torah* is generally regarded as an extension of and integrated with the written *Torah*. This belief is based on the understanding that Oral *Torah* was given to Moses by God on Mount Sinai at the same time He gave the written *Torah*, and that this tradition was to be passed along from one generation of rabbis to the next.

Others would argue that the Oral *Torah* was not given to Moses at Mt. Sinai and instead that it was authored by the rabbis beginning in about 70 CE who used it as a basis of their new Rabbinical Judaism.

One problem with Oral *Torah* is that it is forever evolving. The early Oral *Torah*, consisting of the writings of multiple rabbis, is brought together in a large collection of volumes called the *Talmud*. The teachings of the *Talmud* are then synopsized in a much shorter, but still multi-volume collection called the *Mishna*. Since the *Mishna* was compiled, each successive generation of rabbis has added its own layer of teaching and interpretation. The result has been to create in the Oral *Torah*, an extremely complex, sometimes self-contradictory massive set of writings, so minute in detail and meaning that it has become devoid of spiritual meaning and in some cases even completely nullified it.[4]

In the period of the rise of the synagogue (400-168 BCE.), the written *Torah* was divided into sections for systematic public reading. The first five books came to be divided into 290 "open" and 379 "closed" *parasha*. The "open" marked by a *pe* (p) are paragraphs beginning a new line. The "closed" are shorter and are marked by a *samekh* (s) and preceded by a blank space in the line. The *Mishnah* (200 CE) mentions these divisions, which existed earlier. The *Talmud* (500 CE) distinguishes between the open and closed *parasha*. By the time of Christ, the Prophets had been added to the *Torah* lessons for weekly public reading.[5] This same weekly ritual is followed in traditional synagogues throughout the world, as well as in many of the more conservative Messianic Congregations.[6]

Thus, from a Jewish perspective, the *Torah* consists of two parts: written and oral. The written *Torah* consists of (in the extreme position) all of the Old Covenant; more often, the first five books of the Old Covenant, together with all the major and minor prophetical writings of the Old Covenant. The Oral *Torah* consists of the writings of the *Talmud*, and other selected rabbinical writings.

Most Christian theologians view the *Torah* in its more legalistic aspects; i.e., simply as a collection of legal precepts given by God to His Jewish people. Hence, the translation of "law" for *Torah* has come to be its universally understood reference within the Church.

According to the reckoning of the famous Rabbi Rambam (Maimonides,) there are a total of 613 biblical commandments in the first five books of the Old Covenant. These 613 individual precepts and commandments have in turn, traditionally been separated into three kinds: moral, civil and ceremonial. The moral commands are those which have permanent moral value, and are therefore still binding without further discussion. Civil commands which dealt with the regulation of the life of the nation of Israel, and whose applicability to other contemporary nations is arguable, make their applicability today open to considerable discussion. Ceremonial commands deal with specifically Jewish ritual requirements, such as sacrificial procedures which cannot be applied in the absence of a Temple, as well as dietary instructions detailing which foods can and cannot be consumed, along with other related restrictions.

Since, in several cases, there are disagreements concerning into which of the three categories certain precepts should fall, it is not possible to provide a complete, universally accepted breakdown at this level.

Viewed from a more practical perspective, taking into account that there is no standing Temple, from the 613 commandments and precepts, there are a total of 271— 77 Positive ("Thou shall"), and 194 Negative ("Thou shall not") Commandments which, for Jews, are still applicable today and can be obeyed without restriction. Beyond these 271 universally "doable" precepts and commandments there are another 26 that are applicable only to life within the physical Land of Israel. These too can be complied with today without restriction. Imbedded in these is the Decalogue (the Ten Commandments) written on stone tablets by the finger of God. Beyond the Decalogue, there are commandments, and groupings of commandments that would fall into each of the three general categories: moral, civil and ceremonial.

The 271 more universally applicable "doable" precepts and commandments can, by my reckoning, be about equally divided between "moral" and "ceremonial."

What does the Bible Itself Say about the *Torah*?

As earlier noted, the most reliable interpreter of Scripture is Scripture itself. The Bible offers a great wealth of insight into the nature, meaning, purpose and continued applicability of the *Torah*:

● The *Torah* is the "perfect" (inerrant) Word of God

The law of the LORD is perfect, converting the soul; the testimony of the LORD is sure, making wise the simple; The statutes of the LORD are right, rejoicing the heart; the commandment of the LORD is pure, enlightening the eyes--- (Ps 19:7-8)

As for God, His way is perfect; the word of the LORD is proven; he is a shield to all who trust in Him. (Ps 18:30)

But he who looks into the perfect law of liberty and continues in it, and is not a forgetful hearer but a doer of the work, this one will be blessed in what he does. (James 1:25)

● The *Torah* has not been canceled, annulled or replaced: it has been *fulfilled.*

*"For assuredly, I say to you, till heaven and earth pass away, one jot or one tittle will by no means pass from the law till **all** is fulfilled.*
(Matt 5:17-18)

"And it is easier for heaven and earth to pass away than for one tittle of the law to fail." (Luke 16:17)

Then Jesus came from Galilee to John at the Jordan to be baptized by him. And John tried to prevent Him, saying, "I need to be baptized by You, and are You coming to me? But Jesus answered and said to him, "Permit it to be so now, for thus it is fitting for us to fulfill all right-eousness. Then he allowed Him. (Matt 3:13-15)

Do we then make void the law through faith? Certainly not! On the contrary, we establish the law. (Rom 3:31)

It is time for You to act, O LORD, for they have regarded Your law as void. (Ps 119:126)

● The *Torah* was given to Israel

He declares His word to Jacob, his statutes and His judgments to Israel. (Ps 147:19)

"Now, O Israel, listen to the statutes and the judgments which I teach you to observe, that you may live, and go in and possess the land which the LORD God of your fathers is giving you. (Deut 4:1)

"And what great nation is there that has such statutes and righteous judgments as are in all this law which I set before you this day?
(Deut 4:8)

Moses commanded a law for us, a heritage of the congregation of Jacob. (Deut 33:4)

● The *Torah* was given to enrich, teach and correct as a foundation for us to learn more about God, and develop doctrine as a source of patience, comfort and hope.

All Scripture is given by inspiration of God, and is profitable for doctrine, for reproof, for correction, for instruction in righteousness, that the man of God may be complete, (2 Tim 3:16-17)[8]

For whatever things were written before were written for our learning, that we through the patience and comfort of the Scriptures might have hope. (Rom 15:4)

"This Book of the Law shall not depart from your mouth, but you shall meditate in it day and night, that you may observe to do according to all that is written in it. For then you will make your way prosperous, and then you will have good success." (Josh 1:8)

My soul faints for Your salvation, but I hope in Your word. My eyes fail from searching Your word, saying, "When will You comfort me?"——

Oh, how I love Your law! It is my meditation all the day. You, through Your commandments, make me wiser than my enemies; for they are ever with me. I have more understanding than all my teachers, for Your testimonies are my meditation. I understand more than the ancients, because I keep Your precepts. I have restrained my feet from every evil way, that I may keep Your word. I have not departed from Your judgments, for You Yourself have taught me. How sweet are Your words to my taste, sweeter than honey to my mouth! Through Your precepts I get understanding; therefore I hate every false way. (Ps 119:81-82;97-104)

● The *Torah* is a "shadow," foretelling the coming of Yeshua and the salvation made possible through Him.

For the law, having a shadow of the good things to come, and not the very image of the things, can never with these same sacrifices, which they offer continually year by year, make those who approach perfect.
(Heb 10:1)

So let no one judge you in food or in drink, or regarding a festival or a new moon or sabbaths, which are a shadow of things to come, but the substance is of Christ. (Col 2:16-17)

And beginning at Moses and all the Prophets, He expounded to them in all the Scriptures the things concerning Himself. (Luke 24:27)

They said therefore among themselves, "Let us not tear it, but cast lots for it, whose it shall be," that the Scripture might be fulfilled which says: "They divided My garments among them, and for My clothing they cast lots." Therefore the soldiers did these things." (John 19:24)

"You search the Scriptures, for in them you think you have eternal life; and these are they which testify of Me." (John 5:39)

for he vigorously refuted the Jews publicly, showing from the Scriptures that Jesus is the Christ. (Acts 18:28)

For I delivered to you first of all that which I also received: that Christ died for our sins according to the Scriptures, (1 Cor 15:3)

The written *Torah*, in its Broader Sense, together with *the Neviim (Prophets)*, is a Prophetic Window Looking into God's Plan of Redemption for all Mankind

"To Him all the prophets witness that, through His name, whoever believes in Him will receive remission of sins." (Acts 10:43)

God's incredible plan of redemption began in the Garden of Eden when satan realized that there could be enmity between himself and the woman and between his seed and her seed. From these very first thrilling pages of Genesis, the unceasing struggle between good and evil is woven into the fabric of virtually every page of the Old Covenant. The triumph of good over evil in its every shade and level of intensity can be found in these ancient Hebrew writings: His marvelous ministry, His terrible suffering, His journey to the cross, His burial and the ultimate victory in His resurrection. All of this and more shine forth from the *Torah*. There are more than 300 fulfilled prophesies foretelling the life, death and ultimate triumph of Yeshua to be found in these pages. Consider the following small sampling:

Selected Messianic Prophesies in the *Tanach* (Old Covenant) Fulfilled in the New Covenant

"--- the testimony of Jesus is the spirit of prophecy." (Rev 19:10)

The Foretold Event	Prophesied	Fulfilled
Yeshua would be announced to His people 483 years, to the exact day, after the decree to rebuild Jerusalem	Daniel 9:25	John 12:12-13
Yeshua's hands and feet would be pierced	Psalm 22:16	Matt 27:38 Luke 24:40
The Jew's authority to administer capital punishment would be gone when Yeshua arrived	Genesis 49:10	John 18:31
Yeshua would be killed before the destruction of the temple	Daniel 9:26	Matt 27:50-51
Yeshua would be rejected	Isaiah 53:3	Matt 27:21-23
Yeshua would die for the sins of the world	Isaiah 53:8	1 John 2:2
Yeshua would be born of the "seed" of a woman	Genesis 3:15	Luke 1:34-35
Yeshua would be born in Bethlehem	Micah 5:2	Matt 2:1-2
Yeshua would be killed	Daniel 9:26	Matt 27:35
Yeshua would defeat death	Hosea 13:14	1 Cor 15:55-57
Yeshua would be resurrected and crowned as King	Psalm 2:7	Acts 13:30-33

Yeshua would be resurrected	Psalm 16:8-10	Matt 28:6
Others would rise to life at the resurrection of Yeshua	Isaiah 26:19	Matt 27:52-53
Yeshua would ascend into heaven	Daniel 7:13-14	Acts 1:9-11
Yeshua would be at the right hand of God	Psalm 80:17	Acts 5:31
The Jews would have a hardened heart against Yeshua	Isaiah 6:9-10	John 12:37-40
Yeshua would be God	Isaiah 7:14	John 12:45
Yeshua would be a light to the Gentiles	Isaiah 9:1-2	Luke 2:28-32
Yeshua would come for all nations	Genesis 22:18	Gal. 3:14
Yeshua would be from the everlasting (the "Everlasting Father")	Isaiah 9:6	Revelation 1:8

The Second Coming of Yeshua: Foretold in the *Torah*

While there is much fulfilled Messianic prophecy in the Old Covenant, there are also unfulfilled Messianic prophesies in the "Prophets," most notably those that directly relate to His Second coming, commonly referred to in Scripture as "the Day of the Lord."

The Day of the Lord is the protracted period commencing with the second advent of Yeshua in glory and ending with the cleansing of the heavens and the earth by fire preparatory to the new heavens and the new earth of the eternal state. The Day of the Lord thus comprehends specifically the closing phase of the Tribulation and extends through the millennial kingdom. Apocalyptic judgments [9] precede and introduce the Day of the Lord.[10] While there are several New Covenant references[11] to this much anticipated great day, there are also several Old Covenant references, including:

"For behold, I create new heavens and a new earth; and the former shall not be remembered or come to mind. But be glad and rejoice forever in what I create; for behold, I create Jerusalem as a rejoicing, and her people a joy." (Isa 65:17-18)

257

"For as the new heavens and the new earth which I will make shall remain before Me," says the LORD, "So shall your descendants and your name remain. And it shall come to pass that from one New Moon to another, and from one Sabbath to another, all flesh shall come to worship before Me," says the LORD. (Isa 66:22-23)

For I know that my Redeemer lives, and He shall stand at last on the earth; And after my skin is destroyed, this I know, that in my flesh I shall see God, (Job 19:25-26)

The *Torah* Was Never Intended To Provide Or Maintain Salvation For Anyone

Torah is the very heart and soul of the Old Covenant: a detailed revelation of God's plan for the redemption of mankind. *Torah* announces the forthcoming of a New Covenant: the one and only narrow way. *Torah* was the entire Scripture read and studied by Yeshua, long before the New Covenant was written. *Torah* is a heavenly road map pointing the way to a new and better Covenant and through it to our salvation, by His grace, through our faith in Yeshua.

You search the Scriptures, for in them you think you have eternal life; and these are they which testify of Me. But you are not willing to come to Me that you may have life. I do not receive honor from men. But I know you, that you do not have the love of God in you. I have come in My Father's name, and you do not receive Me; if another comes in his own name, him you will receive. How can you believe, who receive honor from one another, and do not seek the honor that comes from the only God? Do not think that I shall accuse you to the Father; there is one who accuses you—Moses, in whom you trust. For if you believed Moses, you would believe Me; for he wrote about Me. But if you do not believe his writings, how will you believe My words? (John 5:39-47)

Jesus said to him, "I am the way, the truth, and the life. No one comes to the Father except through Me. (John 14:6)

Israeli Messianic pastor, Ariel Berkowitz summarizes this vitally important point:

"The Torah of Moshe was never intended to provide or maintain salvation for anyone upon their obedience to it. It is simply not a salvation document. It is true that, if it is understood properly, one can receive

258

knowledge about how to come into a relationship with the Lord by His grace through faith. But God never gave the document to be obeyed for the purpose of granting salvation through its obedience."12

Torah was given by the Very Hand of God to His Jewish People

The Scriptures themselves make it absolutely clear-the *Torah* was given to the Jews:

For what great nation is there that has God so near to it, as the LORD our God is to us, for whatever reason we may call upon Him? And what great nation is there that has such statutes and righteous judgments as are in all this law which I set before you this day? (Deut 4:7-8)

He declares His word to Jacob, his statutes and His judgments to Israel. He has not dealt thus with any nation; and as for His judgments, they have not known them. Praise the LORD! (Ps 147:19-20)

What advantage then has the Jew, or what is the profit of circumcision? Much in every way! Chiefly because to them were committed the oracles of God. (Rom 3:1-2)

Some Interesting Things The Famous Rabbis Said about *Torah*

Rabbi Hillel (the Elder) writing in Jerusalem in 30 BCE:

"What is hateful to you do not do to your neighbor. That is the whole of the *Torah*. The rest is commentary. Go, learn it."13

Note: Yeshua was Himself a learned Rabbi who was fully *Torah* observant. He would have been very closely acquainted with Rabbi Hillel's teachings. There is a remarkable similarity between this teaching of Rabbi Hillel and Yeshua's own:

Jesus said to him," 'You shall love the Lord your God with all your heart, with all your soul, and with all your mind.' "This is the first and great commandment. "And the second is like it: 'You shall love your neighbor as yourself.' "On these two commandments hang all the Law and the Prophets." (Matt 22:37-40)

Rabbi Gamaliel II writing in Jabneh in 90 CE:

"He who gets a good name gets himself substance; he who gets the words of *Torah* gets himself life in the world to come."14

Note: Rabbi Gamaliel would have been well acquainted with Yeshua's teachings as they were being widely disseminated at the time by the Nazarene's. He may well have also studied the *Gospel According to the Hebrews* (Matthew) and perhaps taken more than just a casual notice of its teaching regarding salvation.

Rabbi Akivah (ben Joseph) writing in Jaffa 135 CE:

"You shall love your neighbor as yourself---This is the great principle of the *Torah*."[15]

Note: There is an interesting continuum here. Yeshua was perhaps influenced by the writings of Rabbi Hillel (the Elder) and, perhaps, He in turn influenced the writings of Rabbi Akivah.

My purpose here is to emphasize that the Bible is truly one book, with a *seamless* division between the Old and the New Covenants - its two major sections.

Does the *Torah* Apply to Christians?

The clear granting of the *Torah* to the Jews begs the question: What if anything in the *Torah* is relevant to Christians? The Scriptures cry out in response: Very much indeed!

The *Torah* is regarded as Holy Scripture by virtually all Christendom: Given their historical predilection to distance themselves from everything Jewish, if any branch of the Christian Church were to reject all or part of the very Jewish *Torah*, one would think it would be the Roman Catholics. Not so!

While the Roman Church has, as earlier noted, interjected the false teaching of replacement theology, and made highly significant, self accommodating deletions and additions to the original *Decalogue*, the remainder of the *Torah*, along with the rest of the *Tanach*, has at least, if not altogether spiritually, materially survived to become a part of the body of canonized Scripture. In fact, the Catholics include several Jewish writings which are not included by most Protestants who rather regard them as Apocrypha.

According to the *Catholic Encyclopedia*, the most explicit definition of the Catholic Canon is that given by the Council of Trent, Session IV, 1546. For the Old Testament its catalogue reads as follows:

"The first five books of Moses (Genesis, Exodus, Leviticus, Numbers, Deuteronomy), Josue, Judges, Ruth, the four books of Kings, two of Paralipomenon, the first and second of Esdras (which latter is called

Nehemias), Tobias, Judith, Esther, Job, the Davidic Psalter (in number one hundred and fifty Psalms), Proverbs, Ecclesiastes, the Canticle of Canticles, Wisdom, Ecclesiasticus, Isaias, Jeremias, with Baruch, Ezechiel, Daniel, the twelve minor Prophets (Osee, Joel, Amos, Abdias, Jonas, Micheas, Nahum, Habacue, Sophonias, Aggeus, Zacharias, Malachias), two books of Machabees, the first and second."[16]

The Council of Jerusalem (49 CE): As previously discussed, Paul brought the pressing case in point before James and the other elders in Jerusalem regarding just what specific requirements of *Torah* Gentiles needed to comply with in order to be converted into the Nazarene Sect: more to the point, for them to share in the same born again salvation enjoyed by the ethnically Jewish and fully *Torah* compliant Nazarenes?

Scripture is very clear, and there is no justification here or elsewhere to add to or subtract from what, under the inspiration of the Holy Spirit, the Word says on this critical point. Out of the 613 specific precepts and commandments operative then, while the temple was still standing, and out of the 271 precepts and commandments that can be complied with today, only *four* were *legislated* by the Council as required of Gentiles:

We have therefore sent Judas and Silas, who will also report the same things by word of mouth. For it seemed good to the Holy Spirit, and to us, to lay upon you no greater burden than these necessary things: **that you abstain from: (1) things offered to idols, (2) from blood, (3) from things strangled, and (4) from sexual immorality.** *If you keep yourselves from these, you will do well. Farewell. (Acts 15:27-29, enumeration and emphasis my own)*

These four requirements are in fact taken from the seven part "Law of Noah," as it is recorded in Genesis, and given by God as a universally applicable standard by which all mankind is to live.

"The U.S. Congress officially recognized the Noahide Laws in legislation which was passed by both houses. Congress and the President of the United States, George Bush, indicated in Public Law 102-14, 102nd Congress, that the United States of America was founded upon the Seven Universal Laws of Noah, and that these Laws have been the bedrock of society from the dawn of civilization. They also acknowledged that the Seven Laws of Noah are the foundation upon which civilization stands and that recent weakening of these principles threaten the fabric of civilized society, and that justified preoccupation in educating the Citizens of the United States of America and future generations is needed. For this purpose, this Public Law designated March 26, 1991 as Education Day, U.S.A."[17]

Following is a synopsis of the seven parts:

1. You shall practice equity, establish and promote justice: We are to be fair, just, and equitable in our dealings with others. We are to love our neighbor as ourselves. This law also commands us to translate the ideals of our personal life into the building blocks of society to uphold the other six laws. A robust and healthy legal system results in a society worthy of God's blessings.

2. You shall not commit Idolatry: We are to believe in God, the Supreme Being. To give life meaning, one has to recognize that there is a Supreme Being who created the Universe. This Supreme Being grants us free choice and is aware of all our deeds. What's more, He desires good, despises evil, and rewards and punishes man according to his actions. The idea of a unique God, which implies the worship of Him alone and obedience only to His will, follows from the very revelation of God and His commandments (Gen. 1:1ff).

3. You shall not commit Blasphemy: We are to respect God and not blaspheme His Name. The most natural inclination is to take credit for our success and blame others for failure. Yet blaming people cannot undo what has been done. Rather, it is a selfish act that can only lead to anger, bitterness, and frustration. Blaming or blaspheming God or cursing in His name is a similarly selfish act; yet one with much greater consequences: it undermines the very foundation upon which society stands.

4. You shall not commit Sexual Immorality: We are to respect the family and not commit immoral sexual acts. Man has the choice of being selfish or selfless. The selfish person is never satisfied. Rather his preoccupation with his own desires leads him to self destruct. What is true of man is true of mankind. The story of the creation of woman and the institution of marriage, presented with such solemnity (Gen. 2:22-24), constitutes a quite solid foundation for the prohibition of forbidden relationships, adultery, and unnatural vices by this law. Those nations that have condoned selfish acts such as adultery, homosexuality, sodomy, and incest have never lasted. True happiness comes when one desires to help another. The family unit is the ultimate expression of that desire. In a wholesome family, man's desires find fulfillment, as his selfish inclination

gives way to selfless love.

5. You shall not commit Murder: We are to respect human life. Man was created in the image of God. Therefore human life possesses sanctity. Everything must be done to preserve life and prevent murder and manslaughter. One who attacks a fellow human being is, in essence, attacking the Image of God. The account of the punishment of Cain, Abel's murderer, is clear evidence near the beginning of Genesis that homicide is a punishable crime. The law which condemns him is laterformulated most explicitly in the covenant established with Noah (Gen. 9:5).

6. You shall not commit Theft: We are to respect others' rights not steal. God not only rules the world, He runs it according to His Infinite Wisdom. An attack upon man is, in reality, an attack on the Creator. Man must realize that he cannot succeed by robbing or cheating others. Whatever gains have been made will ultimately be lost. The prohibition of theft exists in embryo in the distinction made by God as sovereign-master of the earthly paradise between what Adam may take and what is forbidden to him (Gen. 2:16-17).

7. You shall not eat the limb torn from a live animal. Flesh with the life of it, the blood of it, you shall not eat: We are to respect all creatures and not eat the flesh of a living animal. We are caretakers of God's creations. As a result, our responsibility extends beyond our family and beyond society, to the entire world. Removing flesh from a live animal shows that we are insensitive to God's creations. Instead, we must always remember who we are and what we must do to as Partners and caretakers of God's laws given to Noah after the flood world. The commandment of not removing flesh from a live animal and eating it extends to not being cruel to animals. We find this law in full in the. (Gen. 9:4)18

Beyond the Law of Noah, from which they were drawn, there is absolutely nothing further in Scripture that directly adds to or detracts from these four specific requirements levied upon Gentiles by the Council of Jerusalem. Even so, a misunderstanding and poor teaching on this point has recently surfaced and seems to be spreading quickly among Messianic Gentiles, especially in the United States. In brief, the new understanding, as it was recently passionately shared with me by two Gentile brothers in Yeshua, is:

"These four commandments legislated by the Council of Jerusalem are *only the beginning*: much of the rest, if not all other precepts and commandments of *Torah* apply to Gentiles as well."

I can find no direct Scriptural support for this position. However, let me quickly add: non-Jewish believers are in no way restricted by the *Torah* itself, or in any other way of which I am aware, from keeping *Torah* to the extent they may choose. Many Messianic Gentiles participate in the Jewish Feasts, and variously in other ways. There is an important distinction here: Gentiles are *not required* to keep *Torah* (except as noted above): they are *permitted* to do so.

The "clients/sojourners" (*gerim*) who dwell among us: The *Torah* establishes the conditions under which certain Gentiles may dwell permanently in the Land of Israel. A "client" was not simply an alien (*nakri*) or a stranger (*zar*). He was a permanent resident, once a citizen of another land, who had moved into his new residence.

My wife, Donna, born a Gentile, and not converted to traditional Judaism is, to my thinking, a special kind *gera* (feminine), special in that she also is officially a citizen of the State of Israel. There are other mixed couples in Israel where the husband is the Gentile and the wife the Jew. These husbands would likewise be *gerim.*

There are certain other Gentiles (married couples and unmarried individuals) who, I believe, are genuinely called by God to dwell in the Land on a permanent basis. These are rare cases indeed, and the "proof" of their calling is in the fact that they are able to remain in the Land through an extremely rare granting of "permanent residency" status by the government.

While some might not agree, I believe that such Christian *"gerim"* are today subject to the *Torah* in the same way as any Jew (traditional and Messianic). The requirements of *Torah* for *gerim* are quite specific and clear. According to Vine's Expository Dictionary:

> "The *ger* was (is) to be treated as an Israelite, being responsible to and protected by the law: 'Hear the causes between your brethren, and judge righteously between every man and his brother, and the stranger that is with him' (Deut. 1:16); 'ye shall therefore keep my statutes and my judgments, and shall not commit any of these abominations; neither any of your own nation, nor any stranger that sojourneth among you' (Lev. 18:26); 'ye shall have one manner of law, as well for the stranger, as for one of your own country: for I am the Lord your God' (Lev. 24:22) The *ger* also enjoyed (may enjoy) the Sabbath rest (Lev. 25:6) and divine protection (Deut. 10:18). God commanded Israel to love the *ger* as himself (Lev. 19:34). The *ger* could (may, optionally) also be circumcised (Exod. 12:48) and (only then) enjoy all the privileges of the true religion: the Passover (Exod. 12:48-49), the Atonement feast (Lev. 16:29), presenting offerings (Lev. 17:8), and all the feasts (Deut. 16:11). However, the *ger* was (is) specifically forbidden to participate in the Passover Feast if he was (is) uncircumcised."[19]

The Alien (*nekar*): As already noted, there are many Christians who quite sincerely have become persuaded that they have been "called home" to Israel. They believe, for a variety of reasons, they are Jewish. Or, if not Jewish, they believe with certainty they *must* be one of a very few Christians who have been called to the Land, even when there is not one shred of evidence to support that they are Jewish, nor anything like an adequate confirmation concerning their call as Gentiles.

I believe these dear brothers and sisters are best categorized as *nekar*: they are, simply, foreign visitors to the Land, most under the authority of a tourist visa valid for 90 days. They should, by all means, be afforded every courtesy but they, with respect to *Torah*, are in no way different from other Christians. I would never deny that a *nekar* may later be called as a *ger*. Surely, some Christians who are called to permanently reside in Israel are unaware of this call until sometime later during their sojourn in The Land.

However, it is with love and deep concern that I must once again reiterate: Having witnessed the heartbreak and genuine tragedy of many Christians who were thus misled, self deluded and/or ill-advised; who nevertheless persisted beyond all reasonableness in pursuing their "calls" to dwell in the Land permanently; to each Christian who may feel a stirring within your spirit, or otherwise perceive what you may believe is His voice, I urge you be *certain* through multiple confirmations from others in prayer.

God's New Covenant with Israel and the "Grafting In" of the "Spiritual Seed of Abraham" to the "Commonwealth of Israel"

While the *Torah* has not been replaced or otherwise abolished, there nevertheless remains all manner of disagreement concerning several basic issues, not the least of which is: to what degree, if any, do Christians fall under its authority? The answer, as all answers, shines forth from the Word itself: it is the essence of New Covenant theology.

> *For this reason I, Paul, the prisoner of Christ Jesus for the sake of you Gentiles—Surely you have heard about the administration of God's grace that was given to me for you, that is, the mystery made known to me by revelation, as I have already written briefly. In reading this, then, you will be able to understand my insight into the mystery of Christ, which was not made known to men in other generations as it has now been revealed by the Spirit to God's holy apostles and prophets. This mystery is that through the gospel the Gentiles are heirs together with Israel, members together of one body, and sharers together in the*

265

promise in Christ Jesus. (Eph 3:1-6 NIV)

The New Covenant: There is, I believe, a common misconception among believers that the two principle Covenants, Old and New, between God and His people, are separable along both dispensational and ethnic lines. Some might offer a quick definition that the Old Covenant begins with Genesis, ends with Malacahi, and has as its central feature an agreement between YHWH and the Nation of Israel whose central feature is works righteousness. The New Covenant, they might continue in the same vain, begins with Matthew, ends with the Revelation and has to do with an agreement between Yeshua and the Christian Church that is based on salvation through grace. Although the Old Covenant, in my view, is cover to cover all about Yeshua, the foregoing summary of its two major themes: the covenant relationship between YHWH and the Jewish people; and, "works righteousness" is essentially correct. The understanding concerning the New Covenant is not. Once more, Scripture interprets itself:

Behold, the days are coming, says the LORD, when I will make a new covenant with the house of Israel and with the house of Judah—not according to the covenant that I made with their fathers in the day that I took them by the hand to lead them out of the land of Egypt, My covenant which they broke, though I was a husband to them, says the LORD. But this is the covenant that I will make with the house of Israel after those days, says the LORD: I will put My law in their minds, and write it on their hearts; and I will be their God, and they shall be My people. (Jer 31:31-33)

I will give you a new heart and put a new spirit within you; I will take the heart of stone out of your flesh and give you a heart of flesh. I will put My Spirit within you and cause you to walk in My statutes, and you will keep My judgments and do them. Then you shall dwell in the land that I gave to your fathers; you shall be My people, and I will be your God. (Ezek 36:26-28)

For you have not come to the mountain that may be touched and that burned with fire, and to blackness and darkness and tempest, and the sound of a trumpet and the voice of words, so that those who heard it begged that the word should not be spoken to them anymore. (For they could not endure what was commanded: "And if so much as a beast touches the mountain, it shall be stoned or shot with an arrow. And so terrifying was the sight that Moses said, "I am exceedingly afraid and trembling.") But you have come to Mount Zion and to the city of the living God, the heavenly Jerusalem, to an innumerable company of angels,

266

to the general assembly and church of the firstborn who are registered in heaven, to God the Judge of all, to the spirits of just men made perfect, to Jesus the Mediator of the new covenant, and to the blood of sprinkling that speaks better things than that of Abel. (Heb 12:18-24)

Then He took the cup, and gave thanks, and gave it to them, saying, "Drink from it, all of you. "For this is My blood of the new covenant, which is shed for many for the remission of sins. (Matt 26:27-28)

From these four passages of Scripture, can be drawn the following straightforward conclusions about the New Covenant:

● Like the Old Covenant, the New is an agreement between God and the Nation of Israel: not between God and the Christian Church. The Old was mediated by Moses: the New continues to be mediated by Yeshua Himself.

● Yeshua first manifested Himself to the Jewish people, specifically to a Sect who called themselves Nazarenes. Both the Old and New covenants are firmly rooted in the spiritually rich soil of Jerusalem: neither, most assuredly has anything whatsoever to do with Rome.

● Like the Old Covenant, the New begins (figuratively) with Genesis, and it continues on all the way through Revelation. The Prophet Jeremiah wrote down his words from the Lord sometime between 629 and 586 BCE. Most New Testament Scripture was written some 400 years later during a thirty year window that began in about 50 CE. Hebrews was written about 70 CE. Therefore, The "Law" Jeremiah foresaw as being put by God in the minds of men and written by Him on their hearts most assuredly, as the Hebrew word used confirms, was the *Torah*, and it also most likely included a prophetic vision of the New Testament writings that would be recorded several hundred years later.

● Both Yeshua and the writer of Hebrews were talking, at least prophetically, about all sixty-six books of Scripture: or, at the very least the five books of *Torah* and that portion of the New Testament writings that deal specifically with Yeshua's *fulfillment* of the 613 original precepts and commandments of *Torah*.

● The Old Covenant is the promise of redemption through Yeshua *revealed*: the New Covenant is redemption through Yeshua *fulfilled*. There is a "seamless" progression from Old to New. Together, they are a Divine unity: this is what YHWH has placed in our minds and written upon our hearts.

● The New Covenant is a mirror image of the Old. Virtually every precept and commandment of Yeshua has its roots in the *Torah* studies Yeshua did at the feet of the Rabbis. To list them all would fill a huge volume. Following is a small sampling from the Gospel According to Matthew:

Matthew		Old Covenant	
3:15	"Let it be so now; it is proper to do this to fulfill all righteousness"	All	Yeshua refers to all *Torah* precepts and commandments.
5:21	"You have heard that it was said to those of old, 'You shall not murder,' and whoever murders will be in danger of the judgment."	Ex 21:13	"You shall not murder."
5:33	"Again you have heard that it was said to those of old, 'You shall not swear falsely, but shall perform your oaths to the Lord.'	Lev 19:12	"And you shall not swear by My name falsely, nor shall you profane the name of your God: I am the LORD."
10:19	"But when they deliver you up, do not worry about how or what you should speak. For it will be given to you in that hour what you should speak;	Ex 4:12	"Now therefore, go, and I will be with your mouth and teach you what you shall say."
11:28	"Come to Me, all you who labor and are heavy laden, and I will give you rest.	Ex 33:14	And He said, "My Presence will go with you, and I will give you rest."
15:4	"For God commanded, saying, 'Honor your father and your mother'; and, 'He who curses father or mother, let him be put to death.'	Dt. 5:16	'Honor your father and your mother, as the LORD your God has commanded you, that your days may be long, and that it may be well with you in the land which the LORD your God is giving you.

18:10	"Take heed that you do not despise one of these little ones, for I say to you that in heaven their angels always see the face of My Father who is in heaven.	Gen 48:16	"The Angel who has redeemed me from all evil, bless the lads; let my name be named upon them, and the name of my fathers Abraham and Isaac; and let them grow into a multitude in the midst of the earth."
18:16	"But if he will not hear, take with you one or two more, that 'by the mouth of two or three witnesses every word may be established.'	Nu 35:30	'Whoever kills a person, the murderer shall be put to death on the testimony of witnesses; but one witness is not sufficient testimony against a person for the death penalty.
18:22	Jesus said to him, "I do not say to you, up to seven times, but up to seventy times seven.	Gen 4:24	"If Cain shall be avenged sevenfold, then Lamech seventy-sevenfold."
19:17	So He said to him, "Why do you call Me good? No one is good but One, that is, God. But if you want to enter into life, keep the commandments."	Lev 18:5	'You shall therefore keep My statutes and My judgments, which if a man does, he shall live by them: I am the LORD.
22:32	'I am the God of Abraham, the God of Isaac, and the God of Jacob'? God is not the God of the dead, but of the living."	Ex 3:6	Moreover He said, "I am the God of your father—the God of Abraham, the God of Isaac, and the God of Jacob." And Moses hid his face, for he was afraid to look upon God.
23:5	"But all their works they do to be seen by men. They make their phylacteries broad and enlarge the borders of their garments.	Dt 6:8	"You shall bind them as a sign on your hand, and they shall be as frontlets between your eyes.

23:19	"Fools and blind! For which is greater, the gift or the altar that sanctifies the gift? "Fools and blind! For which is greater, the gift or the altar that sanctifies the gift?	Ex 29:37	"Seven days you shall make atonement for the altar and sanctify it. And the altar shall be most holy. Whatever touches the altar must be holy.
24:37	"But as the days of Noah were, so also will the coming of the Son of Man be.	Gen 6:5	Then the LORD saw that the wickedness of man was great in the earth, and that every intent of the thoughts of his heart was only evil continually.

Christian "Branches" are "Grafted In" among "Natural Jewish Branches" so they may be Nourished by their Common Jewish Root, Yeshua: the Living Fulfilled Promise of the New Covenant

For if the first fruit is holy, the lump is also holy; and if the root is holy, so are the branches. And if some of the branches were broken off, and you, being a wild olive tree, were grafted in among them, and with them became a partaker of the root and fatness of the olive tree, do not boast against the branches. But if you do boast, remember that you do not support the root, but the root supports you. You will say then, "Branches were broken off that I might be grafted in." Well said. Because of unbelief they were broken off, and you stand by faith. Do not be haughty, but fear. For if God did not spare the natural branches, He may not spare you either. (Rom 11:16-21)

Some forty years ago, when Donna and I were newlyweds, we rented a small, unpretentious house in Lakewood, Washington, near McChord Air Force Base where I was stationed. We lived there for two of our many wonderful Air Force years.

Lieutenants in those days received precious little compensation: we could scarcely afford to pay our rent, budget for food and meet the ever growing needs of our rapidly expanding family, that within less than these two years had already grown by two precious infant daughters.

It was because of these pressing budgetary problems that we were very grateful for the truly amazing plum tree that flourished in our front yard. This was far from an ordinary fruit tree. It grew from an "Italian Prune" stock: its roots and trunk were clearly "Italian Prune" as were about one third of its thus "natural" branches. There were two grafts about mid-way up the trunk, both from distinctly different varietal scions: one "Green Gage," the other "Santa Rosa."

During our stay, this truly wonderful tree produced two successive bumper crops of three distinctly different varietal plums, each "according to its own kind." Like the fruit they produced, the natural branches and the grafted in branches each had its own distinctly different bark and foliage: yet all three were equally nourished by the same natural root.

We've never seen another tree anything like this one: what a perfect illustration it provided of Yeshua's fulfillment of YHWH's wonderful plan of redemption:

- The roots, the trunk and the natural branches represent the essence of the Nation of Israel and everything Jewish.

- The natural, nourishing sap flowing from the roots, up through the trunk and equally into all the branches represents God's unfailing love in the New Covenant promise of salvation as it is fulfilled in Yeshua.

- The fruit produced by the natural branches represents all Jews who have been born again in Yeshua.

- The fruit produced by the two grafted in varieties, each distinctly different from the other as well as from the natural fruit, represents the many distinctly different denominations of Christianity as well as the generous harvest of redeemed, born again adherents they individually and collectively produce. While the fruit born on the grafted in branches may differ from one branch to another, and all such grafted in fruit may differ from the natural fruit, all of the fruit share two things in common: they came forth from the same tree, and are nourished by the same roots.

Messianic Jews and Gentile Christians are both the "Spiritual Seed of Abraham"

But it is not that the word of God has taken no effect. For they are not all Israel who are of Israel, nor are they all children because they are the seed of Abraham; but, "In Isaac your seed shall be called." That is, those who are the children of the flesh, these are not the children of

271

God; but the children of the promise are counted as the seed. For this is the word of promise: "At this time I will come and Sarah shall have a son." And not only this, but when Rebecca also had conceived by one man, even by our father Isaac (for the children not yet being born, nor having done any good or evil, that the purpose of God according to election might stand, not of works but of Him who calls), it was said to her, "The older shall serve the younger." As it is written, "Jacob I have loved, but Esau I have hated." (Rom 9:6-13)

The metaphorical "Seed of Abraham," I believe, is not properly understood by some Church commentators. A proper exegesis of this particular Scripture is central to understanding relationships: not just between Traditional Jews, Messianic Jews and Christians, but between these three groups and many Muslims (Arabs) as well.

● The "Children of the Flesh" surely refers to Ishmael, Abraham's son born of Hagar, Sari's Egyptian maid, and his many Arab descendants.

● Ishmael's half-brother, Isaac, was conceived by Sari through the supernatural intervention of YHWH. Isaac, therefore was established in the line from which would descend Yeshua and all natural "Children of the Promise."

● Isaac's sons, Jacob and Esau, were to have remarkably different destinies. Esau, who sold his birth right, was, thereafter, hated by God. It was through his brother Jacob, later named *Israel* by God, from whom are descended all natural "Children of the Promise." Esau's descendants are still numbered among the natural enemies of the Nation of Israel.

● Jews in the natural who are "born again" are "partakers of the promise" and as such are "*Spiritual* Seeds of Abraham." The distinction here is that all Jews and many Arabs are in any case also "*Natural* Seeds of Abraham."

● "Born again" Christians are grafted in to this same promise through the New Covenant and are, therefore, also "partakers of the promise" and the "*Spiritual* Seed of Abraham." "--- *that the Gentiles should be fellow heirs, of the same body, and partakers of His promise in Christ through the gospel,* (Eph 3:6)

Together, the "Spiritual Seed of Abraham," Jews and Gentiles alike, are the citizenry of the "Commonwealth of Israel."

Therefore remember that you, once Gentiles in the flesh—who are called Uncircumcision by what is called the Circumcision made in the flesh by hands—that at that time you were without Christ, being aliens

272

from the commonwealth of Israel and strangers from the covenants of promise, having no hope and without God in the world. (Eph 2:11-12)

Please forgive me if I seem to belabor the following essential point:

- The "Spiritual Seed of Abraham" is an entirely spiritual metaphorical appellation: it has nothing whatsoever to do with ethnicity. Ethnically Jewish "Spiritual Seed of Abraham" remain, in the natural, ethnic Jews. Likewise, ethnically Gentile "Spiritual Seed of Abraham" remain, in the natural, ethnic Gentiles.

- "Citizenship" in the "Commonwealth of Israel" is also entirely metaphoric: it in no way carries with it any entitlement, whatsoever, to citizenship in the modern day, physical State of Israel. Jewish and Gentile citizens of the "Commonwealth of Israel" will, most likely on earth, during the millennium, and certainly in Heaven, in another dispensation, cease to be distinguishable from one another as ethnic Jew and ethnic Gentile. Only then, I believe, will they become "One New Man."

What about those "Troublesome" Passages in Paul's Epistles and Hebrews?

There are several Scriptures often used as "proof texts" by the replacement theologists to make their point that the *Torah* has been entirely abolished; the Church has replaced Biblical Israel, and all "true" Gentile believers have become the "true Jews," who are collectively the "True Israel," hence the State of Israel and all Jews in the flesh are irrelevant, etc.

What Paul and the writer of Hebrews really said with respect to the *Torah* is, I believe, quite different from the "replacement" position. The substance of this present chapter up to now has been focused on making this point without getting into a tedious Scripture by Scripture argument: albeit, the relevant Body of Scripture, in my view overwhelmingly demonstrates the continuing vitality and applicability of the *Torah*.

Going right to the heart of the matter, the many references Paul and the writer of Hebrews made concerning the relationship between the Old and the New Covenants and the continuing applicability of the *Torah* can be summed up quite simply:

The New Covenant is the fulfillment of the Old Covenant's promise of redemption in Messiah Yeshua whose once and for all redeeming self sacrifice superseded the sacrificial system of works (Torah/Old

273

Covenant) and thereby negated the requirement for a Temple and its Aaronic priesthood. The Torah remains "holy, just and good." It has not been annulled or canceled but rather upheld, renewed and "upgraded."

As a basis for further study, following are four sub-statements that together encompass all or at least most of the many points Paul and the writer of Hebrews made concerning this centrally important issue:

What Paul and the Writer of Hebrews Taught about the Continuing Relationship between the Old and New Covenants	References
The New Covenant (Messianic Covenant of Grace) replaced the sacrificial works righteousness system of the Mosaic Law (or the Levitical priesthood regulations), while being the fulfillment of the Messianic promise given to the Jews and Gentiles through Abraham. Yeshua said, "I come not to destroy the Law---." It was the sacrificial system and Aaronic Priesthood, not the *Torah* in its entirety that faded away ("soon disappeared") through Yeshua's once and for all sacrifice.	Rom 11:6; 2 Cor 3:11-14; Gal 3:15-17; Heb 7:11-18; Heb 8: 4-6, 13; Heb 10:1-4, 12
To be under the Law is to be under its curse to believe that one can affect his own salvation through good works. Through the New Covenant, the Spirit brings repentance and faith to the heart, and the redeemed is able to confess that his salvation was made possible by grace to have faith in the gospel of Yeshua.	Rom 3:19-24; Rom 6:14; Rom 7:4-6,25; Rom 10:4-9; Gal 3:1-5, 10-13; Gal 5:3-5; Eph 2:14-15
The *Torah* is "holy, and the commandments holy and just and good." "The Law is spiritual." The *Torah* is not made void through faith: on the contrary, faith establishes the *Torah*.	Rom 3:31; Rom 7:7, 12, 14; Gal 3:21; 1 Tim1:8
Not all Jews (circumcised in the flesh) are saved just because they are Jews. Circumcised in the flesh Jews and uncircumcised in the flesh Gentiles are saved in the same way through Yeshua's fulfillment of the New Covenant promise, wherein their hearts have become circumcised. With respect to salvation through grace by faith, there are no differences between Jews and Gentiles.	Rom 2:25-29; Rom 10:12-13; Gal 2:16, 19 Gal 3:7; Eph 2:11-14 Col 3:11 Heb 8:10; Heb 10:16

Summing Up: Two More Points to Ponder

My prayerful hope and expectation is that by now even the most entrenched proponent of replacement theology has succumbed to what seems to me to be an inarguably solid case on the basis of Scriptural evidence alone.

Even so, I offer two more, what I believe are solid proofs, just in case there may still be some who hesitate to believe that Yeshua meant exactly what He said when He proclaimed: "Think not that I have come to abolish the *Torah* or the Prophets, I have not come to abolish, but to ***fulfill***."(Matt 5:17 from "DuTillet" Hebrew Matthew written in original Hebrew.)

Point One: The True Meaning of the Key Hebrew Word

The "DuTillet" Hebrew Matthew is probably the most significant Biblical translation enhancement in many centuries. Before "DuTillet" became available, our study baseline language for all New Covenant writings was Greek. This was fine for those writings which were originally rendered in Greek, but for those, like the *Gospel According to Matthew*, that were originally rendered in Hebrew, the interim translation into Greek introduced all manner of opportunity for translation error.

The key word in point in Matt: 5:17 is *male'* (Strongs #4390), "to fill, fulfill, overflow, ordain, endow." This verb occurs in all Semitic languages (including biblical Aramaic) and in all periods. Biblical Hebrew attests it about 250 times.

Basically, *male'* means "to be full" in the sense of having something done to one. In 2 Kings 4:6, the word implies "to fill up": "And it came to pass, when the vessels were full, that she said...." The verb is sometimes used figuratively as in Gen. 6:13, when God noted that "the earth is filled with violence."

Used transitively, this verb means the act or state of "filling something." In Gen. 1:22 (the first occurrence of the word), God told the sea creatures to "penetrate" the waters thoroughly but not exhaustively: "Be fruitful, and multiply, and fill the waters in the seas." *Male'* can also mean "to fill up" in an exhaustive sense: "...and the glory of the Lord filled the tabernacle" (Exod. 40:34). In this sense an appetite can be "filled up," "satiated," or "satisfied."

Male' is sometimes used in the sense "coming to an end" in the sense of being "filled up." or "to be filled up," to the full extent of what is expected. ***Male' never means to abolish or replace.*** [20]

Hence, Yeshua's intended meaning here seems very certain. He had come

to fulfill the destiny of the *Torah*, to bring it to fruition, to complete its meaning by His own example. By no means did He come to abolish, delete or otherwise obliterate even "one *yod* or one *hook---*." I can't imagine how He could
have made Himself any clearer on this point. Nor can C.J. Koster who offers
his own summary on the matter from a Greek language perspective:

> "This word 'complete' or 'fill'---has different meanings when used fig-
> uratively. *The New English Bible*, the *Modern Language Bible (New
> Berkeley Version)*, Ferrar Fenton's *The Complete Bible in Modern
> English*, *The Jerusalem Bible*, as well the Dutch Canisius Translation,
> all render this word *pleroo* or *plerosai* in Matt 5:17 as to 'complete
> them.' this word *pleroo* or *plerosai* cannot mean "annul" or "abolish"
> here in verse 17, because then Yeshua would have contradicted
> Himself in one and the same verse. Secondly, this same word *plerosai*
> is used in Matt 3:15 and Col 1:25 where it would be preposterous to
> even suggest a meaning of "annul" or 'abolish.'"[21]

Point Two: The Chronology of the Epistles and the Book of Acts

The Pauline Epistles that make reference to the continued viability of the
Torah were written by the Apostle between 53 and 60 CE. Hebrews was written near 70 CE. The earliest date proposed for the writing of the Book of Acts
is 63 CE: most scholars suggest it was probably written in 70 or even later.[22]

In any event, the salient point is that Acts was written well after all of the
relevant Pauline Epistles and Hebrews that have been interpreted by replacement theologists to mean that the *Torah* had been abolished by Yeshua, etc.

In Acts, Chapter 21, we see Paul being admonished by the Council of
Jerusalem who boast to him about " how many myriads of Jews there are who
have believed, and they are all zealous for the law (*Torah*)." Paul was then
instructed to prove to all that he was *Torah* observant by underwriting and
facilitating the taking of the Nazarite vow by four men among them (an act prescribed by the *Torah*).

> *And when we had come to Jerusalem, the brethren received us gladly.
> On the following day Paul went in with us to James, and all the elders
> were present. When he had greeted them, he told in detail those things
> which God had done among the Gentiles through his ministry. And
> when they heard it, they glorified the Lord. And they said to him,* **You
> see, brother, how many myriads of Jews there are who have believed,
> and they are all zealous for the law;** *but they have been informed
> about you that you teach all the Jews who are among the Gentiles to
> forsake Moses, saying that they ought not to circumcise their children*

276

nor to walk according to the customs. What then? The assembly must certainly meet, for they will hear that you have come. Therefore do what we tell you: **We have four men who have taken a vow. Take them and be purified with them, and pay their expenses so that they may shave their heads, and that all may know that those things of which they were informed concerning you are nothing, but that you yourself also walk orderly and keep the law.** *But concerning the Gentiles who believe, we have written and decided that they should observe no such thing, except that they should keep themselves from things offered to idols, from blood, from things strangled, and from sexual immorality. Then Paul took the men, and the next day, having been purified with them, entered the temple to announce the expiration of the days of purification, at which time an offering should be made for each one of them.*(Acts 21:17-26)

If the *Torah* had been abolished or replaced, as some suggest Paul and the writer of Hebrews taught, then the enthusiastic statement made some years later by the Council of Jerusalem boasting about the myriads of *Torah* observant Jewish new believers, as well as Paul's demonstration that he was then *Torah* observant makes no sense at all.

Obviously there can be only one conclusion. Paul and the writer of Hebrews were not teaching according to the interpretation of the replacement theologists. The *Torah* was, is, and ever more shall be the living Word of God.

---

[1] "The DuTillet version of Matthew is taken from a Hebrew manuscript of Matthew which was confiscated from Jews in Rome in 1553. On August 12th, 1553, at the petition of Pietro, Cardinal Caraffa, the Inquisitor General, Pope Julius III signed a decree banning the Talmud in Rome. The decree was executed on September 9th (Rosh HaShanna) and anything that looked like the Talmud, that is, anything written in Hebrew characters was confiscated as the Jewish homes and synagogues were ravished. Jean DuTillet, Bishop of Brieu, Fance was visiting Rome at the time. DuTillet was astonished to take notice of a Hebrew manuscript of Matthew among the other Hebrew manuscripts. DuTillet acquired the manuscript and returned to France, depositing it in the Biblioteque Nationale, Paris. It remains there to this day as Hebrew ms. No. 132." From: Hugh Sconfield *An Old Hebrew Text of St. Matthew's Gospel*, quoted by James Trimm, translator of *"DuTillet" Hebrew Matthew*, Society for the Advancement of Nazarene Judaism, page 1.

[2] Unger's Bible Dictionary, *"Torah."*

[3] Ibid

[4] For example, see: Matt. 15:2; Mark 7:8,18; and, Col. 2:8

[5] Luke 4:16-21

[6] Unger's Bible Dictionary, *"Torah"*

[7] Jamieson, Fausset, and Brown offer an incisive commentary on Matthew 3:15. They say in part: "[To

fulfill all righteousness], [*pasan* (grk 3956) *dikaiosuneen* (grk 1343)]. If this be rendered, with Scrivener, 'every ordinance, ' or, with Campbell, 'every institution, the meaning is obvious enough; and the same sense is brought out by "all righteousness," or compliance with everything enjoined, baptism included. Indeed, if this be the meaning---the import of Circumcision and of Baptism seems to be radically the same.--- He (Our Lord) would seem to have said, 'Thus do I impledge myself to the whole righteousness of the Law--- thus symbolically do enter on and engage to fulfill it all.---." While Yeshua has already ful-filled much of the *Torah*, still much remains to be fulfilled by Him, such as His second coming and the end of the Age.

[8] To those who hold that this reference is from the New Covenant and therefore not applicable to the *Torah*, may they be reminded that there was no written New Covenant at the time Paul wrote this epistle: he clearly had to be referring exclusively to the *Torah*.

[9] Rev. 4:1-19:6

[10] New Unger's Bible Dictionary, "Day of the Lord."

[11] 2 Thes. 2:2; 2 Pet. 3:13; Rev. 21:1

[12] Ariel and D'vorah Berkowitz, *Torah Rediscovered*, page 54

[13] Rabbi Hillel (the Elder), *Babylonian Talmud*, Shabbath 31a

[14] Rabbi Gamliel II, *Mishna*, Aboth 2.4, 7

[15] Rabbi Akivah (ben Joseph), *Midrash*, Siphra 19.28 (89a)

[16] The Catholic Encyclopedia, "Old Testament Canon."

[17] Article: *Comments Concerning the Noachide Law, the Mosaic Law, Judaism and Christianity*, found at: www.auburn.edu

[18] Article: "Comments Concerning the Noachide Law, the Mosaic Law ,Judaism and Christianity," www.auburn.edu

[19] Vine's Expository Dictionary, "Ger"

[20] Nelson's Expository Dictionary of the Old Testament, "*Male'* "

[21] C.J. Koster, *Come Out of Her My People*, page10

[22] *The NIV Study Bible*, From Introductions to the various referenced New Testament Books

Chapter Five

Cleaning Out the Closet
A Rationale Approach to De-Romanizing the Body of Yeshua
and a Balanced Return to the Jewish Roots of the Christian Church

And I heard another voice from heaven saying, "Come out of her, my people, lest you share in her sins, and lest you receive of her plagues. For her sins have reached to heaven, and God has remembered her iniquities. Render to her just as she rendered to you, and repay her double according to her works; in the cup which she has mixed, mix double for her. In the measure that she glorified herself and lived luxuriously, in the same measure give her torment and sorrow; for she says in her heart, I sit as queen, and am no widow, and will not see sorrow. Therefore her plagues will come in one day—death and mourning and famine. And she will be utterly burned with fire, for strong is the Lord God who judges her. The kings of the earth who committed fornication and lived luxuriously with her will weep and lament for her, when they see the smoke of her burning, standing at a distance for fear of her torment, saying, Alas, alas, that great city Babylon, that mighty city! For in one hour your judgment has come. (Rev 18:4-10)

Since I began writing this book some eight months ago, I have become increasingly aware of the fast growing "Return to the Jewish Roots" movement within the Christian Church.

It is difficult to assign any one event as the beginning of this movement, since it really is nothing more than a recognition of Messianic Jewish orientations by the broader Body of Protestantism as well as by a growing number of Charismatic Roman Catholics.

If there is a "textbook" for those who seek to learn more about the pagan roots of the Church, it is to be found in the important work of Dr. C.J. Koster, originally published in 1986 with the title "The Final Reformation." The book was updated and republished in 1996 under the new title, "Come Out of Her My People."

I am also delighted that there are at least several ministries in the United States, and hopefully others elsewhere, that have adopted returning to the Jewish roots of the Church as their central focus. Two such focused ministries are Barbara Richmond's "For His Glory," Woodland Park, Colorado, and Robert S. Somerville's "Awareness Ministry," Huntsville, Alabama.

Just this morning, as I was preparing to begin work on this final chapter, I was blessed with yet another "Godincidence" as Donna excitedly directed my attention to Messianic Jewish Evangelist Sid Roth's June 2000 edition of "Messianic Vision."

Sid, whose anointed ministry is bringing many thousands of Jews to the Lord, devoted this entire edition to the Return to the Jewish Roots theme.

In my spirit, I am certain that all this suddenly implemented and quickly increasing focus is not just a series of coincidences: rather this is a very deliberate campaign orchestrated by the Holy Spirit to put into the minds and write upon the hearts of all Christians the compelling message, "Come out of her, my people."

I am, by no means, advocating that all Christians abandon their various denominational churches in droves. I *am* advocating that every Church leader and every believer very carefully examine the position of his denomination, home church, and the very personal position of his own heart on a number of related points, all of which are constituent parts of the same central "Return to the Jewish Roots" theme.

My prayerful hope and expectation would be that through such self evaluation, individual believers, home churches, and even entire denominations would recognize any apostasy in their current walks, repent, and then restore themselves to their deeply sacred Jewish roots on Mount Zion.

Should individual believers, through this self evaluation, succeed in finding the Jewish origins of their faith, but their home church not so succeed and absolutely refuse to make any further effort in this direction, it is only then, and with great reluctance, that I would suggest, as a very last resort, moving to another church, or even to a different denomination.

Certainly, as already noted, many members of the more liberal denominations are already leaving their home churches and denominations as if they were Christian soldiers taking part in a massive retreat of God's mighty army. While many of these formerly disenchanted believers have found the joy of discovering the Jewish roots of their faith within the rapidly expanding Messianic Jewish movement, I hesitate to recommend this approach as a solution of first choice. **It is a far better thing to restore and rehabilitate than to precipitously abandon a home church or a denomination.**

As the *modes operandi* for such a self evaluation by all Christians I would propose the following program.

Replacement Theology: As a starting point, determine your own current position on the relationship of the Church to Israel. If you retain even the slightest inclination that the Church has in anyway replaced Israel, or that you as a believer have in anyway thus become an ethnic Jew, then stop right there: pray for the truth to be revealed, and you can be certain it will. Then, repent: continue your quest only after you have finally set aside all such false notions.

Talk to your pastor and determine his position as well as the position of your denomination on this seldom discussed by centrally important issue. If even the slightest holding of "replacement" comes forth from such an interface, then dig in and do what you can to bring about change. Pray with your pastor. Share the book you are holding in your hands with him. If for some good reason you can't do so and/or honestly can't afford to buy a copy for this purpose, please write to me about your particular situation so we here in Israel can pray about it too. Also, please include your pastor's name and address and, as the Lord may lead, I will send him a copy personally. I would also suggest that you either give or share with him a copy of Dr. Koster's *Come Out of Her My People*.

Anti-Semitism: Examine your own heart carefully. If you, as certainly many Christians will, find even the slightest lingering anti-Jewish sentiment, then bath these feelings in the cleansing *mikvah* of repentance and prayer, until at last this stain is finally removed.

Determine the position of your pastor and your denomination with respect to Jews, Israel and all other things Jewish. If you find anything anti-Semitic, then attack it head-on: don't relent until you have either succeeded or see that there is no way possible for you alone to do so.

If, even then, such anti-Semitic sentiments linger, only then will you have no alternative but to find someplace else to worship.

Sunday "Lord's Day" Worship: Certainly, in a way, the entire structure of Western civilization revolves around the scheme of Sunday being set aside for Christian worship and/or recreation. It doesn't seem to matter that "Sun-Day" is not in any way justified by Scripture, but is rather a pagan festival, instituted as a day of worship by Constantine.

I am by no means suggesting that Christians should not worship on Sunday. Looking at the example of the Nazarenes, it is appropriate to worship on *any* day of the week. Nor, am I necessarily suggesting that *Shabbat* is the most appropriate day for Church worship. God created *Shabbat* as a day of rest, not necessarily as a day for scurrying about, getting the kids dressed in their best attire, then rushing to get them to Junior Church on time so that you, their parents, can finally collapse in a pew for a time of worship and be at oneness with the Lord.

What I *am* suggesting is that every Christian make an honest effort to keep the *Shabbat* rest as it was first given by YHWH to His Jewish people. Try devoting the day to wholesome family time, be bold enough to experiment with such things as home worship and home communion. You might even try singing praise songs together as a family. But, don't make a religion out of all this: first and foremost, remember to *rest* in Him. I can guarantee from our own personal experience, and the experience of others: if you give even some of these suggestions an honest try for a few weeks, *Shabbat* will become the highlight of all your future weeks. It will heal and restore: it will bring you together as a family in wonderful ways you have either forgotten, or never knew existed. In the words of my delightful, long gone, Yiddish accented Grandmother, Amelia "*Nu*, (so) what could it hurt—try it."

Sid Roth adds some excellent thoughts:

"Many churches have chosen Friday night (the beginning of the Sabbath) as a time for prayer or night watches. Another idea is to have a corporate Sabbath service once a month. Two congregations where I recently shared (a message) are incorporating a monthly *Shabbat* service in addition to a regular Sunday service. On the other Friday nights, why not observe the Sabbath in your homes? The Sabbath was made for man, not man for the Sabbath. This is a wonderful time for families to bond together. Invite unsaved family and friends to join you. What a great way for Jesus to fulfill ("fill full" of Himself) the Fourth Commandment."[1]

Celebrating the Advent of Yeshua on the pagan rooted Winter Solstice (Christmas)

Even my own agnostic Jewish parents taught me to sing "Jingle Bells" and "Silent Night," just before we opened brightly wrapped gifts from under our traditionally decorated Christmas tree each year. Even though I had only the slightest inkling that all this had something to do with a religious event, like so many other Jewish and non-Jewish children, I had no clue about the true meaning of the advent of Yeshua, until I finally met Him in a strictly Christian setting many years later.

Thereafter, I must confess, I exalted Christmas, and its "true meaning" and inculcated the keeping of this holiday into the very fabric of my own children's lives. Even after we were called to Israel seven Christmases ago, I was both shocked and profoundly disappointed that virtually no one in the local Jewish Body even *mentioned* what to me was a greatly treasured holiday, much less celebrated it. We were so desperate during our first Christmas here, that I had a friend pick up a pathetic looking "Charlie Brown"- like tree from Arab Christians in nearby Nazareth. We did the same the second year: by the third, however painfully, we went treeless, having at last begun to transition to the reality of our new surroundings.

There is a real danger, however, in thus totally ignoring Christmas. Most Messianic pastors here give it absolutely no notice, although some, quite inconsistently, make a passing reference to the Advent of Yeshua on *Hannukah.*

I have, in Israel, heard only one resounding message on the Advent of Yeshua given on the *Shabbat* nearest Christmas. It was all about the wondrous aspects of the Birth of Yeshua, contrasted with all the negative things about celebrating this advent on a pagan rooted holiday. (By the way, I gave this message myself in the absence of our regular pastor).

Do we now celebrate Christmas on the 25th of December each year: absolutely not. Would I encourage all Christians to stop celebrating Christmas on December 25th: yes, even though I can empathize how very difficult it will be to give up a life long practice albeit, one based on such great error. Lest your kids start calling me the "Grench who stole Christmas," I suggest that Christians otherwise celebrate the Advent of Yeshua on or at least near *Hanukkah* (the Festival of Lights), not that He was born on that day anymore than He was born on the 25th of December. But *Hanukkah* is a lovely celebration with much traditional Winter seasonal flavor all of its own and *Hanukkah is* scriptural. Such a *Hanukkah* celebration could be a congregational event and/or a family celebration with all the trimmings. So why not?

Celebrating the Resurrection of Yeshua on a pagan rooted festival in honor of *Eostre*, the Teutonic dawn-goddess

I must confess that Donna and I attended the Easter Morning sunrise service of the local Church of Scotland during our first three years in Israel, so deeply ingrained was our nearly life-long practice. Did we teach our own children that rabbits lay eggs, then send them scurrying to find the same hidden about our many various gardens over the years: sadly, we did. We simply didn't know any better. Do we now celebrate the resurrection of Yeshua on "Easter" Sunday: absolutely not! Would I encourage all Christians to stop celebrating this most sacred of events in the history of mankind on a pagan holiday: most certainly, yes!

The Nazarene's celebrated the Resurrection of Yeshua on the historically accurate anniversary of the day that it occurred: three days following the 14th of Nissan, the Jewish Feast of *Pesach* (Passover). There is something incredibly special about a Messianic Jewish Seder oriented around the Resurrection of Yeshua. Most Messianic congregations have such Seders, and I am delighted to learn that more and more Christian Churches are turning to this Biblical way to celebrate the greatest of all events.

In Conclusion

You worship what you do not know; we know what we worship, for salvation is of the Jews. But the hour is coming, and now is, when the true worshipers will worship the Father in spirit and truth; for the Father is seeking such to worship Him. God is Spirit, and those who worship Him must worship in spirit and truth. (John 4:22-24)

I began this book with this Scripture and so let me also conclude:

Salvation is of the Jews. Yeshua was and is the fulfillment of the New Covenant, a covenant His Father, YHWH, made with the Jews, a better covenant, established on better promises: Yeshua was and is the Jewish Messiah. He was and is the Living *Torah* who spent His short life among us teaching His Father's plan of redemption from the pages of the written *Torah*. He treasured the written *Torah* to the point where He took time to emphasize: it would *never* be changed, replaced, or abolished.

By His grace, after He had taken His place sitting at the right side of His Father, He made manifest His intention to include all men, Jews and Gentiles alike, in the Plan of Redemption. He did so through the ministry of His Jewish Nazarene followers, principally through the outreach of the Apostle Paul.

This same Paul taught that each and every believing Jew and Gentile is a member of the Body of Yeshua: each in his own unique way indispensable to the operating of the entire Body. Paul pointed out that each member of the Body, because of his very uniqueness, should "--- remain with God in that state in which he was called." (1Cor 7:24) Jews should be Jews and Gentiles should be Gentiles. Though each has a different calling, never-the-less all should worship their beloved Messiah Yeshua in the same way: in Spirit and in Truth.

We Messianic Jews have come a long way since our predecessors the Nazarenes first worshipped Messiah Yeshua in the Upper Room on Mount Zion. Like the Messianic Seal of the Jerusalem Church, we have shown a remarkable resilience, having emerged to fulfill our sacred destiny after our virtual disappearance for nearly 2,000 years.

Now, by His grace, like the Messianic Seal, we are once again emerging, and we long to do so joyfully, with our Christian Brothers and Sisters by our side.

For those who have not yet heard the Good News of Yeshua, we are, by His sacred command, sending forth His Holy Word from Mount Zion, the place from which we first sprouted from the stump of Jesse. We are reaching out in His love to all people everywhere who do not yet know Him personally.

We are likewise reaching out to all our Christian brothers and sisters, who either have already or who soon will be taking to the heavenly highway leading from the depth of the apostasy of Rome to the glory of the heights of Jerusalem. May we Messianic Jews and Gentile Christians, at the end of this journey back to the Jewish roots of the Christian Church, at last joyfully proclaim together:

Behold, how good and how pleasant it is for brethren to dwell together in unity! It is like the precious oil upon the head, running down on the beard, the beard of Aaron, running down on the edge of his garments. It is like the dew of Hermon, descending upon the mountains of Zion; for there the LORD commanded the blessing—life forevermore.

(Ps 133:1-3)

---

1   Sid Roth, *Sid Roth's Messianic Vision*, June, 2000, page 2

After Word

Another kind of Jihad

Writing this book has been a demanding and consuming challenge: particularly so since it has necessarily been written against the background of a seemingly ubiquitous "peace process," wherein the historic enemies of Israel, encouraged and abetted by the "nations," have been relentlessly zeroing in on the fruition of their unbiblical, even satanic, claim to the Land, the precious, everlasting inheritance given by God to the Jewish people.

Even so, this book *isn't* about the political process. I have tried ever so diligently to avoid sharing the depths of the agony I carry in my own heart about all this; albeit, I have felt it necessary to discuss the general background of this historic and biblical conflict, as well as the hellish collaboration between the Vatican and the "Palestinians" to isolate then "conquer" Jerusalem.

By all means, I believe it is absolutely necessary for every believer in Yeshua to have a good understanding of the *real* nature of this "peace process," which, in point of fact, is not about "peace" at all, but rather about the Jews unilaterally ceding land to the Arabs "piece by piece." In any event, I strongly recommend that *everyone* read and study the two great and monumental works on this subject: *Philistine*, and *The Wall*, both by Ramon Bennett.[1]

Among other poignant issues, Ramon focuses in these books upon the past and the imminently threatened new *Jihad*. Whether or not the ongoing political process "succeeds" or "fails" Ramon believes, and I strongly agree: all hell is about to break loose in Israel, hopefully for the last time, as we Jews once again struggle in a *Jihad* of war and hate with the Arabs for control of the Land.

Jihad is an Arabic word meaning "fight." Webster defines it somewhat differently as "a Muslim holy war against infidels."

Once again, as I neared the end of this work, the Lord provided an amazing "God-incidence" to drive home my understanding of a remarkably important point. To do so, He has, quite miraculously, provided another, entirely different kind of *Jihad*.

This *Jihad*, a common first name among Arabs, is a beautiful brother in the Lord who regularly attends Carmel Assembly in Haifa where we also fellowship. *Jihad*, age 39, is an incredibly on fire believer whose family background has, for several generations, been Greek Orthodox. Getting to know and to genuinely love this Arab brother has had a profound impact upon my life.

About a year ago, when I started thinking about this book, I was then firmly convinced that the term "Arab believer" was an oxymoron. I was very certain that *every* Arab was, in one way or another, rooted in Islam and thus could never *really* embrace the very Jewish foundation of the Old Covenant regarding the Jewish roots of the Church, the Land of Israel, etc. My Arab brother, *Jihad*, just by being himself, has taught me quite differently.

Clearly, it was the Lord who made certain that *Jihad* sat in front of us each Shabbat service: it was *Jihad* who first struck up the beginnings of our mutual outreach, and it was he who initiated our first physical hug as brothers in Yeshua.

I was at once taken with the absolute genuiness of *Jihad's* love for the Jewish Messiah: the sheer joy of his salvation is a glowing aurora that encompasses the man and marks him as someone very special.

Jihad is very proud of the name he bears. He finds for it a very different meaning than "Moslem holy war," in 1 Tim 6:12, where, by his testimony, his eyes first fell when he randomly opened the Word of God for the first time.

Fight (Jihad) the good fight (Jihad) of faith, lay hold on eternal life, to which you were also called and have confessed the good confession in the presence of many witnesses.

Jihad is quite excited to share his remarkable testimony. I marvel at this man, a former drug addict, who, after being hooked on heroin for 21 years now with tears of joy gives full credit to Yeshua for his miraculous salvation, both physical and spiritual.

Our pastor, David Davis, has dedicated his ministry to the concept that unity will finally be achieved when Jew and Arab, as believers in Yeshua, worship together in Spirit and in Truth. The precious relationship the Lord has built between *Jihad* and myself is a living testimony to the anointing of Dave's ministry.

Finally, I ask you all to frequently share my prayer:

May the *Jihad* of peace and love, forever vanquish the *Jihad* of war and hate. May one day very soon all Jews, Arabs and other Gentiles who have been so predestined, at last be united as brothers and sisters in one glorious Body with Yeshua as its head.

RRF
Tiberias, Israel
August, 2000

[1] *Philistine, the Great Deception*, Ramon Bennett, (ISBN 965-9000-1-4) and *The Wall* (ISBN 965-90000-7-3) Arm of Salvation, P.O. Box 32381, Jerusalem, Israel 91322

Bibliography

(The) American Jewish Committee
American Jewish Year Book (1999), Volume 99, New York, 1999

Bacchiocchi, Samuele
From Sabbath to Sunday. Rome: The Pontifical Gregorian University Press, 1977

Bagatti, Bellarmino, O.F.M.
The Church from the Circumcision. Jerusalem: Franciscan Printing Press, 1984

Bagatti, Bellarmino, O.F.M
The Church from the Gentiles in Palestine. Jerusalem: Franciscan Printing Press, 1984

Brown, Francis (and) Driver, S.R. (and) Briggs, C.A.
Hebrew and English Lexicon of the Old Testament. London: Oxford Press, 1951

Bruce, F.F.
New Testament History. New York: Doubleday, 1980

Chadwick, Henry
The Early Church. London: Penguin Books, 1967

Charlesworth, James H. (Editor)
The Old Testament Pseudepigrapha (Volumes 1 and 2). New York: Douobleday, 1983

Cohen, Rabbi Bruce L.
Why Messianic Judaism? (A Position Paper): Congregation Beth El of Manhattan, New York

Concordant Publishing Concern
Concordant Greek Text. Canyon County, California, 1975

Davidson, Benjamin
The Analytical Hebrew and Chaldee Lexicon. Grand Rapids: Zondervan, 1970

Duffy, Eamon
Saints & Sinners, A History of the Popes, Yale University Press, 1997

Dugger, A. N.
A History of True Religion. Jerusalem: Mount Zion Reporter Press, 1972

Dugger, A.N.
Daniel and Revelation. Jerusalem: Mount Zion Reporter Press, 1977

Eisenman, Robert
James the Brother of Jesus. New York: Penguin Books, 1997

Encyclopedia Britannica, Inc.
The New Encyclopedia Britannica, Fifteeth Edition. Chicago: University of Chicago, 1986

Edersheim, Alfred
Life and Times of Jesus the Messiah, Eight Edition, Longmans, Green, and Co., New York, 1915

Flusser, David
Judaism and the Origins of Christianity. Jerusalem: The Magnes Press, Hebrew University, 1988

Fruchtenbaum, Dr. Arnold G.
The Confession of Peter. Ariel Ministries, Tustin, California, 1983

Garraty, John A. (and) Gay, Peter
The Columbia History of the World.. New York: Harper & Row, 1981

Good, Kenneth,
Are Baptists Reformed? Lorain, Ohio: Regular Baptist Heritage Fellowship, 1986

Green, J.P. Sr.
The Interlinear Bible, Hebrew-Greek-English. Boston: Hendrickson Publishers, 1986

Hansen, K.K. and Skjott, B.F., *Facts & Myths About the Messianic Congregations in Israel,* United Christian Council in Israel, 1999

Harper & Row
The Nag Hammadi Library in English. Edited by J.M. Robinson, New York:. 1977, 1988

Hislop, Alexander
The Two Babylons. New York: Loizeaux Brothers, 1959

Juster, Daniel
Jewish Roots. Gaithersburg, Maryland: DAVAR Publishing Co., 1986

Keter Publishing
Encyclopedia Judaica. Jerusalem: Keter Publishing, 1982

Koster, Dr. C.J., *Come Out of Her My People*,
The Institute for Scripture Research, PO Box 4347, 2125 Randburg, Republic of South Africa, 1996

Korin Publishers
The Jerusalem Bible. Jerusalem: Korin Publishers, 1980

Lang, Jovian P.
Dictionary of the Liturgy/No. 273/22. Rome: Catholic Book Pub Co., 1989

Latourette, Kenneth Scott
A History of Christianity. New York: Harper & Row, 1953

Mancini, Ignazio, O.F.M.
Archeological Discoveries Relative to the Judeo-Christians - Historical Survey, Jerusalem: Franciscan Printing Press, 1984

McGrath, Alister E.
Christian Theology. Oxford: Blackwell Publishers, 1994

Noonan, James-Charles, Jr, and Foley, John P.
The Church Visible: The Ceremonial Life and Protocol of the Roman Catholic Church, New York, Viking Press, 1996

Oxford University Press
The New Oxford Annotated Apocrypha. New York: Oxford University Press, 1991

Painter, John
Just James, The Brother of Jesus in History and Tradition. Columbia: University of South Carolina Press, 1997

Peterson, F.Paul
Peter's Tomb Recently Discovered In Jerusalem, P.O. Box 2451, Fort Wayne, Indiana, 1960

Pritz, Ray A.
Nazarene Jewish Christianity. Jerusalem: The Magnes Press, E.J. Brill, 1988

Sanders, Ronald
Lost Tribes And Promised Lands: The Origins Of American Racism, Boston: Little, Brown And Co., 1978.

Schmalz, Reuven E. and Fischer, Raymond R.,
The Messianic Seal of the Jerusalem Church, Tiberias, Israel, Olim Publications, 1999

Schneemelcher, Wilhelm (Editor),
New Testament Apocrypha, (Volumes One and Two) John Knox Press, Louisville, Kentucky, 1991

Schonfield, Hugh
The Pentecost Revolution. Chicago: Element Books, 1985

Schonfield, Hugh
The Essene Odyssey: Element Books, 1984

Stern, David H.
Jewish New Testament Commentary. Clarksville, Maryland: Jewish New Testament Publications, Inc., 1990

Stern, David H.
Messianic Jewish Manifesto. Jerusalem, Israel: Jewish New Testament Publications, Inc., 1988

Terry, Milton S.
Biblical Hermeneutics. Grand Rapids, Michigan: Zondervan, 1974

Testa, Emmanuel
The Faith of the Mother Church. Jerusalem: Franciscan Printing Press, 1992

Tout, T.F.
The Empire and the Papacy. London: Rivington's Publishers, 1924

Trimm, James
"DuTillet" Hebrew Matthew, Society for the Advancement of Nazarene Judaism, Hurst, Texas, 1999

Trimm, James
  Good News According to the Hebrews, Society for the Advancement of Nazarene Judaism, Hurst, Texas, 2000

Wright, George E. (and) Filson, Flyd V.
  The Westminster Historical Atlas to the Bible. London: Westminster Press, 1945

Whiston, William
  The Works of Josephus. Boston: Hendrikson Publishers, 1987

Appendix

Statement of Faith of the Messianic Jewish Alliance of America and the International Alliance of Messianic Congregations and Synagogues

WE BELIEVE:

I.That the BIBLE, consisting of the Tenach (Holy Scriptures) and the later writings commonly known as the B'rit Hadasha (New Covenant), is the only infallible and authoritative word of God. We recognize its divine inspiration, and accept its teachings as our final authority in all matters of faith and practice (Deut. 6:4-9; Prov.3:1-6; Ps. 119:89, 105; Isa. 48:12-16; Rom. 8:14-17; II Tim. 2:15, 3:16-17).

II.GOD – We believe that the Shema, "Hear O Israel, the Lord our God, the Lord is one" (Deut. 6:4), teaches that God is Echad, as so declared: a united one, a composite unity, eternally existent in plural oneness [Gen. 1:1 (Elohim: God); Gen. 1:26 "Let us make man in our image"; Gen. 2:24 Adam & Eve were created to be as one flesh (basar echad)], that He is a personal God who created us (Gen. 1 & 2), and that He exists forever in three persons: Father, Son, and Holy Spirit, as mentioned in Romans 8:14-17 (Father, Spirit, and Messiah – Son) and Matt. 28:18-20 (immersing in the name of the Father, Son, and Holy Spirit).

A.GOD THE FATHER (Abba) – John 6:27b; I Cor 1:3; Gal. 1:1; Rev. 3:5, 21; Jer. 3:4, 19; 31:9; Mal. 1:6; Matt. 6:9, 32; Luke 10:21-22; John 1:14; 4:23; 5:17-26; 6:28-46; Rom. 8:14-15.

B.GOD THE SON (HaBen)

1.God does have a Son [Ps. 2; Prov. 30:4-6 (cf. Heb. 1); Luke 12:35-37; John 1:29-34, 49; 3:14-18].

2.The Son, called Yeshua (Jesus), meaning salvation, came to this world born of a virgin [Isa. 7:14 (cf. Luke 1:30-35)].

3.The Son is God (Deity), and is worshipped as God, having existed eternally [Ps. 110:1 (cf. Heb. 1:13); Isa. 9:6-7; Matt. 28:18-20; Phil. 2:5-11; Col. 1:15-19; Rev. 3:21 (Heb. 1 – worshipped by angels); Rev. 4:8, 5:5-14].

4.This One is the promised Mashiach (Messiah) of Israel [Is. 9:6-7; 11:1; Dan. 9 (esp. verses 20-26); Isa. 53; John 1:17, 40-41, 45, 49; Mark 8:29].

5.He is the root and offspring of David, the bright and morning star (Num. 24:17; Rev. 22:16).

6.He is our Passover, the Lamb of God (I Cor.5:7; Rev. 5; John 1:29).

C.GOD THE HOLY SPIRIT (Ruach HaKodesh)

1.Introduced in Gen. 1:2b.

2.In the Tenach, the Spirit of God came upon individuals during the times of our forefathers, like Moses, David (see II Sam. 23:1-3), and the Prophets, for the specific purposes.

3.In the New Covenant, the Messiah, Yeshua, promised His disciples that "the Comforter" would come to them after He was gone, described as the Spirit of Truth (John 14:17, 26), who was with them and would be in them.Yeshua further declared that the Spirit of Truth, would guide us into all truth and would glorify Him – the Messiah – not Himself (John 16:13-15). He empowers us (Acts 1:8). He seals us [Eph. 1:13; 4:30 (see NIV and Jewish New Testatment versions)]. If we have not the Spirit, we are not His (Rom. 8:9). He leads us and teaches us (Rom. 8:14-17). His indwelling enables us to live a godly life. Acts 2:38 says, "Repent, be immersed, and receive the Holy Spirit."

III.MAN

A.Created in the image of God (Gen. 1:26-27), but:

B.through disobedience, man fell from his first state and became separated from God (Gen. 2:17; 3:22-24). Therefore, according to the Scriptures, all men are born with a sinful nature (Ps. 14:1-3; 49:7; 53:13; Isa. 64:6; Rom. 3:9-12, 23; 5:12).

Man's only hope for redemption (salvation) is through the atonement made by the Messiah (Lev. 17:11; Isa. 53; Dan. 9:24-26; I Cor. 15:22; Heb. 9:11-14, 28; John 1:12, 3:36), resulting in regeneration by the Holy Spirit (Tit. 3:5), which is the new birth (John 3:3-8). For by grace we are saved through faith, it is a gift of God (Eph. 2:8-9)

IV.RESURRECTION AND JUDGMENT

We believe in the resurrection of both the redeemed and the lost: the former to everlasting life and the latter to eternal separation from God, a state of everlasting punishment (Job 14:14; 19:25-27; Dan. 12:2-3; John 3:36; 11:25-26; Rev. 20:5-6, 10-15; 21:7-8).

V.THE MESSIAH – The Redeemer

The Scriptures promised two "comings" of the Messiah:

A.First coming

1.Promised in Dan. 9:24-26.

2.Its purpose was to make an atonement for sin (Dan. 9:24-26; Isa. 53; Rom. 3:21-31; Heb. 9-10; John 3:16-17).

B.Second coming

1.Promised coming in the air to receive the believers to Himself (I Thess. 4:13-18; John 14:1-6; I Cor. 15:51-57).

2.Messiah's return to the earth.

a.The Redeemer shall come to Zion (Isa.59:20-21; Zech. 14:4).

b.Israel's spiritual redemption (Zech.12:8-13:1; Rom. 11:25-27; Heb. 9:28; Jer. 31:31-40; the New Covenant).

c.Israel's national restoration is to recover the remnant of His people Israel from the four corners of the earth, and restor the Davidic Kingdom (Isa. 11 – to re-establish the throne and kingdom of David, which will last forever) [Isa. 9:6-7 (cf. Luke 1:30-33); Jer. 23:3-8].

VI.ISRAEL IN PROPHECY

We believe in God's end-time plan for the nation of Israel and for the world. A central part of Messianic Judaism is the belief in the physical and spiritual restoration of Israel, as taught in the Scriptures. The greatest miracle of our day has been the re-establishment or rebirth of the State of Israel according to prophecy (Ezek. 34:11-31; 36-39; Hos. 3; Amos 9:11-15; Zech. 12-14; Isa. 11; 43; 54; 60-62; 66; Rom. 11:1-34) (see also Scriptures under V. THE MESSIAH).

VII.MESSIANIC JUDAISM

A. We recognize that Jewish people (physical descendants of Abraham through Isaac and Jacob, whether through the mother's or the father's blood-line) who place their faith in Israel's Messiah, Yeshua, continue to be Jewish according to the Scriptures (Rom. 2:28-29). Gentiles who place their faith in Yeshua, are "grafted into" the Jewish olive tree of faith (Rom. 11:17-25) becoming spiritual sons and daughters of Abraham (Gal. 3:28-29).

B. We observe and celebrate the Jewish Holy Days given by God to Israel, with their fulfillment in and through the Messiah Yeshua. We believe that true "Biblical Judaism," the faith of first century believers, which we seek to practice, acknowledges the continuity of faith in the one true God, revealed throughout the Scriptures, and ultimately manifested in God's Son, Yeshua the Messiah. We believe that salvation has always been "by faith," and that works of law, or righteous acts, have never saved anyone (Gen. 15:6; Rom. 2-6; Eph. 2:8-9; Heb. 11:6, 39).

C. We acknowledge that the New Covenant body of believers is composed of both Jews and Gentiles who have received Yeshua the Messiah as the Promised Redeemer. The "middle wall of partition" has been broken down and now we worship the God of Israel together (I Cor. 12:13; Eph. 2:13-14).

Distribution and Contacts

To order more copies of this book, *The Messianic Seal of the Jerusalem Church*, artifact "strike" products, anointing oil, and/or other Olim Creative Products produced by new immigrants in Israel contact:

In Israel:
Immanuel Gift & Book Center

P.O. Box 1693
Tiberias, 14115, Israel
Tel. 972 6 6723620
Fax 972 6 6723195
e-mail: Orders@TheGalileeExperience.com

In the United Kingdom:

Anchor Recordings, Ltd.
72, The Street
Kennington, Ashford,
KentTN24 9HS
United Kingdom
Telefax: 12336 38600

In North America:

For Your Glory, Inc.
P.O. Box 724
Woodland Park CO 80866
(719) 686-5308
www.foryourglory.org

To Contact the publisher or author:

Olim Publications
P.O. Box 2111
Tiberias, Israel
Phone: 972 6720535
e-mail: olim@kinneret.co.il